Plotinus

on BODY and BEAUTY

Frontispiece   Male bust, Tomb of the Aurelii, Chamber III, left wall, mid-third century, Rome, 6¼ in × 4¼ in, wall painting *in situ*.
Source: Archivio Fotographico della Pontificia Commissione di Archeologia Sacra, Rome.

Plotinus

on BODY and BEAUTY
Society, Philosophy, and Religion in Third-century Rome

Margaret R. Miles

BLACKWELL
Publishers

The right of Margaret R. Miles to be identified as author of this work has been asserted in accordance with the Copyright, Designs and Patents Act 1988.

First published 1999

2 4 6 8 10 9 7 5 3 1

Blackwell Publishers Ltd
108 Cowley Road
Oxford OX4 1JF
UK

Blackwell Publishers Inc.
350 Main Street
Malden, Massachusetts 02148
USA

British Library Cataloguing in Publication Data

A CIP catalogue record for this book is available from the British Library.

Library of Congress Cataloging-in-Publication Data

Miles, Margaret Ruth.
    Plotinus on body and beauty : society, philosophy, and religion in third-century Rome / Margaret R. Miles.
        p.   cm.
    Includes bibliographical references and index.
    ISBN 0-631-21274-4 (alk. paper). — ISBN 0-631-21275-2 (alk. paper)
    1. Plotinus. 2. Mind and body—Rome—History. 3. Aesthetics, Ancient. I. Title.
    B693.27M54   1999
    186'.4—dc21   99-32105
                                                                                        CIP

Typeset in 10½ on 12½ pt Sabon
by Ace Filmsetting Ltd, Frome, Somerset
Printed in Great Britain by MPG Books Ltd, Bodmin, Cornwall

This book is printed on acid-free paper.

For Ric

But if someone is able to turn around . . . he will see God and himself and the All; at first he will not see *as* the All but then, when he has nowhere to set himself and determine how far he himself goes, he will stop marking himself off from all being and will come to the All without going out anywhere, but remaining there where the All is set firm. (6.5.7)

[Plotinus] was wholly concerned with thought; and, which surprised us all, he went on in this way right up to the end . . . continuous[ly] turning in contemplation to his intellect . . . He never, while awake, relaxed his intent concentration upon the intellect. (Porphyry, *Life* 8–9)

Contents

Preface

She wanted to be one of those people who found a subject to pursue, then discover a sweet secret about themselves, finally seeing through the filter of what was learned. To take knowledge – facts, stories, equations, whatever it was – and learn to breathe under the water of that place. People who did this found out how alive they were.[1]

The exercise of *thinking with* a mind in which there are no superfluities, no elisions or evasions, every idea examined and its relation to other ideas explored, is both humbling and exhilarating. It is also difficult, not least because it inevitably disorients one from comfortably familiar habits of thought. After reading a great philosopher for a long time, you can stand at a window looking out and see the world as that philosopher saw it.[2]

Plotinus did precisely this exercise with Plato's philosophy. He studied Plato intensively and passionately until he was able to see the world as Plato saw it. Then he tried to explain both what he saw and what helped him to see it. He did not attempt to explain away the points of tension and contradiction in Plato. He even increased the strain and the urgency of these points. Nor did he endeavor to clarify or render more precise Plato's vaguenesses. He defended obscurity on the grounds that what was important was not the idea itself, but the struggle to understand (4.8.1).[3] Plotinus thought of himself, not as a constructive philosopher, even less as a "Neoplatonist," but as a faithful interpreter of Plato.

What *is* a "faithful interpreter" of another author? To be a faithful interpreter in this narrow sense would be simply to read aloud the author's own words. Is it, then, someone who demonstrates the integrity, complexity, and cohesion of that author's thought? Surely this is part of what a faithful interpreter must do. But ultimately, a faithful interpreter is one who relates the earlier author's thought to the present in a way that makes that thought alive, vivid, and directly relevant. Thus, Plotinus tried to supply for his friends and students what he himself had needed in order to see the world as Plato saw it. Inevitably, necessarily, he altered Plato's philosophy in making it his own.

I first read Plotinus for the gentle beauty of his universe and for his aphorisms: "No real being ever ceases to be" (4.3.5). "The universe lies in safety" (3.4.4). "All opposites are entwined together" (3.3.6). "There will be a time when vision will be continuous" (6.9.10). "What does 'really exists' mean? That they exist as beauties" (1.6.5). Gradually I began to sift Plotinus's foundational ideas from those he merely considered and from the views of others, which he sometimes pondered at length. I began to understand, and to delight in, Plotinus's interconnected universe, and to explore the psychological and moral effects of thinking within his universe. What difference does it make, in a daily relationship with the world, if one believes, as Plotinus did, that the world is not made up of a hodge-podge collection of living beings, but that all are intimately related by the same informing soul? What practical effects might it have to believe, as Plotinus did, that the source and energy of everything one sees is spiritual?

The social and economic world of early twenty-first century America does not encourage or support investigation of these questions. Far from it, the media society in which I live urges me to ignore the complex fabric of life on which I am dependent. It incites me to use more than my share of the limited resources of the planet and to turn deaf ears to the cries of misery from the people and animals who suffer so that I may live carelessly. In Plotinus's universe I notice sharp joys and pains I had not noticed formerly, my own and those of other living beings. Plotinus's conceptual universe provides me with a perspective from which I can notice, enjoy, and take responsibility for, the life that circulates through and animates living bodies.

This book is the result of twenty-five years of studying and teaching Plotinus. It represents my effort to know Plotinus so well that I can stand at the window looking out and see Plotinus's world of things and living beings standing in their own light, rich with the precious and unpredictable gift of life. I hope that I am a faithful interpreter of Plotinus, as he was of Plato. I hope that what emerges in my reader's mind is a sense of the generosity of Plotinus's spirit. Mindful of Igor Stravinsky's warning that a sin against the spirit always begins with a sin against the letter, I try not to elide the detailed precision of Plotinus's vision. Nevertheless, in interpreting Plotinus *for readers of the early twenty-first century*, I have omitted some details such as, for example, the school exercises common to philosophical schools of the third century CE.

I have not taken several approaches to Plotinus already mapped by knowledgeable scholars. I do not examine his relationship to Plato, Aristotle, or the Middle Platonists. I do not, in any detail, examine him as representative of a genre of philosophical writing, nor do I attempt to establish the relative commonality or uniqueness of his images and metaphors. The scholars to whom I am most indebted for inspiration, A. H. Armstrong and Pierre Hadot, have primarily placed Plotinus in relation to perennial issues of human life. Orientation to a bewildering and dazzling universe and a spiritual discipline that effectively lives out this orientation in daily life: these are the issues to which Plotinus brought his most focused and forceful thought.

He did not do so, however, in a "perennial" context. The pressing issues of human life do not occur in the abstract, but in notoriously concrete immediacy. Plotinus's remedy for the distractions and embattlements of everyday life does not advocate escape into a mystical timelessness. His instructions in the practice of contemplation, rather, offer a way to place those struggles and sufferings within a conceptual context that diffuses the impressions of uniqueness and targeted victimization they bring.

Moreover, Plotinus constructed his answer to the ancient question, How should we live?, in direct response to other proposals existing in his own intellectual and social situation. There is little that is abstract, timeless, or perennial about Plotinus's philosophy. If it is useful – as a whole, or in part – for the present, that will only be seen when we carefully replace it in its own society, critically examine its function in that setting, and then identify features of our own very different situation to which it may offer usable suggestions.

Pierre Hadot wrote, "It is extremely rare to have the chance to see someone in the process of training himself to be a human being."[4] Yet that is the opportunity offered by Plotinus's writings, an opportunity few of his interpreters have accepted. Reading Plotinus in chronological order of his writings reveals a man who seldom spoke autobiographically, yet in each moment of his life, from the beginning of his authorship, he persistently sought to discern what it meant to be human. As a mature man, free from pain and at the height of his powers, he described body as flawless reflection and embodiment of divine goodness. As an old man, suffering, abandoned by friends, and facing death, he thought of death also as a form of goodness. Read out of the context of his life and present experience, his later statements seem negative and pessimistic. In fact, the philosopher simply seeks the concepts that both explain and compensate his body's defection. Without losing his settled vision of the beauty of the whole, Plotinus found a way to accept death gracefully.

I focus Plotinus on body because body is the point in his philosophy at which the most stress – signaled by apparent contradiction – occurs, the point at which Plotinus struggles to present the beauty and the danger of embodiment, the poignancy and fragility of body, together with its metaphysical significance. I do not refer to "the body," because the phrase implies a generic human body no one has ever seen or touched. While "bodyness," the condition of being body, is a universal trait of humanness, bodies are invariably gendered. They are also young or old, healthy or ill; they are socially located, along with other factors that loudly and intimately affect the experience of body. In short, "the body" does not exist. But body does.

For me, as for Plotinus, body concentrates the mind, making time real and generating my longing to "have it all now." For although life is trustworthy, immortal, and utterly safe, the particular configuration that slides into focus as *my* life will as easily lose focus and dissolve back into the ocean of life. I do not have the luxury of banqueting at ease in Olympia with the blessed immortals. To wish, imagine, or act as if one does, Plotinus said, to be shocked when confronted by old age or death – whichever comes first – is to miss the greatest opportunity we have, the opportunity of realizing our connection to the All and the One, of seeing the great beauty.

Acknowledgements

The chapter I wrote on Plotinus in *Reading for Life* made me aware that, despite a great deal of fine scholarship on Plotinus, a more accessible articulation of what Plotinus's vision can offer the present was needed. I am grateful to Alex Wright, Senior Commissioning Editor in Religion at Blackwell Publishers, for encouraging and shepherding this book. Richard Valantasis gave me his *Lexicon Plotinianum*, an invaluable tool for writing on Plotinus. And my thanks and love to my husband, Owen C. Thomas, who has mastered the delicate art of offering simultaneously critical and encouraging comment.

Quotations reprinted by permission of the publishers and the Loeb Classical Library from *Plotinus: Enneads* (Volumes I–VII), translated by A.H. Armstrong, Cambridge, Mass.: Harvard University Press (1966–1988).

I
Introduction: Seeing Double

When I was a child my family owned a contraption with which I was endlessly fascinated, a stereoscope. You slide a card containing two apparently identical photographs into a slot six inches or so in front of a pair of hooded glasses. The brain refracts the two photographs into a single image so that, holding the glasses to your eyes, you see a single three-dimensional scene. The flat two-dimensionality of the photographs suddenly becomes a living scene in which, it seems, you are present.

Plotinus (205–70 CE) described a conceptual feat comparable to that performed by the stereoscope. He noticed (as had many others before him) that human experience could be analyzed into two components, intellect and senses. But that was only the first step, for he then insisted that, since the two are, in actuality, "entwined together"[1] to see "in the life," one must see as if through a stereoscope. One must see two pictures, but simultaneously: "All things are double, and the one is two and the two come together into one" (5.6.6). The point is to see *the life*, a three-dimensional picture that cannot be grasped by either of the two lenses – intellect or sense – in isolation from the other. To see a body as formed and animated is to see it "boiling over with life" (6.5.12). It is also to see its beauty.[2]

The goal of Plotinus's philosophy is to see the doubleness of the world as a unity. For the impression of doubleness is itself an optical illusion, a bad habit we have acquired and must correct if we are to see that "one and the same life holds the sphere" (5.9.5; 6.5.9). But two further steps remain for which the trained ability to see double is merely a necessary prelude. The penultimate trick is to recognize even the doubleness of seer and seen as an illusion, to "turn around," as Plotinus puts it, and to see, not the whole, but *as* the whole:

> At first he will not see as the All but then, when he has nowhere to set himself and limit himself and determine how far he himself goes, he will stop marking himself off from all being and will come to the All without going out anywhere, but remaining there where the All is set firm. (6.5.7)

Finally, even the metaphor of vision collapses, and Plotinus speaks of an intimate touching more like irradiation than relationship:

> How can one describe the absolutely simple? But it is enough if the intellect comes into contact with it; but when it has done so, while the contact lasts, it is absolutely impossible, nor has it time, to speak. One must believe one has seen when the soul suddenly takes light. (5.3.17)

Plotinus was not a mystic in the Western sense of one who withdraws from society in order to seek and perpetuate a spiritual vision. He was a teacher, and he wrote in order to extend his teaching beyond the intimate circle of his classroom. His writings struggle continuously to find the images and metaphors, the concepts, and the exercises that will help others to see what he saw.

The urgency of Plotinus's attempt to communicate this experience comes from his conviction that all life, whether rational or irrational, plant, or the earth itself, strains towards this vision/touch (3.8.1). It is the quintessential human goal, the profoundly orienting moment that makes the difference between the success or utter failure of a life. "All our toil and trouble is for this: not to be left without a share in the best of visions" (1.6.7). Plotinus's goal, as philosopher and teacher is to help his reader to *imagine the real*, that is, to see the apparent doubleness of oneself and the world as unity, and thus to be "simplified into happiness" (6.7.35). In the pages that follow, I explore his project, seeking to make its present usefulness pop into the reader's eye.

Porphyry's *Life*

Porphyry's *Life of Plotinus* draws a portrait of one of the most unusual people of his – or any – time, a man devoted simultaneously to service of others and to the life of the mind. Teaching in Rome at a time – the mid-third century of the common era – in which one contemporary claimed that there was "an indescribable shortage of philosophy," Plotinus's extraordinary powers of concentration enabled him to be "at the disposal of all who had any sort of acquaintance with him," *and* to be continuously concentrated on philosophy (*Life* 20).

> He worked out his train of thought from beginning to end in his own mind, and then, when he wrote it down, since he had set it all in order in his mind, he wrote as continuously as if he were copying from a book. Even if he was talking to someone, engaged in continuous conversation, he kept to his train of thought. He could take his necessary part in the conversation to the full, and at the same time keep his mind fixed without a break on what he was considering. When the person he had been talking to was gone, he did not go over what he had written . . . He went straight on with what came next, just as if there had been no interval of conversation between. In this way he was present at once to himself and to others, and he never relaxed his self-turned attention except in sleep. (*Life* 8)

Friend of an emperor and of several highly placed public officials, Plotinus shared Plato's dream of a civic society based on philosophical principles. He attempted to organize a "city of philosophers" (to be called Platonopolis). According to Porphyry, his friend and disciple, the emperor's advisors were jealous and squelched the proposal. Plotinus's less ambitious efforts had greater success. His formidable powers of concentration must have been severely challenged by the patient, detailed work he undertook on behalf of the "houseful" of orphaned boys and girls for whom he had accepted responsibility. He "patiently attended to the accounts of their property," taught them (especially if they showed any interest in philosophy), and generally "shielded so many from the worries and cares of ordinary life" (*Life* 9).

Though he had a thorough command of philosophy, Plotinus was apparently not flawlessly educated; his spelling was so-so, and Porphyry, his editor and biographer as well as his friend and disciple, remarks that he consistently confused certain words in writing and speaking. His disciples had to urge him to write, and even then he consented only to write first drafts, not to correct or make revisions in his work. His knowledge was encyclopedic, not only about the work of other philosophers, but also about geometry, mechanics, optics, and music. But philosophy was his passion; whenever he spoke of it, his face lit up. Porphyry describes Plotinus with the attentive affection of a disciple:

> There was always a charm about his appearance, but at these times
> [when he was teaching] he was still more attractive to look at: he sweated
> gently, and kindliness shone out from him, and in answering questions
> he made clear both his benevolence to the questioner and his intellec-
> tual vigour. (*Life* 13)

His teaching style was eccentric. Rather than "speaking in the manner
of a set treatise," Plotinus entertained students' questions, honoring
their perplexities and thinking through these questions with them. Far
from being absorbed in his own thoughts, his generous mind willingly
accepted others' concerns, allowing them to set the agenda for the
classroom. "His lectures were like conversations, and he was not quick
to make clear to anybody the compelling internal logic of his discourse,"
Porphyry writes. Plotinus recognized that, like Plato, he could easily
be misunderstood by anyone who had not grasped the fundamental
premises of his philosophy, but he did little to preclude or correct such
misapprehensions.

Plotinus had two powerful teachers, one dead and one living – Plato
and Ammonius Saccas. He "caught" the love of philosophy – as one
catches a germ – from books and from a living teacher. But he made
his own whatever he discussed. "He expresses himself," Porphyry
wrote, "in a tone of rapt inspiration, and states what he himself really
feels about the matter and not what has been handed down by tradition" (*Life* 14). The originality and independence of his philosophical
thought, however, was not always appreciated. His detractors accused
him of plagiarizing from Numenius, the most popular Platonist of the
second century; others, with less learned objections, simply said that
he was a "big driveller" (*Life* 18). Porphyry thought differently. According to him, Plotinus had found the one thing – the One thing –
that organized and concentrated his attention and affection.

Porphyry gives a wonderfully odd, impressionistic, and personal
biography of his teacher. Without it we would not know many intimate details of Plotinus's life that range from (possibly) irrelevant to
highly significant illumination of his thought. But which is which? It is
not always evident. In addition to the biographical details already
mentioned, Porphyry tells us that Plotinus

- continued to nurse at the breast until he was eight years old
  and someone teased him about it;
- came to Rome to teach when he was 40;
- began to write at about age 50;

- didn't bathe, but had himself massaged every day at home;
- had a disease of the bowels, but would not submit to an enema, saying (in essence) that it was beneath his dignity;
- would not sit for a portrait painter, so Porphyry and his friends brought a famous painter into the school to observe him as he taught and to paint his portrait later;
- had poor eyesight, so did not review or revise his manuscripts;
- practiced vegetarianism;
- attached himself to the Emperor Gordian's campaign against the Persians so that he could travel to Persia to learn about their philosophy; when Gordian was killed, he made a narrow escape, and had to find his own way back to Antioch;
- rejected astrology;
- had male and female students, and taught several physicians, senators, and a rhetorician who later became a philosopher;
- almost walked out of a lecture that advocated "that a pupil for the sake of advancing in the study of virtue should submit himself to carnal intercourse with his master if the master desired it";
- was able to reverse magical attacks against him;
- died in 270 CE at the age of 66.

In the chapters that follow I return to Porphyry's revelations of his teacher's powers and warts from time to time, not because I accept all Porphyry's observations and interpretations at face value, but to examine whether, and how, they may illuminate Plotinus's thought. In fact, I doubt and question Porphyry's memory, his selection of details, and his interpretations as I would those of any disciple/biographer. Biographers routinely select events in their subjects' lives that they think will make sense of those lives. In addition, they inevitably notice and favor features of their subject's life and thought that further their own assumptions and the narrative they seek to construct. If the biographer is himself a philosopher, his agenda may be even more noticeable. For example, the first sentence – and perhaps the most frequently quoted passage, in the *Life* – reads: "Plotinus, the philosopher of our times, seemed ashamed of being in the body." In chapter 4 I examine that claim on the basis of Plotinus's own discussions of embodiment, arguing that Porphyry overstates and distorts Plotinus's careful teaching on body. Why did Porphyry misrepresent his teacher? Why has that misunderstanding been accepted and repeated to our own time? The short answer is that only an informed and subtle mind can make distinctions that do not collapse into separation.[3] The longer and more adequate answer is woven through the topics of this book.

The *Enneads*

Plotinus's philosophical work is contained in a collection of six volumes, each of which has nine treatises. Porphyry edited and arranged the treatises according to subject matter. In addition to the information about Plotinus given in Porphyry's *Life*, this rather slender corpus represents all the evidence there is of the life and work of a thinker whose influence on Byzantine and Western Christianity and Islam has been profound. In the West, Augustine brought Plotinian mysticism into Christianity, ensuring the interest of a long line of Christian thinkers stretching from pseudo-Dionysius, through Renaissance Platonists like Marsilius of Ficino and Nicholas of Cusa, to the Cambridge Platonists of the seventeenth century, the Romantics, and many modern American and British poets and philosophers. Major differences divide Plotinus's philosophy from Christianity, but his emphasis on religious experience, contemplation, and a cultivated vision of the Great Beauty holds perennial attraction.

Greek was the language of high culture in Rome throughout the third century. While Plotinus's use of Greek limited his auditors to the upper classes, it probably did not exclude many of those who wished to study with him.[4]

Although Plotinus's philosophy is orderly it is also complex. It can be approached either by beginning with the world of ordinary experience, as Plotinus usually did, or by beginning with the source, the One, and describing the descent of being, reality, and value from it. Nothing can be said about the One except that it is source. Even to name it God, the Good, or the One – locutions that Plotinus uses interchangeably – is misleading. Nevertheless, one must do so, Plotinus said, even while keeping in mind the imprecision of names of any sort. The One generates intellect without effort or diminishment, and intellect contains in potential the forms of all beings that become embodied at the next level, that of soul. As we will see in more detail in chapter 3, soul is the intermediary, the crucial link between sense and intellect.

Plotinus's universe is, throughout, a universe formed and animated by spirit.[5] Bodies are formed and given life by soul. In fact, anything

that can be seen is already formed. Matter, the limit to which the One
can reach through its intermediaries, cannot be seen until it is formed
into bodies. Anticipating modern scientific ability to identify complex
molecular structures, Plotinus asserted that even rocks and soil have
form and thus are bodies.

Plotinus's universe is also dynamic. Each entity gives being and form
spontaneously and effortlessly to the entity below it. Plotinus's hierarchical language has received much criticism; a careful reading demonstrates that he modifies it by insisting that the entities are so closely
contiguous as to interpenetrate and depend upon each other. His im-
agery of a ladder shows where his interest lies: to be sure, the ladder
has rungs, some of which are higher than others, but it is the uprights
or sides of the ladder that makes the metaphor apposite. The sides of
the ladder hold all the entities together, relating them to one another
and allowing movement and the circulation of energies throughout.

Human beings are composites of body (formed matter) and soul.
They can choose to identify either with body or with soul, and through
soul (whose primary characteristic is life) with intellect (the origin of
form and thus of beauty). The activity of identification with the source
of life, beauty, and goodness (the One) is contemplation.

This summary description of Plotinus's philosophy must suffice for
the moment. In the abstract it gives little indication of the tremendous
passion and energy it has held for many people over almost the last
two millennia. One of the goals of this book, however, is to explore its
attractiveness for the present.

Plotinus for the Present

Why should a third-century philosopher be considered a potential
source of help for the problems and quandaries of the present? But, on
the other hand, why study a thinker who lacks any present usefulness?
Antiquarian interest is not a sufficient reason to devote the necessary
amount of time and energy to the complex task of understanding a
thinker in his own intellectual and social context as well as in our
own. I believe that Plotinus's philosophy reveals a thinker pressingly
concerned with some of the same topics that profoundly interest us,
namely with living and dying. For both personal and philosophical
reasons, Plotinus struggled to think fruitfully and accurately about his
own life and body. His ideas of the relationship of body and soul will,

I believe, help us to think more realistically and affectionately about our own fragile and precious bodies, not because his ideas were timeless, transcending particular social experiences, but because his society and ours display some similarities that make his thoughts relevant to our own social world and historical moment. Indeed, I believe that there is a connection between a widespread modern tendency to misunderstand and caricature Plotinus and some of our most intimate and unexamined loyalties and resentments. If this is true, a more accurate understanding of what Plotinus taught will help us with some pressing contemporary questions and problems. In this sense, the *Enneads* can be thought of as a sophisticated "self-help" manual.

Minimally, listening carefully to an ancient author on issues of perennial interest challenges and revises the reality-picture in which we live. Our actions, and the decisions that intimately affect ourselves and others, rely on assumptions that we are seldom forced to examine because they are shared by many others in our immediate vicinity. Yet these assumptions and the ways we act them out give shape and substance to our lives. Reading an ancient philosopher can help us to imagine our lives beyond the images and social narratives that dominate our society's media. Reading Plotinus "for life" challenges the values that fund our repertoire of instant judgments.[6] It can reveal possible self-identities that are not suggested in the newspapers, magazines, and books we read or the movies and sit-coms we watch.

Yet the discrepancy between our own lives and an ancient author's philosophy is not easily bridged. Plotinus's conclusions cannot simply be detached from *his* life and experience and stapled onto ours. Connecting an ancient author's suggestions with our own lives entails two moments: first, reconstruction of the relevant cultural and intellectual interests and anxieties of his society; second, analysis of the features of our own cultural moment that relate most strongly to the author's particular helpfulness. Many modern authors have expounded Plotinus's philosophical ideas; in the concluding chapter of this book I will try to say why I think Plotinus's vision is usable and important for people living in the West at the beginning of the twenty-first century.

Why has Plotinus's present usefulness not been noticed? Part of the answer to that question lies in the ways he has been studied. Plotinus is usually examined as a philosopher, in relation to other philosophers. I suggest, and will presently describe in greater detail, that Plotinus's ideas of body and soul pop into the eye much more vividly if we consider his teaching first as a direct response to a rich and excited discussion, contemporary with him, about the proper role of bodies in the project of constructing a "self," and second, in relation to his society's fascination with and addiction to the public displays of flesh routinely exhibited in the entertainment culture of third-century Rome.

Approaching Plotinus Historically

The great English interpreter of Plotinus, A.H. Armstrong, once wrote: "There is practically nothing in the whole extent of Plotinus's writings which can be construed as even the remotest allusion to contemporary affairs."[7] While this is mostly true, it is still the case that his thought was intimately shaped by the circumstances of his life, the conversations he shared with others, and the society in which he lived. Plotinus positioned his own proposals within the framework of ancient and contemporary philosophical discussion. He professed his allegiance to Plato and displayed a detailed knowledge of Aristotle. But it can be shown that, while earlier philosophers provided his tools, the philosophical problems he addressed primarily related to urgent contemporary concerns, to other attractive proposals of his own time, and to particular features of his personal and social situation. His teaching methods reflect his interest in immediate questions. He gave priority to the questions people asked him, not only in his classes but also in his writing.

Of course, like studies of Plotinus's philosophy, my approach also highlights some features of Plotinus's writing at the expense of others. But since Plotinus has most frequently been interpreted within a philosophical perspective, examining his philosophical ideas in his historical setting may both reveal some new insights into his ideas and begin to indicate their continuing attractiveness and usefulness.[8]

Like Plotinus's society, but in vastly different forms, American society at the beginning of the twenty-first century is focused on bodies. Whether we are entertained by images of the people considered beautiful by media culture, preoccupied by diet and fitness, or required to choose medical plans and procedures for managing our bodies' vicissitudes from birth to death, our attention is riveted on bodies. Moreover, from the morning newspaper to the television entertainment absorbed by Americans an average of seven hours a day, sex and violence occupy center-stage of most Americans' preoccupations, fears, and amusements. The same was true in Plotinus's day though in very different cultural forms. His philosophy should be read, I believe, in part, as a critique of his society's preoccupation with bodies.[9] The alternative he described may also offer a modification of our society's monomaniacal attention to bodies and give us more choices for self-construction than can be found in our cultural provisions.

Recent scholarship places the relationship of bodies to culture at the center of current interest in ancient societies. For example, Peter Brown's *The Body and Society* interprets the high value of virginity in relation to its cultural setting;[10] Michel Foucault's *The Care of the Self* and *The Use of Pleasure*[11] explore late antique practices of self-definition and self-cultivation. Pierre Hadot's *Philosophy as a Way of Life* approaches ancient philosophies as practical spiritual disciplines. Teresa Shaw's *The Burden of the Flesh* examines the role of fasting in the moralist and medical traditions inherited by early Christianity, and Judith Perkins's *The Suffering Self* argues that attention to physical pain funded and organized the Christian self and Church.[12] These are only a few of the authors who interpret late Roman literary descriptions of physical experience and attitudes toward it. It is largely to their work that I owe the possibility of placing Plotinus in a broader context than that of his philosophical lineage.

Plotinus's Opponents

Historians have often given the impression that Christianity's only rivals in the early centuries of the common era were arid state religions and abstract Hellenistic philosophies. This view does not take into account how thoroughly Roman religions were woven into urban cultural and social life.[13] The "murderous games" of the colosseum are only one arena in which the ancient gods were regularly recognized and honored.[14]

By the mid-third century, Christians were a visible social group. Was Plotinus aware of Christianity? Its rapidly increasingly prominence in Rome would have made it difficult to ignore. By 250 CE, Christians in Rome maintained a staff of 154 clergy, including 52 exorcists. More than 1,500 widows and poor people were said to be supported by the church.[15] New catacombs and churches were being built; by the end of the third century, there were 40 churches in Rome.

By 200 CE Rome could claim (though not without dissent), to be the senior bishopric in both East and West. By 260–9 CE Rome was organized into parishes under presbyters. Moreover, within the Christian community a new type of leader emerged: "Men accustomed to public life and skilled in the exercise of power emerged as Christian bishops."[16] These men stood at the vanguard of the formation of a professional clergy; "episcopal power for good or ill was formidable."[17] Although the ascetic tradition was deeply rooted by the mid-third century, celibacy was not yet a requirement for clergy.

In what social groups was Christianity most visible? According to W.H.C. Frend, Roman Christians formed "a mosaic of ethnic groups, mainly eastern Mediterraneans." And, since the Roman Christian community grew largely out of Judaism, mid-third-century apologetic writings, especially those of the Christian theologian Novatian, still show a preoccupation with Judaism.[18] Moreover, Christianity may have tended to attract young adherents. Peter Brown suggests that Christian preoccupation with virginity as a way to manage sexuality indicates that "Christianity had become a religion for the young."[19] Frend includes ladies of high social standing and civil servants among social groups in which Christianity was prominent in the mid-third century.[20] Although Christianity made the most progress among the urban middle class, Christians comprised no more than an estimated 4–5 percent of total population of empire in 250 CE.[21] In spite of this, the "Christian Church in Rome [was] a body larger than any other voluntary group in the city."[22]

If Plotinus did not notice Christians because of their church buildings and catacombs, they might have come to his attention through the controversies that preoccupied them. In the mid-third century, theological debates over the correct date of Easter and the Monarchian controversy initiated the trinitarian and christological arguments of the fourth century. Hippolytus and Novatian led a small but strong rigorist minority in Rome whose contentions were symbolized by honor for tombs of Peter and Paul.[23] It is noteworthy that Plotinus was able to ignore completely, at least in his writings, a learned group of Christian Platonists in Alexandria.

Because of Plotinus's bad eyesight, he may not have read what was, by his time, a considerable body of Christian literature. There were letters, apologetic tracts against pagans and Jews, commentaries on scripture, sermons, homilies, exhortations, Christian romances, like the Apocryphal Acts of the Apostles, and the ubiquitous *actae* of the Christian martyrs. The revolutionary side of Christian literature was not translated into practice in the third century. Concerned with holding their own in the face of spasmodic but persistent persecution, and with building Christian communities in the variety of ways I have mentioned, the great majority of Christians conformed to society. For example, they accepted slavery and held mixed views on the issue of war.[24]

If he did not notice Christians for their buildings or their controversies, Plotinus might have noticed them for another reason. He lived in Rome during the Decian persecution, the first empire-wide persecution of Christians. The Bishop of Rome was executed on January 20, 250 CE, and church leaders in other major cities, like Cyprian in Carthage, met a similar fate. The shock of a persecution on this scale was enormous: "The Christian Church practically collapsed."[25] The years during which the Decian persecution occurred (248–60 CE) were a "watershed in the church's fortunes."[26]

Printed debates by which rival positions become clear to onlookers were not a part of Plotinus's culture. Thus, he did not differentiate Gnostics from Christians who were rapidly becoming identified as orthodox. He was concerned only to identify beliefs he found deeply antagonistic to Platonism. In the fourth century, Platonism became the rival worldview against which the Christian doctrines of the trinity and christology were argued. In the third century, however, neither Platonists nor Christians fully understood their incompatibilities. Plotinus's student Porphyry would later undertake to respond polemically to what had become the mainstream Christian consensus. In responding polemically to Gnostics, however, Plotinus resisted a worldview he might have heard from a number of ancient sources. Gnostics, Christians, and Platonists appeared to their third-century contemporaries much closer to one another than they do to historians who, with the advantage of hindsight, place them in clearly defined categories.

Plotinus did not consider Roman religions incompatible with his philosophic ideas. He seems simply to have lost interest in the Roman gods. Yet Roman religions did not lack vigor. Mithras was introduced to the Latin West only in the late first century CE, and other Roman religions were still developing in the third century. Cults did not demand their members' sole adherence, and they performed rites without requiring the profession of creeds or doctrines. Robin Lane Fox categorizes Romans' eclectic and syncretistic approach to religion as "religious overinsurance."[27] Romans expressed a great deal of agnosticism, but not much atheism in relation to their gods. Moreover, they had no concept of heresy; *hairesis* meant a school of thought, not false doctrine.[28] It was Christians who gave the motley crew of Roman religions an identity as *pagani*, a colloquial term meaning civilian or rustic.[29]

Emperor worship, the formally established Roman religion had, by the 260s struck a new note. A coin of the time shows Gallienus's investiture by a god, reflecting a new popular trust in emperor's agency based on recent military victories and the "moral and religious tone of their edicts." In 247 CE the "last great festivals of pagan Rome unchallenged by Christianity" were celebrated, the millennial celebrations of Rome's thousandth anniversary which went on for three days and nights.[30]

Plotinus's philosophical rivals in mid-third-century Rome were Hellenistic philosophies. Like Platonism, Stoicism, Skepticism, and Epicureanism, the major philosophies of the imperial age, offered perspective on the pretensions of society and the state. The philosophic piety they advocated coexisted comfortably with established worship.[31] Plotinus seems to have adopted a rather casual attitude toward established Roman religions. He once shocked his students by declining to visit the temples on the occasion of a feast, responding to their invitation by saying, "They ought to come to me, not I to them" (*Life* 10).

Astrology, magic, and numerology all had a firm grip on Roman imagination and practice. Moreover, religion and magic are not easy to differentiate. Magic, the attempt to assert influence for one's own benefit or a rival's harm, can operate within religion or it can take the place of religion. Magic was a recognized feature of third-century religions, woven seamlessly into beliefs and practices. On several occasions Plotinus exhibited his ability to resist and redirect hostile magic. Such demonstrations assured his students and disciples of his authority and power. Both Plotinus and, a century later, Augustine, found it necessary to explain (Plotinus) or refute (Augustine) these beliefs and practices.

Plotinus as Religious Teacher

But there is also another cultural context in which Plotinus taught and wrote. He should be seen not only as a philosopher, but also as a religious teacher, in that he sought orientation to the everyday world of chance events, relationships, and physical need. Arthur Darby Nock and E.R. Dodds have pointed to the continuity between philosophies and religions in the early centuries CE. Similarly, Martha Nussbaum has shown that Hellenistic philosophy was profoundly concerned to provide teaching that oriented, comforted, and challenged people. Both

philosophical schools and religious movements, among them Christianity and various forms of Christian and Jewish Gnosticism, emerged
from esoteric sects to become popular proposals for how to live and
die. Each begins with metaphysical orientation but moves quickly to
practical implications of the advocated worldview. In the first centuries of the common era, the difference between philosophies and religions did not focus on whether the devotee maintains an "objective"
intellectual orientation to a "real" (that is, secular), world or whether
she resorts to "special pleading" for a deity's particular attention and
protection.[32] Both the philosophies and religions of late Roman antiquity sought to provide rational and spiritual orientation to the exigen-
cies of bodied life.

Like their Hellenistic predecessors, the philosophers and religious
leaders of the later Roman empire accepted the challenge of providing
conceptual orientation to the precarious condition of bodied being.
Nussbaum's description of the philosophical schools that flourished
in Rome in the early centuries CE is vivid and compelling:

> The Hellenistic philosophical schools of Greece and Rome – Epicure-
> ans, Skeptics, and Stoics – all conceived of philosophy as a way of ad-
> dressing the most painful problems of human life. They saw the
> philosopher as a compassionate physician whose arts could heal many
> pervasive types of human suffering. They practiced philosophy not as a
> detached intellectual technique dedicated to the display of cleverness
> but as an immersed and worldly art of grappling with human misery.
> They focused their attention, in consequence, on issues of daily and
> urgent human significance – the fear of death, love and sexuality, anger
> and aggression – issues that are sometimes avoided as embarrassingly
> messy and personal by the more detached varieties of philosophy. They
> confronted these issues as they arose in ordinary human lives, with a
> keen attention to the vicissitudes of those lives, and to what would be
> necessary and sufficient to make them better.[33]

Nussbaum argues that Hellenistic philosophies based their therapy for
the soul on medical healing, addressing the individual as a patient,
taking seriously the patient's emotions and fears, as well as her self-
evaluation and her hopes for health and wholeness. Hellenistic philosophers' "central motivation for philosophizing is the urgency of
human suffering, and . . . the goal of philosophy is human flourishing
or *eudaimonia*."[34]

Pierre Hadot has also shown that ancient philosophy was not only
concerned with the set problems discussed in the schools and useful

for training minds; it was also practiced as a way of life.[35] This may be difficult for us to recognize because, from the early modern period in the West to our time, religion and philosophy give an impression of separateness due to their different institutional and social locations. Philosophy is primarily practiced in universities, while people participate in religious communities in synagogues, churches, mosques, and temples. Both, however, continue to offer orientation in a universe that threatens to dwarf human projects, to thwart human longings, and to ignore human suffering. Both ask: How should we live? Both endeavor to define ethical action in a bewildering and complex world. Both engage their participants at the level of belief, whether belief in a rational process or belief in gods (or a God) who orders and sustains the universe. Both philosophers and religious people wager (in Pascal's term) their precious, short, pressured, and dazzling human lives on a conceptual picture of "reality." Even in our own time, and certainly in antiquity, religion cannot accurately be described as limited to "prayers and wishes"; nor is philosophy accurately defined as rational process, unaffected by longing and emotion, by prejudices both personal and social, and by social location.

In Plotinus's time, two centuries after the heyday of the Hellenistic schools Nussbaum wrote about, the perennial issues of human life had not changed, but approaches to them had. Instead of conceiving the soul's healing on a medical model, an essentially religious model prevailed. The goal of philosophy is now salvation, a stronger form of healing addressed primarily to the soul.[36] Instead of conceiving psychic health on a physical model as a balance of humors in the body, religious thought of the mid-third century tended to regard body as problem, tool, or condition of the soul's salvation.[37] Plotinus shared this focus on soul, defining his own position in relation to the proposals of his contemporaries.

Plotinus should be read in part as a religious teacher and also, in modern terms, as something like a psychotherapist, that is, as someone interested in integrating a metaphysical/cosmological worldview with practices of everyday life. He advocated the therapeutic, ultimately salvific, effects of an adequate comprehension of the source and goal of one's life, an orientation to the universe that is simultaneously personal and intimately shared with other living beings. He also defined a practice designed to weave this orientation to the universe into experience.

In this project of transformative philosophy, Plotinus's opponents were not primarily other philosophers, either those of his own time or of philosophical traditions. Although he was familiar with other philosophers' arguments and he often considered them as he formulated his own positions, he never wrote a treatise addressed to refuting them. His explicit opponents, rather, were people who advanced religious claims, namely Gnostic teachers whom he seems to have thought of simply as Christians.[38] Four lengthy treatises of his middle period consider Gnostics' ethical, religious, and philosophical claims, ultimately rejecting these proposals with as much acrimony as Plotinus ever permitted himself. In addressing Gnostic teachings, scorn and sarcasm occasionally sharpened his usually gentle argument. Using vivid metaphors, he sought to undermine Gnostic claims to esoteric knowledge of the universe and how best to live in it. Without naming the names of particular teachers, Plotinus deconstructed Gnostics' values, rhetoric, and credibility, building his own by contrast.

Plotinus's place on a continuum from Christian emphasis on body's centrality to Gnostics' understanding of body as unredeemable must be carefully located. His philosophy addresses the question of the role and significance of body but it insists that body is not, as Tertullian had called it, "the pivot of salvation," either by its rejection (Gnostic) or by its redemption (Christian).[39] In chapter 4 I examine what it was about Gnostic teachings that Plotinus found so uniquely irritating and, therefore, why the only polemical treatises of his entire corpus are addressed to Gnostics. Minimally, his rivalry with them reveals the similarity of their religious tasks and goals.

Plotinus in Third-century Roman Culture and Society

Like several earlier Hellenistic philosophers who wrote in Greek, the social and political context in which Plotinus's teachings were discussed was not primarily Greek, but Roman. It is, then, to Roman philosophical and religious preoccupations in the mid-third century that we must look if we are to identify Plotinus's interests and interpret his project. What were the most salient and relevant elements of the cultural conversation within which he spoke? Ultimately, answers to this question will lead me far from the gentlemanly conversations of rival philosophers, but let me begin with those conversations.

What was the pressing question or problem engaged by *all* the speakers? Porphyry put it quite directly in a question to Plotinus during one of the class sessions of the school: "Once I, Porphyry, went on questioning him for three days about the soul's connection with the body, and he kept on explaining to me" (*Life* 13). Plotinus recognized the importance of Porphyry's question and persisted in dealing with it, even though others were annoyed.

> A man called Thaumasius came in who was interested in general state-ments and said that he wanted to hear Plotinus speaking in the manner of a set treatise, but could not stand Porphyry's questions and answers. Plotinus said, "But if when Porphyry asks questions we do not solve his difficulties we shall not be able to say anything at all to put into the treatise." (*Life* 13)

Porphyry gives no further details of the development of this three-day-long inquiry. Perhaps the question was refined in the discussion. Per-haps its relevance to contemporary religious and philosophical issues and practices was specified. Plotinus's discussions of the relationship of body and soul in the *Enneads* offer the only available clues as to what was said in those three days. But the *Enneads* does not provide a reconstruction of the context of Plotinus's concerns about body and soul, for Plotinus, like so many other authors, declined to tell readers what was most evident and taken for granted. The hard work of his-torical reconstruction lies largely in identifying these assumed ques-tions, problems, and values. One must be alert to occasional hints and suggestions, such as Plotinus's evident preoccupation with Porphyry's question. Body was evidently "big" in mid-third-century discourse. How did this come to be?

Two volumes of Michel Foucault's *The History of Sexuality* – *The Use of Pleasure* and *The Care of the Self* – make the persuasive claim that, several centuries before Plotinus and among a certain class of educated and moderately wealthy men, carefully designed "practices of the self" were used to create a consciously chosen, intentionally developed, counter-cultural "self." These practices ranged from di-etary regulations to the strict governance of sexual pleasure. They rep-resented, Foucault writes, a deliberate "attempt to transform oneself into the ethical subject of one's behavior."[40] Practices addressed to the body were identified as the best method for creating and cultivating a carefully designed self.[41]

The "practices of the self" undertaken by some late Roman men included not only disciplines of diet and periodic sexual abstinence, but also assumed a "combative attitude toward the pleasures" in gen-eral.[42] As Geoffrey Harpham has demonstrated in *The Ascetic Impera-*

tive, pleasures were not to be eliminated but neither should they be thought of simply as relaxation and relief. Instead, pleasures were understood to provide an invaluable occasion for practicing the self-control that strengthened and energized the conscious and rational self.[43] *Aphrodisia* are a force that "could not be used in the moderate way that was fitting unless one was capable of opposing, resisting, and subduing them."[44]

To this end, all pleasurable, or potentially pleasurable, features of life – food, marriage, erotic and sexual attractions, economics, and social relationships – were scrutinized and shaped according to principles of moderation and self-control. In the process, pleasure was redefined. No longer the unthinking, socialized pleasures of "eating, drinking, and making merry," pleasure was understood as the satisfaction inherent in a chosen style of living and acting.[45] The stronger and more accessible the pleasure, the more opportunity it offered for deliberate self-construction. The attention of these "self-masters" was directed to the body as the privileged site for establishing and performing the self.

Practices and attitudes relating to and affecting the body were also given a central role in the early centuries CE in nascent Christianity. However, these should not be confused with the forms of body-management Foucault discussed. In the earliest Christian movements, the prominence of bodies was at least partly dictated by the ever-present threat and frequent occurrence of persecution, torture, and martyrdom.[46] Oddly, far from discouraging converts to Christianity, the threat of martyrdom seems actually to have attracted converts. The North African Christian Tertullian gave a forceful description of the effectiveness of suffering for generating imitation. Anticipating Foucault's axiom that coercion always generates resistance, Tertullian addressed the Roman state:

> But nothing whatsoever is accomplished by your cruelties, each more exquisite than the last. It is the bait that wins people to our school. We multiply whenever we are mown down by you; the blood of Christians is seed . . . That very obstinacy with which you taunt us is your teacher. For who that beholds it is not stirred to inquire, what lies within it? Who, on inquiry, does not join us, and joining us does not wish to suffer, that he may purchase for himself the whole grace of God? [47]

Alongside the attention to bodies brought about by persecution and martyrdom, another focus on bodies grew as Christianity itself expanded numerically and spread geographically, namely, the ascetic movement. Christian asceticism in Plotinus's time was, as yet, embryonic and informal. A half-century later, after Constantine's 312 CE Edict of Toleration, the ascetic movement would replace state persecution with the "daily martyrdom" of ascetic practice. In Christian asceticism, as in philosophical asceticism, the pleasures of everyday life were deliberately scrutinized and reconstituted, and the unexamined pleasures of everyday life became "the pleasure of no pleasure."[48] Skeptical as contemporary North Americans may be of the pleasures of asceticism, there is evidence that "the pleasure of no pleasure" worked powerfully in Roman culture.[49] By the late fourth century, hordes of ascetics flocked to the Egyptian desert to grapple alone with the demons of lust, anger, and boredom, while other ascetics lived in community, committed to virginity, unquestioning obedience to a leader, and poverty. In Plotinus's time, the ascetic movement was on its way to becoming a strong force in the Christian movement.

Christian asceticism, though differently articulated in practices, differently reasoned theoretically, and differently socially located, had common features with Roman philosophical "care of the self." Both identified one's own body as the site upon which identity can be constructed. But the argument for the centrality of body to the practice of Christianity has recently been taken further. Judith Perkins's book, *The Suffering Self: Pain and Narrative Representation in the Early Christian Era*, argues persuasively that it was not simply the body, but more particularly, the *suffering* body that became the foundation of the Christian self and the Christian Church.[50] Perkins shows that early Christian narrative representations consistently point to suffering as a uniquely resonant occasion for the construction of self and community.

Incitement to imitation was the explicit purpose of these narratives, whether martyrdom *actae* or hagiography. The circulation of such literature in liturgical and devotional contexts made it widely accessible and its effects can be documented: martyrs-to-be quote earlier martyrdom accounts and ascetics report that they were inspired by reading or hearing of other ascetics. As late as the end of the fourth century, Augustine described his conversion to celibate monasticism as inspired by hearing and reading with great excitement accounts of others who had made this choice. Vivid representations not only inspired contemporaries to imitation, they also help the modern historian to identify, for particular times and locations, the aspects of human experience most likely to be the spots at which alternatives to socialization were fashioned.

Foucault's and Perkins's descriptions of self-making at different times and among different classes in Roman society state the case for the power and effectiveness of *social* definitions of meaning, circulated by example, by word-of-mouth, and, perhaps most importantly, by narrative representation. The superior capability of the "suffering-self" model over the "self-mastery" model to multiply converts and to create the Christian Church is due at least in part to the perennial and democratic accessibility of pain and suffering. By contrast, the conditions necessary for self-mastery were rare and relatively inaccessible to large numbers of people in Roman – or in any other – society. In both cases, individuals were addressed, but the energy and commitment for defining the *project* and for identifying the location and the tools were provided by communal consensus. Both elite Roman men and later, Christians of all classes created counter-cultures that understood body as the locus and focus of practices that generated, sustained, and empowered the self.

Where do Gnostics belong in third-century conversation about the body's significance? Although they are usually seen as the most extreme and explicit voices denying that body has any role in identity and salvation, the more amply documented Gnostics of late antiquity call this assumption into question. Were "Gnostic feelings and beliefs about the world . . . in fundamental conflict with that conviction of the essential goodness of the cosmos and the rational necessity for its existence that was most basic in most Hellenistic philosophy"?[51]

If doctrinal statements were the only evidence, this conclusion would be inevitable. But if the *effects* of Gnostic teachings are taken into account the picture changes, and the vehemence of Gnostic rejection of body can be read as "strategic overstatement."[52] For example, the poignant hymns that express Gnostics' vivid sympathy for the suffering and struggle of all living beings, and their richly articulated longing for humanity's perfection and completion reveal a different, and in some ways contradictory, picture of Gnostic values.[53] In this context it is apparent that the Gnostics' flagrantly dualistic beliefs resulted, at least in some Gnostic groups, in the most intellectually profound, deeply felt, and tenderly expressed compassion for living beings to be found in the literature of the early centuries of the common era.

In short, far from representing defined locations from body-aversive to body-affirming on a pre-set scale, the philosophies and religions of the early centuries CE each sought to articulate an understanding of body and soul that produced a "sharp quick sense of life."[54] And all – Christians, Gnostics, and Platonists – succeeded, appealing to different audiences. Like Epicureans, Gnostics were misunderstood in their own time, and modern intellectual historians simply adopt the attitudes of their ancient opponents when they attend only to Gnostic rhetoric, ignoring its effects.[55]

Bodies in Plotinus's Society

Intellectual historians describe a rich and complex cultural discourse about body in late antiquity. Social historians reconstruct another highly important form of social attention to bodies, popular Roman entertainment. The Roman empire was a warrior state that routinely socialized its population to enjoy the cruelties of battle by creating, at enormous expense, spectacles of violence. Sociologist Keith Hopkins remarks that "bloodshed and slaughter joined military glory and conquest as central elements in Roman culture."[56]

Military values are revealed in Pliny's remark that gladiatorial shows "inspired a glory in wounds and a contempt of death, since the love of praise and the desire for victory could be seen, even in the bodies of slaves and criminals."[57] The gladiatorial combats of the colosseum taught the whole population, not only professional soldiers, to support Roman military aggression. This was accomplished by the systematic desensitization created by witnessing one killing after another until any feeling of empathy for those wounded and killed was overwhelmed by identification with the strength and skill of the victors. In this sense, "public killings were a Roman rite."[58]

After witnessing a day-long blood-bath in the colosseum, one thoughtful Roman, the Stoic philosopher Seneca, remarked that he went away feeling "more callous and less human."[59] At the end of the fourth century, Augustine vividly described a friend's addiction to these events: Alypius was determined to deny himself the excitement of the bloody spectacles, but after being dragged to the amphitheater by his friends, he could not keep his eyes closed when he heard the crowd roar at the sight of a killing.[60] The Roman historian Tacitus noted that "children seem to absorb" a passion for public spectacles "almost in the mother's womb."[61] The scale and popularity of these "murderous games" should not be underestimated. They were attended by emperors and senators, shopkeepers, philosophers like Seneca, and women and children. The enormous size of the amphitheaters in which they were held attests their popularity;

the colosseum in Rome seated 50,000.[62] Since the expense of collecting the animals and gladiators who fought in these shows was prohibitive, they were relatively infrequent "special events." An official calendar from the fourth century lists ten gladiatorial shows each year, the most spectacular of which were given by emperors as part of their campaigns for public support.

> At the dedication of the Colosseum in AD 80, Titus gave games that lasted 100 days and included the slaughter of 5,000 or 9,000 animals in a single day . . . plus individual and mass gladiatorial fights and pitched battles, including a naval battle on an artificially flooded site. One day's fighting alone involved 3,000 men . . . Trajan, to celebrate his conquest of Dacia, gave games in 108–9 lasting 123 days, in which some 11,000 animals wild and tame were killed and ten thousand gladiators fought.[63]

The financial resources of the empire were regularly drained to provide these spectacles, and so were its resources of bodies, human and animal. Condemned criminals were purchased from other towns and cities for grisly public execution in the amphitheaters of the empire; potential gladiators from every walk of life were seized for training; there were even occasions on which slaves and bystanders were forced to fight. "One day, when there was a shortage of condemned criminals, Caligula commanded that a section of the crowd should be seized and thrown to the wild beasts instead."[64] Although nobles and even emperors occasionally acted as participants in the gladiatorial contests, almost all who fought were from the lowest sector of the steeply stratified Roman population. Tacitus remarked casually that those who were destroyed in the spectacles of the Roman colosseum were "worthless."[65]

The bodies of people and animals were vividly in view in Roman entertainment culture. As we have seen, body was also, for different reasons, the subject of philosophical and religious attention. Gnostics may have represented the most extreme philosophical alternative to Christian affirmations of body, but Roman popular entertainment that regularly presented bodies as spectacle – naked, torn, and bleeding – framed philosophical and religious discussion of the meaning and value of body.[66] Social practices and religious and intellectual discourse surrounding human bodies were in sharp and evident conflict within third-century Roman society. In the context of wildly conflicting evaluations of body's meaning and worth, Plotinus articulated an appraisal of body that steered between both exaggerating and undervaluing body.

Plotinus on the Care of the Self

The notion of self-identity as intentionally created and cultivated was already apparent in Greek philosophical discourse five centuries before the common era. By the third century of the common era it had crossed class lines and traversed vast geographical distances from Greece to Rome, Alexandria, and North Africa.[67] As we have seen, Plotinus addressed the question of the relation of body and soul in a cultural world in which regard for body was defined by two extremes, body as spectacle, and body as the privileged "spot" on which to create self-identity.

Plotinus embraced the project of self-creation and cultivation as essential to human flourishing and central to the philosophic quest. The human self, however, far from being an end in itself, could only be understood accurately when its intimate consanguinity with the universe was deeply interiorized.

> What is really worth aspiring to is our selves, bringing themselves back for themselves to the best of themselves; this is the well-proportioned and beautiful, and the form which is not part of the composite and the clear, intelligent, beautiful life. (6.7.30)

The goal of Plotinus's metaphysics was practical: he sought to define a place for human beings within a universe whose rich pulsating variety might easily overwhelm and erase them. He incited his hearers and readers to focus and strengthen a consciously chosen and intentionally developed and exercised self. A lengthy passage is worth quoting in this regard:

> How then can you see the sort of beauty a good soul has? Go back into yourself and look; and if you do not yet see yourself beautiful, then, just as someone making a statue which has to be beautiful cuts away here and polishes there and makes one part smooth and clears another till he has given his statue a beautiful face, so you too must cut away excess and straighten the crooked and clear the dark and make it bright and never stop working on your statue till the divine glory of virtue shines out on you, till you see self mastery enthroned upon its holy seat. If you have become this, and see it, and are at home with yourself in purity, with nothing hindering you from becoming in this way one, with no inward mixture of anything else, but wholly yourself, nothing but true light, not measured by dimensions, or bounded by shape into littleness,

or expanded to size by unboundedness, but everywhere unmeasured, because greater than all measure and superior to all quantity; when you see that you have become this, then you have become sight; you can trust yourself then; you have already ascended and need no one to show you; concentrate your gaze and see. This alone is the eye that sees the great beauty . . . For one must come to the sight with a seeing power made akin and like to what is seen. No eye ever saw the sun without becoming sun-like, nor can a soul see beauty without becoming beautiful. You must first become all god-like and all beautiful if you intend to see God and beauty. (1.6.9)

Clearly, Plotinus accepted the philosophical project of consciously constructed selfhood, but it is evident in this passage that he also criticized the methods he heard proposed. He objected to a consensus that body was an adequate and appropriate basis for self-construction. Instead of working one's body in order to create an intentional self, he proposed a different location for the construction of selfhood and a different method. *Soul*, he said, is the trustworthy basis of identity; thus, soul should be cultivated directly. As an alternative to asceticism he developed a method, which he described in some detail, for contemplative practice.

Was Plotinus's proposal simply a return to a traditional "Greco-Roman image of the soul/mind controlling the body"?[68] I think not, for his suggestions occurred in quite another cultural and religious context than did Plato's or Aristotle's. Plotinus's much-remarked intellectual "disdain" or over-looking (literally: "looking over") of the body addressed the problems he saw in contemporary philosophical, religious, and social forms of attention to body. His philosophy, effectively if not explicitly, provided an alternative to Christian doctrinal affirmation of body, to Gnostic allegations that body is the evil creation of an evil demiurge, and to the spectacles of the colosseum. He countered exploitation and vilification of body as well as what he considered unrealistic philosophical and religious claims for body as site and symbol of the self.

In fact, however, Plotinus was not primarily interested in body. He was interested in life, and he talked a great deal about body because body bears a peculiarly intimate relation to life. A century after Plotinus, Augustine described this relation. One cannot see life, Augustine said, but seeing the movements of bodies we infer life. Bodies and their movements constitute the best immediate evidence available to us for the presence of life. Therefore we tend to identify life with an animated body. Both Plotinus and Augustine said, however, that life should not be identified with body, just because it is body that makes life visible and vivid.

The tendency to identify life with body has increased in the centuries between Plotinus's time and our own. Contemporary conflations of life and body create predictable difficulties for reading ancient texts. Before Descartes, body – without the animating presence of soul – was thought to consist of nothing but the corpse that is buried at death. After Descartes, body is conceptualized as having a life of its own that includes involuntary processes (like digestion) as well as affective faculties. Because we tend to conflate "life" with physical and affective activity, we find it difficult to grasp Plotinus's understanding of life as a spiritual entity identified with soul but permeating and animating body. According to Plotinus, at body's demise life departs, ready to form and inform other bodies or, ultimately, to retire to union with the universe.

Plotinus's contemporary, Origen, also thought that life goes on when body can no longer contain it. Christians like Origen believed that life is strong enough to repossess body on the day of resurrection. Though both Plotinus and Origen felt the need to define body carefully because of the common careless identification of body with life, what interested them was not body, but life. God "takes away from us the irrationality and deadness," Origen said.[69] And Plotinus wrote, "Nothing of real being is ever cancelled" (4.3.5). In chapter 3 I describe his argument for the indestructibility of life in spite of its close association with the biodegradable body.

Plotinus's interpreters agree that he thought of philosophy as salvific. But they often emphasize his occasional disparagement of body without attention to textual context. In doing so, they ignore his insistence that identification with soul is the most effective and trustworthy way to see the startling beauty of bodies and of the natural and social worlds.

Yet, far from allowing his attention to soul to make him a resolute ascetic, Plotinus explicitly rejected this relation to the world. According to Porphyry, Plotinus lived thoughtfully and responsibly, but he pointedly eschewed both ascetic and ritual practices. Instead, he practiced and advocated contemplation. For him, contemplation was a natural activity, participated in by all living beings, and he thought of contemplation as consummately practical, producing real effects in a specific quality of attentiveness to people and objects. For all his alleged "transcendence" of body, Plotinus's philosophy was commonsensical and empirical. In his *Life* of Plotinus, Porphyry admitted that, in a bad moment, he had considered suicide. On hearing of this, Plotinus chided Porphyry briefly for his irrationality, but his advice was simple and practical; he urged Porphyry to take a vacation. Porphyry did, and his "longing for death" evaporated.[70]

The chapters that follow take up the primary themes of Plotinus's alternative to his contemporaries' various preoccupations with body. He did not simply deny the value of his opponents' suggestions; rather, he constructed a cosmology, worldview, and psychology that articulated and supported his advocacy of contemplation as self-making – and more directly so – than philosophical or Christian asceticism, or Gnostic rejection of body. Chapter 2 begins where Plotinus began his authorship, that is, with *Ennead* 1.6, "On Beauty," in which he discussed the role of sensible beauty in alerting people to the Great Beauty that forms and fills the sensible world. I then explore Plotinus's idea of soul, examining its pivotal role as the hinge that connects intelligible and sensible (chapter 3). Next I discuss Plotinus's idea of body and matter, which can be accurately understood only in relation to his idea of soul (chapter 4). Plotinus's answer to the perennially poignant question: Does the universe care for humans – for *me*? – is the topic of chapter 5. What is providence for Plotinus? The answer he gives is, I believe, important to consider, for it offers a simultaneously realistic, experientially resonant, and generous picture of the way the universe works. The penultimate chapter concerns Plotinus's description of contemplation and the suggestions he makes for a method of contemplation (chapter 6). The concluding chapter focuses on the practical usefulness of Plotinus's philosophy for people who live and think at the beginning of the twenty-first century (chapter 7).

Plotinus as Writer

Plotinus was a self-conscious writer. Writing was difficult for him and he analyzed why this was so. He did not suffer from writing blocks, nor did he find it hard to organize his thoughts. But he was profoundly uncomfortable with his tools. Language seemed to him a crude tool for communication. He commented on the problems inherent in language from time to time throughout his writings, repeatedly urging his readers to take these problems seriously. Before discussing his teaching, we need to consider his instructions on reading.

Perhaps Plotinus was originally sensitized to the limitations of writing by Plato's well-known objections to the written word:

That's the strange thing about writing, which makes it truly analogous to painting. The painter's products stand before us as though they were alive, but if you question them, they maintain a most majestic silence. It is the same with written words; they seem to talk to you as though they were intelligent, but if you ask them anything about what they say, from a desire to be instructed, they go on telling you just the same thing forever. And once a thing is put in writing, the composition, whatever it may be, drifts all over the place, getting into the hands not only of those who understand it, but equally of those who have no business with it; it doesn't know how to address the right people, and not address the wrong. And when it is ill-treated and unfairly abused it always needs its parent to come to its help, being unable to defend or help itself.[71]

Plotinus's objections to writing, however, are somewhat different and more fundamental than Plato's concern about misinterpretation. Plotinus doubts the adequacy of words to communicate meaning. One of his most frequently used words is *hoion* (so to speak), and he advises his readers that when, for example, he speaks of the Good, *hoion* should always be understood, whether or not he says so explicitly: "But one must go along with the words, if one in speaking of that Good uses of necessity, to indicate it, expressions which we do not, strictly speaking, allow to be used; but one should understand 'as if' (*hoion*) with each of them" (6.8.13). Frail and rough as they are, words must nevertheless be used.

Moreover, the philosopher's responsibility to inspire his reader sometimes outweighs the value of speaking as accurately and precisely as possible: "But now we must depart a little from correct thinking in our discourse for the sake of persuasion" (6.8.13). At the end of a lengthy discussion on the One's generative power, Plotinus again reminds the reader that his discussion, full of metaphors and images, is less than adequate to the subject: "For this is how one has to speak of him since one is unable to speak as one should" (6.8.18).

Naming misleads, and Plotinus also feared the power of metaphor to direct and, quite possibly, to distract and to distort interpretation. Nevertheless, his writing abundantly demonstrates that he incorporated Plato's method, "I strain after images" (*Republic* 488a), and that Plotinus was himself master of the apposite metaphor.[72] "This has been mentioned for the sake of something else," he nervously reminds his reader in one passage. He was keenly aware of the limits of analogy. Strictly speaking, he says, "analogies from elsewhere should not be used in speaking of the intelligible world" (4.4.5).

Simple declarative language worried him no less than names, images, metaphors, and analogies. "Abandon the verbal signification and grasp the meaning," he advised as he attempted a description of his concept of the "All" (6.4.2). "One must not stop at the word," he urged in another passage, "but understand what the one who says it has in mind" (6.8.9). In other words, the reader must perform the considerable feat of reading what the author *means*, not what he says.

But even the distorting potential of language is not as serious a handicap as is the notorious difficulty and fragility of the very most important knowledge. Immediately after his only description of an experience of contemplative unity with the divine, Plotinus hastens to say that teaching cannot produce experiential knowledge. Always an optimist, he nevertheless sees benefit for the active reader in the apparent disadvantage. Using Heraclitus as a example, Plotinus says, "He has left us guessing, since he has neglected to make clear to us what he is saying, *perhaps because we ought to seek by ourselves*, as he himself sought and found" (4.8.1). Knowledge is not a matter of grasping concepts, but of a cultivated ability to relate concepts to our world, to be able, eventually, to stand at the window looking out and to see the rational principles of the intelligible pulsating in the sensible.

Plotinus wrote reluctantly, feeling Plato's strong sense of the risk of misunderstanding and misrepresentation endemic to any written communication. He would not, then, have been completely surprised by many twentieth-century authors' identification of "Neoplatonism" as the source of many problems they associate with Christian philosophy and theology. Late twentieth-century theological villains like "dualism" and "hierarchy," hatred of body and the natural world, and, more generally, a predilection for abstraction and for neglect of pressing social problems: all are confidently, and with varying degrees of legitimacy, placed at the gate of "Neoplatonism."

Twentieth-century misapprehensions of Plotinus and his followers demonstrate the importance of reading a philosopher *historically*. A committed effort to learn from the intellectual, institutional, and social context, and from what we can find about the particular conditions of her/his life will reveal a great deal about why that philosopher chose those particular topics and why she or he treated them as she or he did. Intent on communicating insights they have been led or forced to by the circumstances of their life, by their reading and thinking and by their conversations, authors usually omit mention of the circumstances that motivate their authorship. They usually do not omit this information through purposive concealment. Like other human beings (and often more so), philosophers are intimately and pressingly aware that their lives are short, and that if they are to communicate what they consider important for others to know, they must get straight to the point. Yes, but if their readers are to evaluate the usefulness, for our own lives, of the philosopher's insights, this means minimally that we must not only understand texts, but that we must also be very competent and attentive social and cultural, medical and institutional historians.

Authorship, for Plotinus, entailed moral commitments. Distinguishing his own commitments from those of his rivals, he wrote with unaccustomed immodesty:

> The kind of philosophy which we pursue, besides all its other excellences, displays simplicity, straightforwardness of character along with clear thinking, and aims at dignity, not rash arrogance, and combines its confident boldness with reason and much safeguarding and caution and a great deal of circumspection: you are to use philosophy of this kind as a standard of comparison for the rest. (2.9.14)

By contrast, Plotinus accused his opponents of overlooking their own inconsistencies while inventing "a new jargon to recommend their own school" (2.9.5). I will discuss elsewhere his other objections to what he takes to be self-serving and crowd-pleasing strategies.

Several fundamental procedures define Plotinus's philosophical method. First, he tells his readers, he will necessarily distinguish in thought what is "together" in experience and in actuality (4.3.9). He says this in order to caution against naive readings of philosophy that interpret analytical distinctions as, in some mysterious way, creating separations in fact. He should, no doubt, have emphasized this point more, for the resentments and objections brought against "Neoplatonism" in the twentieth century testify to precisely this form of misunderstanding.

For example, although Plotinus analytically distinguishes body and soul, in actuality body is not separated from soul until it decomposes in the grave. In fact, the intimate integrity of body and soul is the most fundamental "fact of life": body is formed by the soul's prerogative – life, and soul is body's life (4.5.7). The philosopher's task, however, is to *articulate* the unity of the whole, to "divide in such a way" that the hearer can grasp how the parts contribute to and fit in the whole (6.4.4). For a uni-verse is not composed of various entities swirling in chaos, but of distinct powers and entities in relation to others. The philosopher's distinctions do not affect the universe; they simply attempt to highlight its internal connections. Plotinus is clearer than most philosophers in insisting that distinctions are not to be thought of as separations.

Distinct but not separate

The second procedure Plotinus habitually employed in philosophizing was to examine the assumptions on which propositions are
grounded. He said, for example, that the primary evidence for the
existence of intellect is the rich variety of sense objects. The beauty we
see requires the real (permanent) existence of an informing beauty;
beauty must exist if the phenomena of the world are beautiful.[73] In
intellect, the same beauties exist without the transience and vulnerability of their sensible offspring.

Turning over propositions to uncover the assumptions beneath them
served Plotinus well in polemic and also in his positive philosophy.
Referring to Gnostics' rhetorical disdain for the sensible, he writes,
"But one should notice that they would not give themselves airs if they
despised something ugly; they do so because they despise something
which they begin by calling beautiful: and what sort of a way of managing is that?" (2.9.17).

Third, in several passages in which Plotinus has difficulty speaking
of the topic at hand, he suggests that it is possible to "come to some
idea" of the thing discussed by considering things opposed to it. If, for
example, one wants to understand the nature of the Good, one might
consider evil and, by means of the vivid contrast, get closer to an understanding of the Good.

Fourth, Plotinus found it useful, when exploring a metaphysical
or theological question, to "first inquire about ourselves" in relation to the question. For example, in *Ennead* 6.8.1 he wishes to
explore the gods' power, but first inquires, "as we usually do," what
happens to be in our power. Even before this, however, he asks what
is meant by the phrase "being in our power." His purpose is to clarify
and simplify the inquiry by focusing on what is at stake for human
beings.

Plotinus was continuously aware of the limits of philosophical
thought. Having explored at length and from several different perspectives the question, "What is this [being] which did not come to
existence?," he writes,

> We must go away in silence and inquire no longer, aware in our minds
> that there is no way out. For why should one even inquire when one has
> nothing to go on to, since every inquiry goes to a principle and stands
> still in it. (6.8.11)

Finally, he rejects metapositions: "there is no principle of the universal
principle" (6.8.11).

Notes on Style

I usually resist citing Greek words and phrases because they intimidate non-Greek-readers and distract from the momentum of arguments. I rely on the late A. Hilary Armstrong's translation of the *Enneads* for the Loeb Classical Library, modifying it occasionally as noted. I especially correct his tendency in some passages to emphasize the valuelessness of the sensible. For example, Armstrong sometimes translates as "*only* an image" what appears in Greek simply as "an image." Since Plotinus says repeatedly that an image is its original's most proximate and consanguineous kin, this apparently innocent addition substantially distorts Plotinus's meaning.

I have abandoned the academic custom of capitalizing the names of the hypostases that follow the One. The risk, that of confusion over whether it is individual soul or intellect that is referred to or whether it is the cosmic entity, seems to me worth taking in the interest of maintaining Plotinus's insistence that the cosmic and the individual are not separated, but are transparently intertwined. I also resist referring to the hypostases as "worlds" for the same reason. These usages carry distinctions to implied separation that distort Plotinus's meaning. The accuracy of Plotinus's fear of language is fully demonstrated in the frequent and widespread misrepresentation of his thought, but perhaps this can be minimized by rejecting language that reifies distinctions. My usage, however, creates some dissonance with passages quoted from Armstrong's translation which retains capitalization of the hypostases. I hope that this dissonance, rather than confusing my reader, helps her to notice the effect of apparently innocent capitalizations in a translation. In contrast to Stephen MacKenna's earlier translation of the *Enneads*, Armstrong has retained only those he thought necessary.[74] I do not think that even these are necessary, and I do think that they are misleading.

I have already indicated that I focus on Plotinus's central organizing concepts, omitting his occasional technical discussions of set problems common to the philosophical schools of late antiquity. These discussions are not uninteresting; they usually bring the "academic" discussion to a characteristically Plotinian interpretation and reveal, if nothing else, the consistency of a fine mind. But Plotinus's discussions of vision, numbers, guardian spirits – even his late short treatise on love – will not be explored except insofar as they provide perspective on the central concerns of his philosophy.

Rather than interrupting discussions of passages from the *Enneads* by too-frequent citations, I have usually reserved citations for the end of the paragraphs in which I discuss them. All emphases in quotations from the *Enneads* have been added.

It is probably an exaggeration to claim that Plotinus's *Enneads* is a self-help manual. Yet that claim is accurate in two senses. In fact, most philosophers and religious teachers instruct their followers in the techniques of self-help. They advocate a fruitful orientation to the universe of human experience, instruct in the attitudes and behavior that embody the recommended principles and beliefs, and encourage their readers and hearers to make the most of the richness, beauty, fragility, and brevity of human life. Plotinus is no exception. He wrote because Porphyry convinced him that his ideas were needed, that his contemporaries were writing what Porphyry disdainfully called "occasional works," rather than philosophies that provided orientation in life and retained their grip in the face of death.[75]

After a relatively short acquaintance with Plotinus, Porphyry recognized that Plotinus offered such a philosophy, and he urged Plotinus to commit to writing what would otherwise have remained – or been lost – only as the crude lecture notes of his disciples. But the surest testimony of the staying power of a philosophy is not the skill and persuasiveness of its presentation but its demonstration in life. Porphyry suggests that the strength of Plotinus's philosophy was decisively exhibited by the report of a mutual friend who, having been away for some time, returned to find Plotinus on his deathbed. Plotinus was consumed by a disease so repugnant that his friends, to a man, had abandoned him. Even in this condition, Plotinus's last words were simultaneously those of a teacher and a practitioner. "Try," he said, "to bring back the god in you to the divine in the All!"[76] Then he died.

2
Beauty: the Stepping Stone

It is difficult to get the news from poems,
Yet men die miserably every day
   for lack of what is found there.[1]

What does "really exists" mean? That they exist as beauties.

Ennead 1.6.5

Plotinus's World

Plotinus lived in Rome during what is commonly called the "crises of
the third century," a time of social collapse, bankruptcy, demise of
traditional religion, and political instability.[2] Peter Brown describes
"a sharpening of the division between the classes, the impoverishment
of town councilors, and the accumulation of wealth and status into
ever fewer hands."[3] Yet the later third century was also an age of
ambition. In Rome's colosseum culture competition for wealth, for
imperial favor, and for power took the form of lavish expenditure on
gladiatorial and wild beast shows. Wealth could be ostentatiously displayed without fear of jealousy and reprisals when it was done under
the guise of benefiting the public, acknowledging the ancient gods,
and pleasing the people.

The population of Rome in 200 CE was at least a million, a population unmatched in Europe until the early nineteenth century.[4] Food
was a major focus and anxiety in the Mediterranean world, a world in
which the 10% of the population "who lived in the towns and have
left their mark on the course of European civilization, fed themselves
... from the labours of the remaining 90% who worked the land."[5]
Utterly dependent on the annual grain shipments from North Africa,
Rome was an uneasy society. A population on the brink of starvation
is one in which plague can find easy victims, as did the plague of the
250s. "Spectacular inflation" is evidenced by the debasement of Roman coinage between 250 and 280 CE.[6]

In addition, "with the rise of Persia in 224, the formation of the

Gothic confederacy in the Danube basin after 248, and the pullulation of war-bands along the Rhine after 260, the empire had to face war on every front."[7] It was not equipped to do so. Between 245 and 270 every frontier collapsed. There were 25 emperors in 47 years, only one of whom died in his bed. Professional soldiers became the new aristocracy as the senatorial aristocracy was excluded from military commands in about 260. The army doubled in size to become the largest force the ancient world had ever seen. It also more than doubled its cost, requiring an expanded bureaucracy to serve its needs.[8]

What relationship did Plotinus's social and political world have to the universe he conceptualized? This is a difficult question but one that must not be evaded. I return to it at the end of this chapter.

Plotinus's Universe

Plotinus began his authorship with the suggestion that no one can adequately understand the world who has not been startled and instructed by its beauty (*Ennead* 1.6). For Plotinus, beauty was not an aesthetic category, in the usual sense of the word. To notice beauty is not to make a judgment about a particular object. To perceive beauty is to experience the universe as gift. In this chapter I sketch Plotinus's universe before focusing on his understanding of beauty and its role in organizing and revealing the universe's essential nature.

Plotinus's concept of the universe provides a framework within which to imagine living beings. Clearly, Plotinus worked within a Platonic tradition and with certain doctrines he did not dispute. Nevertheless, as Porphyry said in the *Life*, he never simply reiterated the thoughts of others. Although his writings are informed by Stoic and Peripatetic doctrines as well as Platonic thought, he "states what he himself really feels about the matter and not what has been handed down by tradition" (*Life* 14). Thus, Plotinus's universe was not only inherited from tradition; it was also informed by his own experience and perspective. It describes what must be the case if people experience the universe as we do.

In Plotinus's universe each entity has a place where it may stand in its own light, protected from either being flooded by chaos or marginalized by stronger realities. Plotinus's worldview has frequently been diagramed as a ladder: matter lies at the bottom, supporting the ladder, body is on the first rung, and so "on up" through soul to intellect and to the One, source of the whole (4.9.4). However, this image meant something quite different to Plotinus than it did to many twentieth-century people who are suspicious of hierarchies of all sorts. It presents Plotinus's thought accurately only if one focuses on the uprights or sides of the ladder that hold the whole together, rather than on the rungs. Although he had no difficulty saying that some entities are higher and some are lower, it was the interconnection of the whole that interested Plotinus.

Each entity, informed to the full extent of its capacity by the being, goodness, and reality that emanates from the One, participates in a common life force. The commonality of the various entities is the basis for Plotinus's theory of the continuous circulation of being through all living beings. Each entity catches, absorbs, and is formed by reflecting the being above it. It's all done with mirrors. The One emanates its undifferentiated rays to intellect effortlessly, spontaneously, and without diminishment. In intellect, thoughts as well as the forms of everything that exists originate. Far from being a realm of abstraction, intellect "reduces" – as a cook reduces a sauce to its most potent flavors – the powerful but undefined energy of the One, using it to make the world we see and experience. Plotinus twice describes intellect as "boiling with life" (6.5.2; 6.7.2).

The One gives birth to intellect spontaneously, effortlessly, without losing anything of itself. But almost nothing further can be said about the One, for it is beyond being; it has no thoughts or activities; it plans nothing; it has no movement or rest (6.9.3). It does not love as an act of intention, since it has no activity of any kind. But there is a sense in which the One *is* love: It is pure gift, supplying to every living being its own particular life, intelligence, and beauty. Plotinus frequently characterizes the One as the "great beauty" (*mega kalos*: 1.6.9), the origin of every sensible and moral beauty: "Who, then, will not call beautiful that which is beautiful primarily, and as a whole, and everywhere as a whole when no parts fail by falling short in beauty?" (5.8.8).

Intellect contains thoughts, differentiations, movement and rest, qualities and quantities. Intellect, in turn, beams its myriad forms to the common soul of all living creatures. At the level of soul, a further differentiation occurs; soul transforms the forms it receives from intellect into bodies.[9] Bodies are created and supported in life by the One's continuous creative power circulating through the universe: "The One does not give, and pass, but gives on forever" (6.9.9). The energy and animating power of the One reaches its limit in matter. The person is a composite of soul and body, and intellect contains the form of each individual as well as that of the cosmic soul.

Life never perishes. At an individual's death it lifts off from the used-up body to animate other forms. Like light, life depends on its source, not on the body animated and illuminated by it.

> When the body perishes – for nothing can exist without a share of soul – . . . how could the life still remain? Well, then, has this life perished? No, certainly not, for this too is the image of a radiance; it is simply no longer *there*. (4.5.7)[10]

A.H. Armstrong says that of all ancient thinkers, pagan or Christian, Plotinus "is the least interested in life after death and escape from the body."[11] For Plotinus, the world of human experience is a perfectly adequate index of reality, for the world perceived by the senses contains all the forms of life existing in intellect (4.8.1). Plotinus insists on this in some detail: "Does the world there have everything that is here? Yes, everything that is made by forming principle and according to form." His misleading way of putting this is that the condition of (sensible) existence "here" is presence "there" (in intellect). Lest his reader miss the point, he enumerates:

> Certainly the sky there must be a living being, and so a sky not bare of stars . . . But obviously there is earth there too, not barren, but much more full of life, and all animals are in it . . . and, obviously, plants . . . and sea is there, and all water in abiding flow and life, and all the living beings in water . . . and air, and aerial living things. (6.7.11)

Plotinus's vision of the universal life is expansively inclusive; even rocks have life: "The growth, then, and shaping of stones and the inner patterning of mountains as they grow one must certainly suppose take place because an ensouled forming principle is working within them and giving them form" (6.7.11).[12] Plotinus's universe is the arena of life, in which "these things here below are carried along with those things in heaven, and those in heaven with these on earth, and both together contribute to the consistency and everlastingness of the universe" (3.3.6).

Because the universe would not be complete without the sensible, intellect beams its thoughts and forms into soul, and soul uses its infused energies to create and animate living beings. In addition to the creation of bodies, a further definition occurs within soul: although soul does not, strictly speaking, have parts, Plotinus says that "part" of the soul "remains above," contemplating intellect, while "part" maintains the integrity of physical life.

The individual soul, midway between intellect and body, has choices. It can lean, by its directed attention and affection, toward intellect, the source of its existence, or it can spill over into body, identifying itself with body and seeking to possess the bodies and objects that cross its path. Plotinus's universe is a mobile, volatile universe in which souls, if not always in motion, are poised at any moment to move in one direction or another. This dynamism is both intimate and cosmic, at once happening in a person's most secret interiority and in cosmic space. Body is ambiguous, simultaneously the starting point or first step – and lowest in value. But Plotinus has much more to say about body which I examine in chapter 4.

This short sketch of Plotinus's universe will be further elaborated in the chapters that follow. For now it will suffice to orient us to Plotinus's understanding of beauty and its significance. Something fundamental is known about the nature of the universe when we recognize and take seriously Plotinus's insistence that nothing produces awareness of the interconnectedness of the universe as effectively as seeing its beauty.

Seeing Beauty

The universe is beautiful. Intellect's beauties "sally out and come into matter and adorn it and excite us when they appear" (1.6.3). Those who do not see this beauty are clueless. But a capacity for perceiving beauty can, and must, be trained. In Plato's *Symposium*, Diotima's exposition on love instructs the seeker to begin by devoting himself "to the beauties of the body."[13] He cannot begin too early, she says. He should fall in love with a beautiful body; when he notices that there are many beautiful bodies, his love for one will expand to all beautiful bodies. The seeker next understands that "beauties of body are as nothing to the beauties of the soul," and proceeds to the discovery of the beauty of laws and institutions, academic disciplines, and ways of life. Noticing that there is a constant feature in these diverse occurrences of beauty, an emotionally toned quality he can identify only as beauty, he is now prepared to perceive a "sea of beauty," the open secret of the universe.[14]

Commenting on this passage, Plotinus moves much more rapidly than does Plato from sensory beauties to asking whether there is "any beauty prior to these." He seeks a unifying ground, a "stepping stone," a leg-up.[15] What makes every beautiful thing beautiful? he asks. What, in a beautiful sight, attracts, draws, and creates the viewer's enjoyment?

He considers several answers to these questions proposed by other philosophers, ultimately discarding them as partial or misleading suggestions. Returning to his initial question, he asks again "what the primary beauty of bodies really is." This question leads him to observe the soul's affinity with whatever it is that makes bodies beautiful. On first glance at a beautiful object, the soul recognizes and welcomes it; correspondingly, the soul shrinks from anything ugly. Plotinus explains that this occurs because souls are related "to the higher kind of reality in the realm of being [so that] when it sees something akin to [that reality, soul] is delighted and thrilled and returns to itself and remembers its own possessions." Perhaps, then, the right question to ask is: "What likeness is there between beautiful things here and there?" (1.6.2). Plotinus answers, "We maintain that the things in this world are beautiful by participating in form." Form is the link between the "realm of being" (intellect) and (sensible) beauty.

Here Plotinus is simultaneously a profoundly Platonic thinker, and at his most innovative, stating "what he himself really feels about the matter." At this point, Plato invoked mathematics as the connecting link between intelligible and sensible. Above the door to the Platonic academy in Athens was inscribed the phrase, "Let no one enter who is not thoroughly versed in mathematics." Because mathematics and geometry (measure and proportion) are both *in* sensible objects and detachable from them, mathematics *mediates* between sensible objects and intellect. Thus Plato claimed that study of mathematics "plainly compels the soul to employ pure thought with a view to truth itself." It "naturally conduces to the awakening of thought;" it "really does tend to draw the mind to essence and reality" (*Republic* 7. 522d–523a; 544d; 527e). Mathematics is useful "not for buying and selling . . . but for facilitating the conversion of the soul from the world of generation to essence and truth" (*Republic* 526b). For Plato, mathematics both *connects* intellect and the sensible and provides a *route* from one to the other.

Plotinus largely ignores mathematics. Yet, having distinguished intelligible and sensible, Plotinus, like Plato, needed to demonstrate their connection. What, in Plotinus's philosophy, takes the place held by mathematics in Plato's? The short answer, one that will be examined in the rest of the chapter, is that for Plotinus, sensible objects' link with intellect is so intimate as to need no intermediary other than sensible beauty, the unmistakable signal of the presence of intellect. Plato described mathematics as beautiful (*Greater Hippias* 303). Plotinus believed that sensible beauty speaks for itself; it does not need mathematics to express its source.

But we must ask: Why imagine another world that guarantees the beauty, reality, and value of our world? And what is the effect of imagining this? Does imagining a permanent beauty bleach our world of its colors, reducing its objects to dim and distorted reflections of a perfect world somewhere else? "Why set the pear upon that river bank, or spice the shore with odors of the plum?" Or does that doubling support and augment and intensify "the silken weavings of our afternoons"?[16]

Why does our experience of the sensible require the presence of intellect? What does form do? Our awareness of the source of the sensible world enables us to perceive some of its most salient features, namely its beauty, order, and unity. When we recognize that "the beautiful body comes into being by sharing in a formative power which comes from the divine forms" (1.6.2), we better understand reality. Our understanding does not alter the world; the benefit is ours.

Soul recognizes beauty because soul participates in form, albeit at a greater intensity than do bodies. So we see something *as beautiful* when it matches the beautiful form that *is* ourselves, that is, soul. We detect beauty by kinship, whether beauty in bodies or beauty in ideas, virtues, or ways of life:

> When sense perception, then, sees the form in bodies binding and mastering [matter] . . . it [sense perception] gathers into one that which appears dispersed and brings it back and takes it in, now without parts, to the soul's interior and presents it to that which is within as something in tune with it and fitting it and dear to it. (1.6.3)

It is important to notice that seeing the beauty – seeing the life – of people and objects, occurs *at the level of perception*, not by adding concepts. Plotinus's examples of this immediacy are light (which he thought of as incorporeal) and fire (which he calls "close to the incorporeal" 1.6.3). Light and fire give color and warmth, qualities that are indistinguishable from the lighted or enflamed objects themselves. Similarly, soul immediately recognizes and enjoys a kinship of beauty wherever the person looks, whether within itself or in sensible objects.

But perhaps we should not too hastily accept this claim. How is it possible to understand the universe without the mediation of language and concepts? On one level, it is not possible. If it were, Plotinus would not have written or taught. But something more, and more fundamental, than comprehension of concepts is needed. The ability to see beauty is the result of a strenuous and patient spiritual discipline, a discipline that cumulatively embeds a particular way of seeing into a person's feeling and thinking. I discuss that discipline shortly.

Plotinus concludes his discussion of sensible beauty by remembering that the things we see, hear, or otherwise perceive as beautiful, exciting as they are, are "images and shadows" of intellect. We must not linger with them, but go on to the "beauties beyond," seen by the eye of the mind rather than the bodily eye. Bodily beauties come to us; they "sally forth." But we must, with considerable effort, "go on up" to invisible beauties. The more beautiful one's own soul is, the more readily it relates to the beauty in sensible objects. Affinity is crucial. "These experiences must occur whenever there is contact with any sort of beautiful things, wonder and a shock of delight and longing and passion and a happy excitement" (1.6.4).

This "wild exultation" is at its most intense when the soul's beauty is revealed "*in yourself or in someone else*," when "greatness of soul, a righteous life, a pure morality, courage, dignity, and modesty, . . . the godlike light of intellect" are evident (1.6.5). These qualities are called beautiful because anyone who sees them must say that "they are what really exists."[17]

Plotinus pictures an ugly soul in order to understand, by contrast, what characterizes a beautiful soul. Even the ugly soul pursues beauty, but mistaken about what beauty is, it pursues "a dim life and diluted with a great deal of death . . . dragged in every direction towards the objects of sense." Its fetishistic and addictive choices make soul "ugly by mixture and dilution and inclination towards the body and matter" (1.6.5). At any moment, however, the possibility exists of scouring off the acquired "mud" and revealing the underlying gold.

Plotinus's description of the virtuous soul owes much to the philosophical tradition within which he worked. Like many philosophers before him, he understood the virtues of self-control, courage, and wisdom as purifications of the soul. Each virtue, he says, entails refusal to identify one's "self" with one's body. For example, self-control consists in "not keeping company with bodily pleasures, but avoiding them as impure and belonging to something impure." He sums up, "greatness of soul is despising the things here." But this is shocking advice! What has happened to that respectful appreciation Plotinus has described as the right attitude toward the sensible world?

Indeed, the translation distorts: Plotinus's word for "despise" is literally "look over" – a differently toned word than "despise." To "look over" objects of sense is conceptually to see their essential form. For example, although the animating presence of soul can be "seen" only in bodies' movements, it is possible by an exercise of imagination, to strip soul to "form and formative power, altogether bodiless and intellectual and entirely belonging to the divine."[18] Intellect, Plotinus says, is the soul's essence and therefore its beauty: "The soul's becoming something good and beautiful is its being made like to God . . . or rather, beautifulness is reality" (1.6.6). "The beauty [in intellect] is overwhelming" (2.9.17).

What, then, is the role of beauty in Plotinus's universe? Sensible objects in all their fragility and impermanence are the link between sense and intellect. Plotinus concludes his investigation of "the primary beauty in bodies":

> Our explanation of [the beauty of bodies] is that the soul, since it is by nature what it is and is related to the higher kind of reality in the realm of being, when it sees something akin to it or a trace of its kindred reality, is delighted and thrilled and returns to itself and its own possessions . . . the things in this world are beautiful by participating in form. (1.6.2)

Plotinus reverses his usual method of starting with experience and observation to describe the awesome derivation of the familiar sensible beauties we so often take for granted:

> For God the qualities of beauty and goodness are the same, or the realities, the good and beauty . . . First we must posit beauty which is also the good; from this immediately comes intellect, which is beauty, and the soul is given beauty by intellect. Everything else is beautiful by the shaping of soul, the beauties in action and in ways of life. And soul makes beautiful the bodies which are spoken of as beautiful . . . it makes everything it grasps and masters beautiful, as far as they are capable of participation. (1.6.2)

The momentum of the argument is dizzying and swift; it can go either way, from bottom to top, or from top to bottom. Like a roller coaster, the argument ascends and descends *in order to show the connectedness of the whole*. The ascent is a process of stripping accretions until "one sees with oneself alone That alone, simple, single, and pure, from which all depends and to which all look and are and live and think" (1.6.7).

To see the universe as beautiful is to understand *at the level of perception* that the beauty one sees is precisely the One's informing emanations.[19] Again, it is crucial to distinguish *seeing as beauty* from what we normally call "aesthetics," namely, an intellectual judgment that an object is beautiful. To see *as beautiful* is to perceive that their beauty is supplied by the great beauty. Plotinus's metaphor for such seeing is something like Emily Dickinson's "certain slant of light." When the soul "sees the beauties here flowing past it, it *already knows completely* that they have the light which plays on them from elsewhere" (6.7.31).

In Plotinus's universe, the act of seeing beauty integrates sensibilities we might analyze as religious and aesthetic. Two assumptions may prevent our understanding Plotinus's insistence that seeing beauty is a spiritual discipline. First, if we think of aesthetic appreciation as a capacity one is either born with or else simply does not possess, we will miss Plotinus's advocacy of committed exercise to strengthen one's capacity to see beauty. Second, if we think of religious understanding as primarily conceptual, we will miss Plotinus's integration of sense and intelligence in what he believed to be the only activity by which reality can be adequately grasped.

Beauty as Discipline

Pierre Hadot has identified the definition of "a way of life," a spiritual discipline, as a common and central feature of ancient philosophies.[20] Every philosophical school also had thought exercises, set questions on which students whetted their minds. But philosophy as a practice differed from discourse about philosophy.[21] Both thought exercises and spiritual disciplines contributed to training the person to avoid being "deceived in our everyday lives by false representations." The object of philosophy as an ethical discipline was the range of human affairs that lie within our power, and "what depends upon us is the acts of our own soul."[22]

> We shall desire only that which *does* depend on us – moral virtue – and shall also avoid only that which depends on us – moral evil. We are to regard everything which does *not* depend on us as indifferent; that is to say, we must not make any *difference* between such things.[23]

Philosophical writings in the context of spiritual disciplines were

> written not so much to inform the reader of a doctrinal content but to
> form him, to make him traverse a certain itinerary in the course of which
> he will make spiritual progress . . . [In short,] one must always approach a
> philosophical work of antiquity with this idea of spiritual progress in mind.[24]

Plotinus's writings exemplify the concern with spiritual progress that
Hadot has discussed: "How shall we find the way?" he asks in the first
treatise he wrote (1.6.8). Can you get there from here? Is there a trustworthy method? He began writing at about the age of 50, when his
philosophy had been thoroughly worked out in his mind. It is, then,
highly significant that he began with a treatise "On Beauty," a treatise
in which he begins by inquiring about different forms of sensible beauty
and goes on to posit a beauty that both informs and out-shines the
beauties accessible to human senses. A critical feature of Plotinus's
spiritual discipline is seeing beauty.

Sensible beauty is the starting point because we are surrounded by
it. In a Plotinian spirit, Iris Murdoch wrote:

> The appreciation of beauty . . . is not only (for all its difficulties) the
> easiest available spiritual exercise; it is also a completely adequate entry
> into (and not just analogy of) the good life, since it is the checking of
> selfishness in the interest of seeing the real . . . Beauty is that which
> attracts this particular sort of unselfish attention.[25]

For Plotinus, however, there is still an important step between the
appreciation of sensible beauty and apprehension of the origin of "these
beauties here." For the "inconceivable beauty" does not "sally forth"
as do sensible beauties, but "stays within" where the unprepared cannot see it. Plotinus proposes a method. It is not an easy method; not
for nothing is it called a spiritual discipline!

> Let the one who can, follow and come within, and leave outside the
> sight of his eyes and not turn back to the bodily splendours which he
> saw before. When he sees the beauty in bodies he must not run after
> them; we must know that they are images, traces, shadows, and hurry
> away to that which they image. (1.6.8)

Sensible beauty provides the impetus and the energy for a deeper and
more concentrated look, not beyond, but within visible beauties, for
they are an image of the great beauty.

The myth of Narcissus illustrates the impossibility, indeed, the danger, of attempting to embrace and possess an image. We must not drown in images (enchanting as they are), but must return to intellect, the "country from which we came." The return trip, however, is not a hike; "we cannot get there on foot." Ultimately, sensible "images" must be seen as the vibrant and radiant representatives of the great beauty by which they exist. "Shut your eyes, and change and wake to another way of seeing, which everyone has but few use" (1.6.8).

Plotinus recalls Plato's metaphor of the cave when he tries to describe this unfamiliar "inner sight." At first the light is blinding; exercise is needed, and extensive training. But the most riveting information of all comes from looking at oneself with the new vision. The passage, quoted at length in chapter 1, advocates the vigorous activity of a spiritual discipline:

> How then can you see the sort of beauty a good soul has? Go back into yourself and look; and if you do not yet see yourself beautiful, then, just as someone making a statue which has to be beautiful cuts away here and polishes there and makes one part smooth and clears another till he has given his statue a beautiful face, so you too must cut away excess and straighten the crooked and clear the dark and make it bright and never stop working on your statue till the divine glory of virtue shines out on you, till you see self mastery enthroned upon its holy seat. (1.6.9)

The perception of beauty is a discipline requiring training and exercise. Plotinus describes an intensely concentrated activity similar to giving birth. Like birth-giving, the exercise requires a combination of hard labor and patient waiting.[26] To seek the vision is not to seek something alien or external, but to bring forth what is most intimately one's own. The vision, when it comes, is a vision of the source of the seer's own being, an awareness of her own life and light. There is no separation between vision and seer: one "sees suddenly, not seeing how, but the vision fills his eyes with light and does not make him see something else by it, but the light itself is what he sees" (6.7.36).

> There must be those who see this beauty by that with which the soul sees things of this sort, and when they see it they must be delighted and overwhelmed and excited much more than by those beauties we spoke of before, since now it is true beauty they are grasping. These experiences must occur whenever there is contact with any sort of beautiful thing, wonder, and a shock of delight and longing and passion and a happy excitement . . . you feel like this when you see, in yourself or in

someone else, greatness of soul, a righteous life, a pure morality, courage . . . he who sees them cannot say anything except that they are what
really exists. What does "really exist" mean? That they exist as beauties. (1.6.4)

As we have seen, ugliness, by contrast, is caused by an "admixture of
evil living, a dim life and diluted with a great deal of death" (1.6.5).
Extending the visual metaphor he has used throughout his discussion
of beauty, Plotinus suddenly speaks of *moral* ugliness:

> Suppose, then, an ugly soul, dissolute and unjust, full of all lusts and all
> disturbances, sunk in fears by its cowardice and in jealousies by its pet
> tiness, thinking mean and mortal thoughts as far as it thinks at all,
> altogether distorted, loving impure pleasures, living a life which con
> sists of bodily sensations and finding delight in its ugliness. (1.6.5)

Plotinus finds even ugliness poignant. In a misguided search for beauty
the soul clutches compulsively at everything that crosses its path, seeking to possess it by joining it to itself. "The soul becomes ugly by
mixture, and dilution, and inclination toward the body and matter . . .
just as pigs, with their unclean bodies, like that sort of thing."[27]

For humans, the Good and beauty are not identical as they are from
the God's-eye-view. Beauty is a feature of the intelligible world, while
the Good is beyond intellect, the "spring and origin of beauty."

Every society trains its members to recognize certain kinds of beauty.
Early twenty-first-century media culture is technologically equipped,
as no society has ever been, to direct Americans to certain repetitive
identifications of beauty. We have only to see babies, brides, roses,
and basketball shots to know that we are expected to think them beautiful. And these sights *are* beautiful. But why these stereotypes of beauty
at the expense of an expansive and inclusive repertoire of beautiful
things? To see accurately is to see *as* beautiful, Plotinus says.

How is beauty seen? What lens selects for beauty? Plotinus's answer
is paradoxical: A person or an object (we are not socialized to see as
beautiful) is nevertheless seen *as* beautiful "by those passionately in
love with the invisible," by an "inner eye" trained to see a nearly unbearably fragile, poignant, and transient beauty of structure or, in Plato's and Plotinus's word, form.

To see beauty is to see an object *in its* life. Plotinus says that because
an object localizes and radiates its form (intellect) and its life (soul), to
see its beauty is to grasp the connections that give it existence. He
asks:

> Why is there more light of beauty on a living face, but only a trace of it on a dead one? And are not the more lifelike statues the more beautiful ones, even if the others are better proportioned? And is not an uglier living man more beautiful than the beautiful man in the statue? Yes, because the living is more desirable; and this is because it has soul; and this is because it has more the form of good; and this means that it is somehow colored by the light of the Good, and being so colored wakes and rises up and lifts up that which belongs to it, and as far as it can, makes it good and wakes it. (6.7.22)

Seeing beauty depends on us. It is not inborn, inherited in the genes, or automatically acquired in the process of socialization. The practice by which the spiritual discipline of seeing beauty is trained and exercised is contemplation. Contemplation, however, is not uninformed and unfocused meditation, but a precise practice. In addition to providing a conceptual orientation to the universe, Plotinus assists the one aspiring to contemplation by giving some rather detailed exercises in imagining the real. I discuss these in chapter 6.

What is the relationship of beauty to human arts? Can music, the visual arts, and drama play a role in helping a person to see beauty? Or is a painting one step deader than a corpse, which at least *has been* alive?

Beauty and Art

Plotinus nowhere offers a theory of why some objects are – or appear to be – more beautiful than others. He comments, however, that it is possible for works of human art to alert their viewers to the great informing beauty. Again, religion and aesthetics are inextricably blended in his description of artworks. Like natural objects, they have the capacity to integrate sense and intellect in an activity of seeing:

> The wise men of old, who made temples and statues in the wish that the gods should be present to them, looking to the nature of the All, had in mind that the nature of Soul is everywhere easy to attract, but that if someone were to construct something sympathetic to it and able to receive a part of it, it would of all things receive soul most easily. That which is sympathetic to it is that which imitates it in some way, like a mirror able to catch a form. (4.3.1)

Works of art, however, are not the only representations of reality; objects of sense also represent reality, not as the presence of an absence but as the presence of a presence.

> Yes, the nature of the All, too, made all things in imitation of the intelligible realities of which it had the rational principles, and when each thing, in this way, had become a rational principle in matter, shaped according to that which was before matter, it linked it with that god in conformity with whom it came into being and to whom the soul looked, and whom it had in its making. (4.3.1)

Art historian André Grabar thought that Plotinus's cosmology held some implications for artists. He suggested that the artist who wishes to paint realistically – to paint the real, in Plotinus's sense – must eliminate the dimension of material depth. Optical illusions occur in the third dimension because that is where matter exists, in the volume and separateness of bodies. If three-dimensionality reflects the depth (*bathos*) of matter, then "realistic" figures should be flattened. They should also have uniform lighting, eliminating shadows.

Grabar pointed out that, perhaps in response to Plotinus's ideas, the naturalistic art of the classical tradition was largely abandoned in late antiquity in favor of an art that showed the true size, uncorrected for distance, the true color, and other characteristics of objects. He claimed that Plotinian aesthetics informed the new Christian iconic art of catacombs, church walls and apses, and panel painting in late antiquity.[28]

More recently, Eric Alliez and Michel Feher have corrected and refined Grabar's interpretation. They propose that although the depth associated with materiality was to be avoided in a Plotinian aesthetic, a different kind of depth – a fourth dimension – was sought. True depth is to be found in

> the luminous intensity of which the One is the primordial source ... Extension and the bodies that inhabit it can now be seen to be effects of the luminous radiance that emanates from the One and seem to well up from the depths of the soul.[29]

The Plotinian painter must, then, aim at a "translucent world in which the internal light passes through bodies, and, as it propagates itself, can thereby abolish the distances that three-dimensional space creates between the bodies ... His task is to celebrate radiance of mind as he represents bodies."[30]

According to Alliez and Feher, the Plotinian painter also strives to

"dispel the state of dispersion in which physical bodies live." The trans-
lucency of the painted figures must evoke the transparency of souls.
But "the separation that it is the artist's task to overcome is a lack of
unity not simply between the various components of his picture but
above all between that picture and whoever looks at it." The spectator
of a Plotinian artist's painting discovers in it "reflections of a light
from which not only the work of art but he himself proceeds."[31]

Alliez and Feher's description of Plotinus's aesthetics moves attention from the beautiful object – the painting – to the viewer's act of
perceiving beauty. They argue that Grabar's stylistic specifications are
irrelevant to Plotinus's interest in sensible beauty's role in alerting one
to the great beauty (1.6.4). In fact, Grabar acknowledged that there is
no evidence that Plotinus had any interest in Roman figurative painting or that artists contemporary with him were aware of his philosophy. In fact, so-called illusionistic painting was still done when the
resources and skill of the painter permitted. Lacking evidence that third-
century artists considered these issues, it is probably best to curb speculation and content ourselves with considering a work of art exactly
contemporaneous with Plotinus's residence in Rome.

The mid-third-century Tomb of the Aurelii in a catacomb on the
Viale Manzoni in Rome bears a figure that may be a better example of
Plotinian aesthetics than either contemporary catacomb images with
their cartoonish quality, or Byzantine icons (see frontispiece). This bust
of a young bearded male figure is naturalistically rendered. The head
is striking. The mouth and nose are modeled by shadows; the eyes and
brow, however, are modeled by light and the eyes gaze piercingly into
the middle distance. Matter, the third dimension, has not been eliminated but it has been deeply penetrated and transformed by the light
of intellect. A more accurate description would be that the sense has
been drawn up into the potent intellect which blazes through the "win-
dows of the soul," the eyes.[32]

In being lifelike, the bust meets Plotinus's criterion for beauty. The
"more lifelike" images are the more beautiful. Similarly, in painting, it
is not the flat unshaded figures of many catacomb paintings of the
mid-third century that best enable the viewer to recognize the represented figure's life, but the naturalistic depiction of fruits and flowers,
and portraits that seem to breathe, that best represent the figure's life.
In Plotinian aesthetics, there is no reason why representation should
not be naturalistic. Indeed, "what other fairer image of the intelligible
world could there be [than the familiar sights of this world]?" (2.9.4).

There is another way in which this fresco exemplifies Plotinus's philosophy. Matter, according to Plotinus, should be neither denied nor hated, but simply ignored. It is a necessary part of the universe and bodies participate in matter, but bodies must not absorb an unwarranted share of attention. The light playing about the figure's eyes draws the viewer's attention to the upper part of the face, the location of vision and intellect, rather than to the heavily shadowed lower face.

Works of art are fully capable not only of recalling the viewer to life and beauty but even of providing more direct access to intellect than do natural objects. Plotinus's strongest statement about the potential value of art works is completely consonant with naturalistic portraiture. It is quite possible for a portrait painter to represent a balance of the physical features and spiritual life of the subject.

> But if anyone despises the arts because they produce their works by imitating nature, we must tell him, first, that natural things are imitations too. Then he must know that the arts do not simply imitate what they see, but they run back up to the forming principles from which nature derives; then also that they do a great deal by themselves, and, since they possess beauty, they make up what is defective in things. (5.8.1)

Yet Plotinus declined, according to Porphyry, to have his own portrait painted. As I have already suggested, Porphyry's interpretation of Plotinus's objection to being painted need not be accepted. Porphyry quotes Plotinus (from memory, many years after the event) as saying, "Why really, is it not enough to have to carry the image in which nature has encased us, without your requesting me to agree to leave behind me a longer-lasting image, as if it was something genuinely worth looking at?" (*Life* 1). Indeed, placed in the same paragraph in which Porphyry describes Plotinus as "ashamed of being in the body" as support for this interpretation, the statement is suspect in its quite unPlotinian scorn for "image." Plotinus may not have wanted to be painted simply because he was shy or because he did not want his students' attention distracted from his philosophy to his personal characteristics.

Porphyry reports that one of Plotinus's best students, Amelius, outwitted him in his desire to remain portraitless. He brought "the best painter of the time," Carterius, to observe Plotinus's lectures and to paint Plotinus from memory. In this way, an "excellent portrait" of Plotinus was painted without his knowledge. If Carterius had listened to Plotinus's lectures in addition to committing to memory his physical characteristics it is not unlikely, for the reasons I have given, that he would have painted something very similar to the Aurelii bust!

However, Plotinian aesthetics has a larger than aesthetic role to play in Plotinus's moral universe. Indeed, for Plotinus, the ability to perceive beauty is the foundation of ethical judgment and behavior. I turn, in the following section, to Plotinus's description of moral accountability.

Beauty as Moral Responsibility

Plotinus's "most serious consideration of the problem of evil," *Ennead* 3.2, is the setting for "one of his most beautiful expressions of [his] enjoyment of the endlessly outspreading richness of the diverse beauty of this world."[33] His high esteem for sensible beauty is evident throughout the treatise, for example:

> This [universal] order extends to everything, even to the smallest, and the art is wonderful which appears, not only in the divine beings but also in the things which one might have supposed providence would have despised for their smallness, for example, the workmanship which produces wonders in rich variety in ordinary animals, and the beauty of appearance which extends to the fruits and even the leaves of plants, and their beauty of flower which comes so effortlessly, and their delicacy and variety, and that all this has not been made once and come to an end but is always being made as the powers above move in different ways over this world. (3.2.13)

In the context of this beauty of order and exquisite detail, evil is a "falling short of good" – disorder. Yet even disorder, as represented by bodily illness, poverty, and vice can be useful for instruction and for "waking up the intelligence." For "nothing is bad for the good person and nothing, correspondingly, good for the bad" (3.2.5–6).

Beauty is a primary characteristic of reality; evil is not. Beauty characterizes the whole, and while each part is "stationed where it ought to be," "each by contributing its own sound helps toward the perfection of a single melody . . . the notes of the pipe are not equal, but the melody is complete, made up of all" (3.2.17).

Plotinus says that the recognition of beauty occurs not at the level of judgment, but at the foundational level of perception itself. Seeing beauty is a profoundly moral act, an "ethical ability."[34] But this sounds deceptively simple; it is more accurate to say that Plotinus derives a complex metaphysics, morality, and what we might call a spirituality

from his conception of the universe as beautiful to the core. I have said
that perception of the truly beautiful, for Plotinus, requires training,
concentration, and an eye adapted to the vision. If, however, one is
content with placing beautiful objects – art – before one's eyes, "you
may fall out of beauty into what is called beauty" (6.7.33).

The direct apprehension, *at the level of perception*, of the
interconnectedness of the universe is the quintessential human activity, the insight it would be tragic to miss. Because "we are what we
desire and what we look upon," the formative effects of contemplation of beauty are crucial to human integration (4.3.8). Inability to see
beauty is a moral failure, since cultivating the ability to see beauty is
"within our power." Seeing beauty is an achievement, namely, the
integration of intelligence and feeling by which we participate in beauty.
Because perceiving beauty defines human happiness, misjudgments
about what is beautiful are the greatest human danger.

The vision of "That alone" is the ultimate energizer.[35] Plotinus paraphrases Plato's description of the affect accompanying the sight: "If
anyone sees it, what passion will he feel, what longing in his desire to
be united with it, what a shock of delight!" He speaks of wonder,
delight, shock, love, and "piercing longing." The sight of this primary
– or ultimate, depending on your perspective – beauty "makes its lovers beautiful and lovable." In fact, sighting (not merely desiring) the
great beauty is the criterion for a "successful life": "The one who attains [the vision of the "inconceivable beauty"] is happy in seeing that
'happy sight', and the one who fails to attain it has failed utterly."
Plotinus emphasizes this: "A man has not failed if he fails to win beauty
of colours or bodies, or power or office or kingship, even, but if he
fails to win *this* and only this" (1.6.7).

Plato had similarly identified the goal of rational exercise as a vision
of the beautiful. In his treatise on beauty, the *Greater Hippias*, he set
out to find, "not what seems to the many to be beautiful, but what is
so." Yet at the end of the treatise he was forced to admit, as the only
fruit of his labor: "So Hippias, . . . I seem to myself to know what the
proverb means that says, 'The beautiful things are difficult'."[36] But
Plotinus saw, as Plato did not, that an aesthetics that seeks only to
identify the beautiful properties of an object is fundamentally misguided. One must, instead, exercise and develop one's capacity to see
beauty in its myriad forms. At their best, beautiful objects train the eye
to perceive beauty; at their worst, they present economically or socially "interested" identifications of what *counts* as beauty, blocking
perceptions of livelier and more surprising beauty.

Plato's method in the *Symposium* described a process by which, starting with bodies, the most immediately evident beauty, one proceeded
to less visible beauties such as lifestyles, laws, and conceptual schemes.
Plato's invisible beauties were, however, not part of the soul. Plotinus
finds the source of the perception of beauty not in beautiful objects,
nor in the socialized eye, but in the beholder's soul. So far from being
an inherently dualistic venture in which the seeker attempts to find
beauty outside herself, in social practices or institutions or in some
fantasized heavenly realm, it is, rather, in a process devoted to exploring her own life that she discovers the source of her being.

> If, then, a soul knows itself . . . [it] knows that its movement is not in
> a straight line [but] in a circle around something, something not out-
> side but a centre, and the centre is that from which the circle derives,
> then it will move around this from which it is and will depend on this.
> (6.9.8)

While Plato's method consisted of abstracting the quality of beauty
from the many objects and practices that exhibit it, Plotinus's method
entailed a systematic and cumulative movement from attention to external things to one's own life. For Plato, beauty depended on and
resulted from virtue. For Plotinus, perceiving beauty is more fundamental; it underlies and supports the practice of virtue so that the
primary effects of an active and alert perception of beauty are ethical.
The one who has "become sight" understands intimately the irreduc-
ible connection of all living beings that is the basis of ethical feeling
and activity. Plotinus discusses at length the apparent absurdity of
believing that all living beings share the same soul:

> It must, no doubt, seem strange that my soul and that of any and every-
> body else should be one thing only: it might mean my feelings being felt
> by someone else, my goodness another's too, my desire her desire, all
> our experience shared with each other and with the one universe, so
> that the very universe itself would feel whatever I feel. (4.9.3)

But this "strange" sharing, Plotinus insists, exists, and we already recognize it, if we think more profoundly and honestly about everyday
experience:

> We are in sympathetic relation to one another, suffering, overcome at
> the sight of pain, naturally drawn to forming attachments; and all this
> can be due only to some unity among us. (4.9.3)

Soul is the source of that unity. It is because "all souls derive from the same from which the soul of the All derives too, [that] they have a community of feeling." But we also know from experience that every individual does not share the feelings of every other individual. This occurs because human beings do not consist in soul alone, but in the composite of body and soul. Thus they are differentiated from one another in two ways: by different bodies, and by the objects of their active attention and affection: "Different souls look at different things and are and become what they look at" (4.3.8). Plotinus urged that the most fruitful direction one might look is toward the One, and that what one sees when one does so is her own participation in the all-pervasive beauty of the universe:

> But if someone is able to turn around . . . he will see God and himself and the All; at first he will not see *as* the All but then, when he has nowhere to set himself and determine how far he himself goes, he will stop marking himself off from all being and will come to the All without going out anywhere, but remaining there where the All is set firm. (6.5.7)

At first three entities seem to be present in the vision: God (or the One, or the Good), oneself, and the All, the existing world. When the seer stops saying, "up to here, and no further, it is I," however, seer and seen blend into unity. The most immediate effects of this inclusive vision appear in the seer; the great beauty "makes its lovers beautiful and lovable" (1.6.7). But the vision's effects go beyond personal enhancement.

The perception of beauty is an activity; it is, furthermore, an activity that flows spontaneously from our most fundamental gift, our aliveness. Plotinus was able to picture with equanimity human vulnerability to crushing loss, even to the fact that a moment will inevitably come in which life itself is "simply no longer there" (4.5.7). Could Plotinus's vision of a vitally interconnected universe provide a basis for activist concern for the natural world? Is it true that while one is absorbed in "seeing" one cannot simultaneously be struggling to make the world and human society a better place to live for more human beings? Is perception of beauty and struggle for justice inevitably at odds? These questions are not foreign to Plotinus's own concerns.

Cultural critic Ian Hunter has argued for understanding aesthetics as inevitably and irreducibly political. He advocates what he calls a "politicizing aesthetics." He acknowledges that aesthetics, the study of beauty as a property of objects, has seemed to many contemporary cultural critics to be at odds with social and political responsibility. But this judgment, he says, rests on defining aesthetics as elitist interest in museum art works. A more comprehensive definition of aesthetics could examine art works' political functions in their material and economic roles, in the social assumptions they communicate, and in the way they inform our lives. He urges that aesthetics be understood as an activity interwoven with, and deeply informing, the material realities of life.[37] An even broader definition of aesthetics than Hunter's could examine the sources of our individual and communal designations of beauty and the ideological, political, and economic interests these serve.

Or perhaps the answer to the question of whether perceptions of beauty distract from, or contribute to, social responsibility depends at least partly on one's theory of vision.

The Loving Eye

Plotinus's favorite metaphor, seeing, does not emphasize the distance between the seer and object as do most twentieth-century theories of vision.[38] Plato had articulated a theory of vision that emphasized the viewer's activity and the strong connection of viewer and object in the moment of vision. The so-called visual ray theory pictures vision occurring when a quasi-physical ray, created by the same fire that animates and warms the body and is at its most intense in the eyes, touches its object. An image of the object then travels back along the ray to imprint itself on the memory.[39] Seeing connects viewer and object through the viewer's activity. Obviously, visual ray theory did not emerge from an entertainment culture, a culture that thinks of seeing as passive and largely without consequence; rather, it assumes active engagement with the object of vision.

Plotinus accepted the ancient claim that vision touches its object, but he found the crude physicality of the visual ray theory incompatible with intellectual/spiritual vision. Intellectual vision occurs when the individual directs her concentrated longing to intellect. But it is not, in our sense or in Plotinus's, an intellectual experience: "that which touches does not think" (5.3.10). Through the part of the soul that has "remained above," vision touches the One. The medium of this connection is love: "since the soul is other than God but comes from him it is necessarily in love with him" (6.9.9).

Plotinus discusses the experience of touch as "a passionate experience, like that of a lover resting in the beloved" (6.9.4).

> The soul by a kind of delight and intense concentration on the vision and by the passion of its gazing generates something from itself which is worthy of itself and of the vision. So from the power which is intensely active about the object of vision, and from a kind of overflow from that object, love came to be as an eye filled with its vision, like a seeing that has its image with it. (3.5.3)

Midway through his discussion of the vision of the One, Plotinus suddenly changes from speaking of the One in abstract terms – "simplicity," "indivisible," "power," "the principle of all things," – to using a personal pronoun: "he." As if to demonstrate the necessity of interweaving both abstract and personal terms, however, he soon returns to the abstract: "something extremely self-sufficient," "the cause" (6.9.4). Difficult as it is to cultivate the energy of love for an abstract force, Plotinus never goes very far toward personifying the One. His description of providence and prayer, discussed in chapter 5, reveals the reasons for his reluctance.

We have come full circle: the longing for beauty, originally inspired by "one beautiful body," creates and sustains the love that ultimately touches its object.

> And if someone assumed that the origin of love was the longing for beauty itself which was there before in people's souls, and their recognition of it and kinship with it and unreasoned awareness that it is something of their own, he would hit, I think, on the truth about its cause. (3.5.1)

In his late treatise on love, Plotinus insists that his account of spiritual vision does not disparage, but rather enhances, the beauty of the visible world: "If anyone delight in something and is akin to it, he has an affinity also with its images" (3.5.1). Recognition of soul's kinship with the One generates love for its images, together with an attitude of enjoyment of, and gratitude for, the beauty of the visible world.

Language, which can only say one thing at a time, is severely limited when it tries to express the intimate and the cosmic effects of the One. The One is at once "the spring of life, the spring of intellect, the principle of being, the cause of good, [and] the root of the soul." Yet the

One is no less active in maintaining an individual's life: "for we are not cut off from him or separate . . . but we breathe and are preserved because that Good has not given its gifts and then gone away but is always bestowing them as long as it is what it is" (6.9.9).

Over six centuries before Plotinus lived, Plato had endeavored to see the world as Socrates saw it. Through Socrates' eyes, he saw a world in which death stole nothing of importance from the living soul. In fact, death brought the soul closer to real existence by stripping off the biodegradable body. Plotinus, in turn, trying to see the world as Plato saw it, understood that Plato had found human vulnerability intolerable and had tried to articulate a world in which it didn't matter. But, standing on his shoulders, Plotinus also saw that both vulnerability and the capacity to receive the universal circulation of life depend on the same condition – consanguinity, interconnection, the great beauty. Unlike Plato, he was not primarily concerned with death. He sought, rather, to understand life. His philosophy seeks to demonstrate his conviction that one life, marked by beauty, circulates throughout the universe. This is what he endeavored to communicate to his friends and students.

Finally, how did Plotinus's universe relate to his social, political and cultural world? I discuss similarities between Plotinus's stratified and orderly universe and the firm distinctions among social classes in his society in chapter 4. In chapter 5, his appropriation, at a crucial point in his philosophy, of the rhetoric of the colosseum will become evident. A broader and more speculative suggestion, however, is that the political turmoil, instability of food supply, and rapid social change of his time may have prompted him to find in the unity and trustworthiness of the Platonic universe an attractive alternative to the frightening disorder of Roman society. This is *not* to say that Plotinus's philosophy derives from wishful thinking. He did not, as earlier Platonists had done, insist that a person ought to be able so to divorce himself from painful events that he could maintain a balanced and optimistic disposition even while being roasted alive. He called that claim silly. Nor did he urge that philosophy supplied an escape from pressures and pains. But he advocated a disciplined perspective that alters the quality of experience. He presented his philosophy as a way of regarding the universe and one's experience realistically and calmly as part of one great beauty.

3
"Choice and Chance": Soul as Pivot of the Universe

One and the same life holds the sphere, and the sphere itself is set in one life; and so all things in the sphere depend on one life: and so all the souls are one, but so one that it is also an unbounded soul.

Ennead 6.5.9

There were many proposals in mid-third-century Rome about the nature of the "real self" and the methods by which this self could be focused and strengthened. Plotinus's claims for the lineage and capacities of soul reveal his confidence that soul is the "real self," the center of human personhood. Some of his most elegant and persuasive prose occurs in describing soul and its powers. His emphasis on, and enthusiasm for, the beauty and integrity of soul seems to signal his awareness that others in his society were identifying "real self" differently and were suggesting other focusing and strengthening exercises.

Early in his authorship, Plotinus wrote a series of treatises on the nature, activity, and power of soul. As we have already seen, his first treatise, "On Beauty" (1.6.9), presents soul as an active fulcrum, a hinge connecting intellect and sense. Soul is the pivot on which the universe revolves, for soul can see deeply into the sensible objects with vision informed by intellect. "The ultimate power of soul begins at the earth [from one perspective] and is interwoven through the whole universe" (2.2.2).

His second (chronological) treatise, *Ennead* 4.7, "The Immortality of the Soul," turns to a direct discussion of the nature and role of this all-important link, soul. Since Plotinus began writing only when he had worked out the main tenets of his thought, his early attention to soul and its powers reveals his sense of the foundational importance, for his whole philosophy, of understanding soul's role.

In *Ennead* 4.7 Plotinus's ultimate concern is to determine whether or not the soul is immortal, but he begins with a prior question.[1] Why should human being – a unity – be analyzed into two entities, body and soul? Plotinus recalls Plato's reminder that "divisions" of unified entities (for example, "dividing" the universe into intelligible and material spheres, or human being into soul and body) is done in concept only and for purposes of discussion.[2] These divisions can never be observed in life, but are useful for thought.

Since human being is a composite unity, he says, it is possible that one part could survive death while another part might not. It seems to him immediately and evidentially obvious that body cannot be immortal. Since body is itself a composite, it cannot be expected to hold its parts in the necessary delicately balanced tension forever and thus to achieve immortality. Body is in a state of evident and perpetual change, growing and diminishing, "dissolving" and "wasting away." The precision tricks it performs – breath, digestion, heartbeat, and circulation of blood – depend on soul's animating and energizing function. Clearly, then, the whole human composite is not immortal. Rather, body should be thought of as soul's instrument or tool, expected to last for a roughly specified time.[3] Because it is biodegradable, then, body is not the most important part; soul is the self.

Soul's Nature

What is soul's nature? Is soul a kind of body? Plotinus decides immediately that it cannot be body for it forms body. In fact, soul's first responsibility is to produce body by shaping matter. Body cannot shape itself, nor can it supply its own continuing life. If it were not for soul, "all things would stick in matter." If there were nothing to shape it, "this universe of ours would be dissolved [or] perhaps there would not even be any matter at all . . . But if soul exists, all these bodies serve it for the maintenance of the world and of each individual" (4.7.3).

Soul has powers that distinguish it from body. If soul were a body, "neither perception nor thinking nor knowing nor virtue nor anything of value will exist," for each of these activities presupposes the ability not simply to respond, but to perceive and remember wholes (4.7.6). Plotinus concludes that soul is "real being . . . prior to bodies and stronger than they are" (4.7.4).

Plotinus pictures soul in relation to body as a center charged with registering and organizing sense perceptions that come to it through body. For example, when a face is seen, it is soul which collects and organizes the disparate features into the unity, face. If the eye could see only parts and pieces (like a neonate's eye), how could it see landscapes, elephants, and galaxies? Plotinus gives examples that support his conclusion that "it would not even be possible to think if soul was any kind of body" (4.7.8).

In the context of his project of identifying soul as source of form and life, Plotinus dramatizes the power of soul by minimizing the importance of body. In order to apprehend concepts like circle, triangle, line, and point, he says, soul must disengage from body, because material objects never perfectly reflect them. This is even truer of concepts such as justice, courage, virtue, self-control, and beauty. Take beauty, for example: in order to perceive a person as beautiful, we necessarily import "a kind of shapeliness in impressions, by which we say, when we see them that people are fresh and young and beautiful in body." The judgments built into and informing our perceptions are stable; their instantiations come and go: "the whole nature of bodies does not abide, but flows away" (4.7.8).

But why distinguish soul from body? Clearly, both are necessary to a living being. Plotinus is concerned that the human habit of conflating soul and body hides soul's all-important role. Observation reveals bodies acting; it does not, without a further step, reveal that which enables bodies to act, to breathe — in short, to live. If body and soul are not clearly distinguished, "the powers of bodiless realities [are transferred] to bodies," leaving no role for soul. The resulting misapprehension of reality has consequences, disorienting the one who misapprehends and misdirecting his/her attention to transient and fragile bodies rather than to soul, the real source of body's life and action. Soul vivifies and sensitizes whole bodies and each part of body, a role it could not play if it *were* body, or part of body, belonging to body, or a kind of body.

Soul's mobility through bodies is another evidence of its priority and power in relation to body: "the same soul belongs to one living thing after another." Plotinus rejects Aristotle's claim that soul is "the form of the body," because this makes soul dependent on body. Soul *informs body*, but exists before – and after – any particular body. Soul is "real substance" – the only worthy holder of that title, "for everything bodily should be called becoming, not substance" (4.7.8[5]). Body participates in soul's being, but soul is not its own source of being.

John Donne

Soul's Powers

Satisfied with his discussion of soul's distinction from body, Plotinus waxes eloquent about soul's abilities and powers. Soul originates motion, gives – but cannot lose – life, being "indestructible and immortal of necessity." Soul is "kin to the diviner and to the eternal nature" (4.7.10). It is also an accessible source of reliable information about the universe. Since soul comes from and shares characteristics with intellect, a person can begin to understand the universe by examining her own soul to "find out what sort of nature it has." But this examination is limited by the fact that "soul, in the great majority of people, is damaged in many ways." It has accumulated encrustations of evil and developed dependencies and addictions. In most people, soul cannot be observed "in itself," in which case one must "consider it by stripping," that is, by *conceptually* distinguishing it from body. What will the committed observer see when this is done?

> He will see an intellect which sees nothing perceived by the senses, none of these mortal things, but apprehends the eternal by its eternity, and all the things in the intelligible world, having become itself an intelligible universe full of light, illuminated by the truth from the Good, which radiates truth over all the intelligibles . . . For it is certainly not by running around outside that the soul "sees self-control and justice," but itself by itself in its understanding of itself and what it formerly was, seeing it standing in itself like splendid statues all rusted with time which it has cleaned . . . seeing itself isolated, it wondered at its worth, and thought that it needed no beauty brought in from outside, being supreme itself, if only one would leave it alone by itself. (4.7.10)

"Who with any sense could doubt that a thing of this kind is immortal," Plotinus concludes. "It has life of itself," and life is substance, the same substance as soul. Soul *is* life, the spiritual substance of the universe.

Moreover, the "soul of the All" is indistinguishable from individual souls: "the soul is a single and simple nature which has actual existence in its living" (4.7.12). Plotinus will make much of the unity of soul. It entails a fundamental kinship between living beings, and it guarantees soul's indestructibility; because it is not body, soul cannot be chopped up into parts and dispersed. Soul is immortal.

Another early treatise, *Ennead* 4.2, builds on Plotinus's previous discussions of soul's immortality. This very short treatise explains that soul's position in the universe, simultaneously the product of intellect and the source of body's life and unity, makes soul not only the pivot of human life, but the hinge of the universe. Soul possesses double potential; it is, on the one hand, indivisible, but it also has a natural inclination to, and capacity for, division. Plotinus stretches language to cover his claim that soul is both divisible and indivisible; it is, he says, "indivisibly divided." In intellect, souls are without bodies and thus indivisible. Yet soul is also in bodies and divided by bodies. Soul does not completely leave intellect when it comes to body; "something of it did not come down," but remains "above." Even when soul is embodied it brings with it the character of the All-soul, for it is both undivided and divided; it both "gives itself whole to the whole [body], . . . and it is present in every part" (4.2).

If soul is indivisible, how then does soul come into body while simultaneously remaining in intellect? Plotinus's answer is that its activity in the sensible reflects and depends upon its intelligible existence. Soul comes into body in order to produce the kind of order and beauty with which it is familiar in intellect. Strikingly, Plotinus's metaphor is pregnancy and birth: "As if pregnant by the intelligibles and labouring to give birth," soul strains toward the sensible world, eager to care for the All by investing itself in a part of the All, a body. Even when this occurs, however, "some part of soul" remains in intellect, invulnerable to the changes to which bodies are susceptible, for "nothing of real being perishes" (4.7.13–14).

Soul, as life, migrates through bodies, forming them and maintaining them until those bodies fatigue. Soul can animate any and all kinds of bodies for all living beings "started from the same origin," but Plotinus believes that soul has a special affinity for human bodies (4.7.14). The accuracy and frequent helpfulness of prophetic utterances at oracular shrines, he says, testify to soul's on-going interest in the human sphere.

The third treatise Plotinus wrote, "On Destiny" (*Ennead* 3.1), argues that the universe is directed not by physical necessity but by spiritual force. What is destiny, he asks, and how does causation work? After demonstrating soul's immortality he is ready to describe its activity and responsibility.

He begins by making an assumption explicit: everything that exists – actions as well as entities – owes its existence to a cause. Neither spontaneous lurches of bodies nor random impulses of the soul can account for the phenomena of the universe. If they did, soul would be subject to irrational compulsion. And this would be intolerable for Plotinus.

He gives an example: "The cause of the child is the father, and perhaps some external influences . . . [like] a wife well adapted to bearing children."[4] Plotinus's point is not to glorify the father's role at the expense of the mother's, for he reduces the father's role to being merely a local cause. The child's existence can be traced beyond and behind the father to "Nature," and beyond nature ultimately to the One. To the question, where do babies come from *really*, he has a firm answer: "the ruling principle in each living thing" (3.1.2). He postpones saying what he means by this until he has considered others' opinions.

Ordinarily thorough and meticulous in considering others' views, Plotinus gives very short shrift to those who would answer the question of the child's origin in physical terms, dismissing this view as "absurd and impossible." He hurries to another proposal, namely, that one soul, "permeat[ing] the universe, accomplishes everything, each individual thing being moved as a part in the way in which the whole directs it." But this proposal carries the difficulty of entailing "an excess of necessity and of destiny." If all developments are coerced by an overriding and irresistible momentum, this leaves no room for "thoughts and actions that are *our own*" (3.1.4).

Plotinus insists that "each one's good and bad actions must come from himself, and that we must not attribute the doing of bad actions to the All."[5] This matter is close to the bone for Plotinus; it involves soul's agency. In spite of his earlier assertion that the universe is not governed by chance, he must create some elbow room for acts which are "our own." Neither spiritual forces nor physical exigency must usurp this "narrow own little strip of orchard in between river and rock."[6] We must not be "stones set rolling, but people who have work to do of ourselves." Our lives will be intimately and dramatically affected by whether or not we succeed in making a distinction "between what we do ourselves and what we experience of necessity" (3.1.5). Moreover, the stars do not determine who we are and how we will act; at best, and quite incidentally to their real purpose, they may suggest analogies.

What Plotinus seeks is complex; it is a cause that will "leave nothing causeless, and will preserve sequence and order, and [still] allow us to be something." But he has a candidate: "Soul, surely, is another principle which we must bring into [our picture of] reality – not only the soul of the All but also the individual soul along with it as a principle of no small importance; *with this we must weave all things together*" (3.1.8).

He considers soul's qualifications for this enormous role. Soul initi-
ates activity, but its freedom is somewhat limited by its association
with body; apart from body, "it is in absolute control of itself and free
and outside the causation of the physical universe." Even embodied, it
is possible for soul to master the chance events that surround it "and
lead them where it wishes" (3.1.8). The same circumstances and emotions that derailed the less concentrated soul – lust, anger, poverty, or
power – will not affect the strong soul. The strong soul will make
choices; sometimes it will yield to circumstances, sometimes it will
alter them.

Human life supplies a rich and complex mixture of choice and chance.
One can "choose" through laziness to think of oneself as perpetually
at the mercy of whatever happens, but actions based on "the violence
of passions" are nothing but "passive responses." Or, on every occasion, one can exercise maximal choice within the parameters of chance
situations. Human freedom is the result of choosing to respond and
act on the basis of soul's "own pure and untroubled reason." Such
action requires premeditation and a great deal of practice. It is anything but automatic. The "best actions come from ourselves" (3.1.9).

Soul's Ascent

Plotinus's agenda in *Ennead* 5.9, "Intellect, the Forms, and Being," is
to describe the strength and beauties of intellect, soul's origin. He considers different methods of achieving his goal:

> One must therefore speak in two ways . . . if one is going to turn [peo-
> ple] round to what lies in the opposite direction and is primary, and to
> lead them up to that which is highest, one, and first. What, then, are
> these two ways? One shows how contemptible are the things now hon-
> oured by the soul . . . but the other teaches and reminds the soul how
> high its birth and value are, and this is prior to the other one and when
> it is clarified will also make the other obvious. (5.1.1)

If one's goal is to encourage the listener to recognize soul's grandeur
and integrity, one can either, Plotinus says, draw invidious contrasts
between the vulnerable and transient body and the immortal soul or
one can simply attract the listener by narrating the beauty and power
of soul. The first strategy could be misunderstood, but Plotinus says

that he will use it elsewhere. He *never does so in a systematic way* in the *Enneads*. It was clearly not his preferred method. Other than asides on the relative worthlessness of body in relation to soul and intellect, Plotinus's method of choice is simply to emphasize the glory of the realm that is the source of our world.

Plotinus had a reason for avoiding the other method: his only polemical treatise, "Against the Gnostics" (*Ennead* 2.9), reveals his opposition to those who regard the sensible world, including the sensible world nearest home – the body – with unrelieved contempt. Plotinus never expressed sympathy with this view. Indeed, his own position on the relative value of body and soul was framed in opposition to it. Even in the process of prompting identification with soul and its origin in intellect, Plotinus cannot bring himself to vilify body.

His own position is that the sensible world is an admirable and beautiful image or reflection of intellect. But the sensible is not intellect's equal in beauty, reality, or value. One who sees this world with clarity and accuracy, sees it *as* image and lets its beauty provide motivation and energy for pursuit of the great beauty of the One. Ascent to intellect never simply "happens." If it is undertaken at all, it requires strong conscious intention. On occasion, it is even necessary to sacrifice "the pleasant [for] a greater beauty" (5.9.1).

The ascent requires strong motivation: the one who "comes home after long wandering to his own well-ordered country," must be "a lover and truly disposed to philosophy from the beginning, [and] in travail over beauty." She or he quickly learns the lessons to be learned from attention to beautiful bodies and turns to "the beauties of soul, virtues and kinds of knowledge and ways of life and laws, and . . . to the cause of the beauty in souls," coming finally "to the ultimate which is the first, which is beautiful of itself" (5.9.2).

From where will the enormous energy needed for the ascent come? Plotinus returns to Plato's account of the ascent in the *Symposium*. The pivotal recognition – simultaneously motivation – is that "the beauty of bodies comes from elsewhere." Beauty "rests on" bodies; they do not possess beauty, because they are vulnerable at any moment, and certainly across time, to losing their internal coherence, and thus, their beauty. But the beauty of bodies is nonetheless *real*; it is not illusory, false, or misleading. No, it is real – even more real than the bodies on which it rests. Unlike bodies, it is lasting because its source is not susceptible to change, alteration, and decay.[7]

This point cannot be overemphasized, given the frequent misreading of Plotinus as one who condemns body and the sensible world.

Plotinus could not take more seriously and emphasize more clearly his view that the beauty seen (and heard) by the senses is connected to the great beauty, the most intimate and vivid characteristic of the universe. In short, the sensible objects in which beauty appears change and vanish before our very eyes. Their beauty is *really* that of the informing soul, a stable beauty derived in turn from soul's source, intellect and ultimately from intellect's source, the One. Since the One is beyond all predication it is intellect which is "beautiful of itself," "genuine reality and true substance" (5.9.2–3).

Plotinus explores intellect, soul's immediate origin, in order to better understand soul. He first notes that everything we are familiar with is a "compound of matter and what forms it." He remarks, somewhat puzzlingly, that even soul has traces of a compound, with "something in it like matter and something in it like form." What he means is that like body, soul is not, after all, self-sufficient but receives its powers from intellect, in turn passing them along to body. Despite his high esteem for soul's powers, Plotinus is careful to insist that soul too must be kept in perspective, for it is "matter to the first reality which makes it," while intellect's realities are "actual and without deficiencies and perfect."

Describing intellect and its activity is a considerable challenge, even for Plotinus! Intellect thinks itself, having its objects within itself. Human discursive thinking is not a good model for intellect's thought, for the objects of our thought are things that are not part of our own substance. In intellect, however, the objects of thought are not separate from the thinking. Moreover, separation of "things of that higher world" from "things in our world" is a bad human habit, one that must be overcome when we try to imagine intellect. By thinking "the real beings," intellect "establishes them in existence. It is, then, the real beings." Plotinus's criterion for real being is permanence; real beings "undergo no alteration or destruction"; "they are unchanging" (5.9.5).

In intellect, (Plotinus quotes Plato), "all things are together and nonetheless they are separate." Plotinus illustrates his point: seeds contain minutely differentiated capacities but yet are "undistinguished in the whole." Differentiating knowledge of objects of sense and knowledge of intelligible objects, he calls knowledge of sensible objects "opinion." Knowledge of sensible objects can never be exact since sensible objects change before our very eyes. Knowledge of intelligibles, because it does not rely on objects of sense, is the only genuine knowledge.

Intellect thinks its own contents, but it does not think things into physical existence, as soul does. Plotinus believed that intellect thinks something like Plato's Ideas. Yet intellect is "active actuality," which *is* being. Again, confusion is caused by our habits of thought. Active actuality and being "are thought of by us as one before the other because *they are divided by our thinking*, but . . . both are one thing." Intellect is undivided, "but we must bring [its contents] forward, as one examines in order the contents of a unified body of knowledge" (5.9.8).

The universe we see is a living being; its source and archetype is intellect. Living creatures, each having its own rational forming principle, are also "formed into the order and beauty of the universe." In intellect the apparent divisions – "humans in one place and the sun in another" – are canceled for "the forming nature has all things in one" (5.9.9).

The unity of the universe is guaranteed by intellect which is, after all, nothing but an articulation of the One. "All things, then, which exist as forms in the world of sense come from that intelligible world," and "all things are here below which are in the intelligible world" (5.9.14). Elsewhere he eulogizes in detail the perfect match of sense and intellect. Here his interest is in demonstrating that nothing but goodness and perfection exists in intellect. There is no form for evil in intellect, "since evil here is the result of want and deprivation and failure and is a misfortune of matter and of that which becomes like matter" (5.9.10).

Surveying the contents of intellect, Plotinus remarks that it contains many kinds of art. He differentiates the "imitative arts" – painting and sculpture, dancing and mime – and those arts that rely on precision measurement. But if any artistic skill starts from the proportions of living things and goes on from there to consider the proportions of living things in general, it would be a part of the power which also in the higher world considers and contemplates universal proportion in the intelligible. Music, building and carpentry, rhetoric and administration, geometry and, most importantly, wisdom, are Plotinus's examples of arts of this sort. He disqualifies farming, medicine, and body-building because they entail physical effects rather than intellectual principles.

Do the forms of individuals exist in intellect, soul's origin and home? In 5.9.12, where he is speaking only of bodily differences, he says that there is a form of humanity, but there is "no form of Socrates." But in the somewhat later treatise 5.7.18 he asserts the existence of forms of individuals. Moreover, in this passage, where he urges readers to pursue intellect, he also suggests that certain qualities of soul, derived from intellect, are not images of intellect, but themselves exist in actuality:

> Not all things which are here below ought to be thought of as images of archetypes. There must belong to an individual soul which is really a soul some kind of righteousness and moral integrity, and there must be true knowledge in the souls which are in us, and these are not images and likenesses of their Forms as things are in the sense-world, but those very Forms themselves existing here in a different mode. (5.9.13)

This is a startling claim. Virtues and strength of character are not reflections (even strong ones) of the integrity and goodness of intellect, but the very qualities themselves "existing in a different [i.e. temporal, embodied] mode."[8] Unlike sensible objects which necessarily take up space and are in one place, "the intelligible world is everywhere" (5.9.13), localized through soul.

Soul's Descent

Plotinus's only description of what we might call "mystical experience" occurs in the treatise he wrote next after "Intellect, the Forms, and Being," discussed above. *Ennead* 4.8, "The Descent of the Soul into Bodies," begins with a completely uncharacteristic autobiographical note. Immediately *after* his short description of that experience, he comments that investigation of the most important topics should not be foreshortened by ready answers. Heraclitus, he says, taught in riddles, leaving his readers guessing, neglecting to make clear to us what he is saying, perhaps because *"we ought to seek by ourselves, as he himself sought and found"* (4.8.1). Empedocles and Plato, he says, were similarly less than clear about their teachings on essential points, and for the same reason. The account of his mystical experience links his consideration of "Intellect, the Forms, and Being," and "The Descent of the Soul into Bodies":

> Often I have woken up out of the body to my self and have entered into myself, going out from all other things; I have seen a beauty wonderfully great and felt assurance that then most of all I belonged to the better part; I have actually lived the best life and come to identity with the divine; and set firm in it I have come to that supreme actuality,

setting myself above all else in the realm of Intellect. Then after that rest in the divine, when I have come down from Intellect to discursive rea-soning, I am puzzled how I ever came down, and how my soul has come to be in the body when it is what it has shown itself to be by itself, even when it is in the body. (4.8.1)

Plotinus is puzzled: Why in the world does soul desire the entangle-ments of bodily existence, when it has the potential revealed by this experience? He notes that Plato seemed to feel a similar ambivalence. Sometimes he said that soul is "fettered and buried" in body; at other times, he "praises the universe and calls it a blessed god and says that the soul was given by the goodness of the Craftsman, so that this All might be intelligent." Plotinus says that Plato implied that the soul of the All was *sent* into the physical universe so that the sensible would be intelligent; individual souls are sent "that the All might be perfect" (4.8.1).

Because Plato was evidently ambivalent and certainly obscure, his successors, instead of simply accepting authoritative teaching, must "undertake a general inquiry about soul . . . and about its maker." Because of the slippery and problematic nature of bodies, "souls had to sink deep into the world . . . if they were going to control them." Which of his readers (of mature years) – then or now – could quarrel with Plotinus's description of "the problem with the body"?

> Our individual bodies need a great deal of troublesome thought, since many alien forces assail them and they are continually in the grip of poverty, and require every sort of help as being in great trouble. (4.8.2)

The ultimate goal of a virtuous and intelligent life is to migrate no longer from one body to another, but to join the soul of the All in effortless direction of the universal body. In this ideal condition, soul has an administrative position; the hands-on service that was once required of it is now done by simple authority. It is not, therefore, general care of body that compromises and distracts soul, but the di-rect and constant engagement required in caring for a *particular* physical body.

Plotinus sees two primary reasons why soul's entailment with body is problematic. First, sensory experience can hinder thought by gener-ating models that do not apply to intellect. Second, experience in the sensible world stimulates passions, filling the soul with "pleasures, desires, and griefs."

Even the necessity of caring for a particular body, however, is not necessarily a burden. The good news is that neither bad habits of thought nor irrational passions can "happen to a soul which has not sunk into the interior of its body, and is not anyone's property, and does not belong to the body, but the body belongs to it." Soul is not necessarily defined either by body *or by ascetic resistance to body and its needs and desires*, but by its attention to "those higher realities." Such a soul handles the necessities of this world "with a power which requires no active effort" (4.8.2).

How should Plotinus understand body? He interprets an author – Plato – to whom he feels great respect and loyalty, but who has simply not been clear in his teaching about body's role in human being. And he lives in the midst of a confusing and conflicted cultural conversation about body. Is body to be thought of as fundamentally worthless, a spectacle in the gladiatorial shows of the Roman colosseum? Is it to be considered the enemy nearest home against which one must struggle to achieve salvation as Gnostics taught? Or, should management of body's needs and habits be thought of as "practices of the self," by which, by careful intentional construction, the edifice of self is built?

Educated readers expect to be able to detect, and to describe, the self-consistency of an author's ideas. But often, as in Plato's writings, the most interesting and revealing features of a philosophy are its points of tension or even contradiction. Those moments occur when language fails to express the complexity of the world or when different contextual interests make necessary virtually contradictory statements. At many points, language is strained and inadequate; opposites must be said, and awkwardly and stubbornly *held* without modification or resolution. Eventually, one must see that these points of awkwardness, of clumsy tension, must occur in philosophy because they are in the world, and philosophy reflects the world.

Plotinus resolved his dilemma skillfully. He refused both extremes of Plato's ambivalence about soul's role in relation to body, maintaining their tension but opting for an arguably Platonic insouciance about body. Animating, organizing, and caring for body is perhaps not ultimately irreconcilable with soul's primary activity, contemplation, but there is inevitable competition for soul's attention and energy: "when it looks to what comes before it exercises its intelligence, when it looks to itself it sets in order what comes after it and directs and rules it" (4.8.3).

This competition for soul's attention can foster the habit of putting first the body's comfort, effectively dislodging soul's connection with intellect. If this happens, soul "becomes a part and is isolated and weak and fusses" over its body. It then "has left the whole and directs the individual part with great difficulty." The individual soul sacrifices the effortless spontaneity of the All-soul in directing the whole. It is now "fallen," "caught," and "engaged with its fetter."

Its degradation, however, is not final. At any moment it can turn and ascend "when it is started on the contemplation of reality by recollection." Soul, Plotinus says, is "amphibious, compelled to live by turns the life there and the life here" (4.8.4). Plato is not inconsistent, Plotinus says; he simply comments in different textual contexts on different "moments" in soul's life cycle. Come to think of it, he continues, Heraclitus and Empedocles were similarly "inconsistent" in their descriptions of soul's responsibility to body. By definition, "everything that goes to the worse does so unwillingly, but since it goes by its own motion, when it experiences the worst it is said to be punished for what it did." But in this case, in which "it is eternally necessary by the law of nature . . . that in descending it meets the need of something else, if anyone said that a god sent it down, he would not be out of accord with the truth or with himself" (4.8.5). The ambiguity and the tension exist *in experience*; to resolve them too neatly *in philosophy* would be to distort. Plotinus does so only to the extent that he urges that the soul who quickly rebounds from anxious preoccupation with the care and nourishment of body "takes no harm" from the sensible world. Soul is even benefitted by acquiring a knowledge of good and evil and by being placed in concrete situations that exercise its power to choose.

Plotinus's own loyalty to body and the sensible world is evident when he describes the "richly varied" universe (a phrase he uses repeatedly) as an advance over the solitary unity of the One. Soul's descent articulates and actualizes all things that would, without descent into bodies, have remained "hidden, shapeless within that one." He speaks of a "power unspeakably great . . . which sends them out and cannot leave anything without a share of itself." The same power holds all things together forever, "those which exist intelligibly and those which exist perceptibly" (4.8.6).

Soul is the pivotal point of the universe, the spot at which the intelligible and the sensible converge: "it occupies a middle rank among realities." Soul can go either way. It can "plunge into the interior," or it can identify, through contemplation, with intellect. Its position is not easy; its task of holding together these crucial facets requires knowledge, skill, and concentration. But when the feat works, the perceptible world can, in fact, actually inform and enrich soul's repertoire:

it is possible for [soul] to emerge again having acquired the whole story of what it saw and experienced here and learnt what it was like to be There, and, by the comparison of things which are, in a way, opposite, learning, in a way more clearly, the better things. For the experience of evil is a clearer knowledge of the Good for those whose power is too weak to know evil with clear intellectual certainty before experiencing it. (4.8.7)

This is Plotinus's most forceful argument for the value of soul's descent. It is thoroughly congruent with his metaphysics and compatible with his values. For he insists on the inextricable interweaving *in reality* of intellect and sense; things perceived by the senses "receive their existence forever by participation in them, imitating the intelligible nature as far as they can" (4.8.6). They are distinguished only for the purpose of articulating their unity. The connection of intellect and senses is intimate; not only are they interwoven, but the senses depend on the intellect as source and as support. Plotinus posits a clear hierarchy, but one that gives their full value to both intellect and the senses. The All-soul, like the efficient administrator it is, does not condescend to handling "in person" the myriad minute daily adjustments necessary for the maintenance of the whole, but "considers what lies beneath it contemplatively and remains attached to the realities before it forever" (4.8.7). Since particular human souls "do not altogether come down, but there is always something of [them] in the intelligible," they can "receive from There and at the same time distribute here" (4.8.8).

Soul's Unity

Continuing his account of soul and its powers and responsibilities in *Ennead* 4.9, Plotinus explores the amazing implications of his doctrine of the descent of all things from a single origin. If it is true, he begins, that soul is one, "present as a whole everywhere," at all parts of the body, then could we go further to say that "my soul and your soul" are one, and "all the souls are one?" He answers: "if my soul and your soul come from the soul of the All, and that soul is one, these souls also must be one." This is a very radical statement and one to which objections must be considered. He imagines an interlocutor responding:

For it would be absurd if my soul and anyone else's were one soul: for if I perceived anything another would have to perceive it too, and if I was good he would have to be good, and if I desired anything, he would have to desire it, and in general we should have to have the same experiences as each other and as the All, so that if I had an experience the All would have to share in the perception of it.

This does seem questionable, but Plotinus replies to the objection: "if we are not going to make that assumption [i.e. that all souls are one] the All will not be one." Clearly, for Plotinus, this is an impossible conclusion. But there is a problem closer to experience: How can souls be one but nevertheless have different perceptions, feelings, desires, and experiences?

First, Plotinus says, although souls are one, the human composite of body and soul makes everyone different. Even within the body, parts experience differently from one another, and many experiences escape the conscious attention of the whole person. Certainly the whole is affected by the experience of a part, but it need not be a conscious impression. Second, soul integrates multiplicity; it is a unified entity that is multiple in its dealings with the world.

There is plenty of room for difference among entities sharing a common soul. But oneness of soul is also something we experience:

> We do share each other's experiences when we suffer with others from seeing their pain and feel happy and relaxed [with others] and are naturally drawn to love them: for without a sharing of experience there could not be love for this reason . . . And a word spoken quietly acts on what is far off, and makes something separated by an enormous distance listen; from this one can learn the unity of all because their soul is one. (4.9.3)[9]

Even the fact that we can speak of a rational and an irrational soul should not imply the existence of two souls. Soul has many powers, but these do not threaten its unity. No, the arguments for separate souls are not persuasive, Plotinus decides. He wants to "prevent astonishment at the bringing back of all souls to one," but it still remains to investigate *how* they are one.

Quite uncharacteristically, Plotinus introduces the discussion of the oneness of soul with a prayer for assistance. Having done so, he asserts (rather than argues) that "there must be one which is prior, if there are many, and the many must come from this." All this would be impossible, he says, if the universe were founded on bodies, for the One would need to be broken into myriad tiny pieces to provide the rich variety of living beings. In a spiritual universe, however, "one and the same soul" can be in many bodies, "and before this one in the many bodies, another exists which is not in many bodies, from which derives the one in the many" (4.9.4). Soul is substantial and incorporeal, the "stuff" of the universe sought, but not found, by the pre-Socratic philosophers because of their materialism.

The incorporeal foundation and sustenance of the universe is one of Plotinus's most fundamental doctrines. Spiritual substance can remain "an undiminished whole" even when divided by matter. The problem of sensible experience is that it tends to obscure the fact of spiritual substance. From the vantage-point of intellect, however, this fact is clear and evident.[10]

In the *Enneads* thus far discussed, Plotinus's agenda has been to urge his readers to ascend. His task is practical and educational. He does not survey the metaphysical map for its own sake. In *Ennead* 5.1, "On the Three Primary Hypostases," he covers similar ground, but with a different intent, one that allows him to exhibit soul from a different perspective.

He begins with soul's descent. He has considered this in an earlier treatise, but it must be considered afresh in this context because this is the point at which human beings come into the cosmic picture. Here his picture of the descent of soul into the body is more negative; souls descend because they "forget their father, God." They are "ignorant of themselves and him" and this failure is the "beginning of evil." He piles on overlapping and sometimes conflicting reasons for the descent: "audacity," "wishing to belong to themselves," "delighted with their own independence," "ignorant," "admiring everything rather than themselves," "astonished and delighted and dependent on these things." He summarizes: "Their honour for these things here and their contempt for themselves is the cause of their utter ignorance of God" (5.1.1).

Soul is the proper investigator of realities, Plotinus states; "it has an eye of the right kind to see them." The investigation is made possible by the soul's creation of, and inner connection with, intellect: "For if the objects are alien, what is the point? But if they are akin, the investigation is suitable and discovery is possible." The kinship theme provides Plotinus with a starting point consistent with his esteem for the soul's power. The shift is dramatic: "Let every soul first consider this, that it made all living things itself, breathing life into them" (5.1.1). Whatever is alive is alive because it is informed and invested by soul. In Plotinus's universe, soul clearly stands prior to, and higher than, the created entity. The power to give life is "more honourable" than the things enlivened.

In order to locate soul's role in the universe Plotinus introduces a thought experiment.[11] He asks his reader to instruct body and its "raging sea," earth, sea, and air to be momentarily silent and at rest. Then he instructs her to picture soul "flowing in from outside, *so to speak* (*hoion*), . . . giving life and immortality and waking what is inert." Before the presence of soul, even heaven was "a dead body." This exercise is designed to jar the mind habituated to sensible composites into understanding the life-giving power of soul. Because it is a spiritual power, it extends to "every stretch of space" without being cut up or diluted. "All things live by the whole, and all soul is present everywhere." And because soul is one, "by admiring the soul in another, you admire yourself" (5.1.2).

Soul's kinship with the divine is the basis for the confidence that one can "attain God." Indeed, Plotinus emphasizes, "you will not look far; and *the stages between are not many.*"[12] In fact, divine intellect is the "soul's upper neighbour," so one must not imagine stretching toward something distant across vast expanses of time or space, but of an intimately known but often neglected neighbor. Soul derives its powers directly from "divine intellect." The only difference between them is that "around Soul, things come and go one after another"; intellect, however, "is all things . . . at rest . . . all things stationary for ever" (5.1.4). The universe is fundamentally spiritual: "these things which have thickness come afterwards, and sense perception thinks they are realities" (5.1.5).

Returning to the question of the one and the many, Plotinus repeats the precaution he had used earlier in the context of the same question (4.9.4). He calls upon divine assistance: "Let us speak of it in this way, first invoking God himself, not in spoken words, but stretching out with our soul into prayer to him, able in this way to pray alone to him alone" (5.1.6). Even as he invokes "God himself" Plotinus reminds his readers that to do so is to turn *ourselves* toward reality, not to move the One to response. The One remains as always, its power continuing to radiate the whole universe. No, the point of prayer is ourselves: by praying, *our* attention is focused in a fruitful direction, the direction of our origin. Plotinus's metaphor of the One's presence is fragrance, which diffuses itself into the surrounding air.

Plotinus complains of the difficulty of describing the relationship of the One to "what has come into being." Because the origin and source of a living being is the One, the living "must be in a way that Good, and retain much of it and be a likeness of it, as light is of the sun." Having said that, however, Plotinus immediately adds, "But Intellect is not that Good," but *is* its "seeing" (5.1.7). Intellect's ability to see is the result, "so to speak," of distinguishing itself from the One's undifferentiated power.[13] Being resides in intellect because it "must not fluctuate, so to speak," as it obviously does in living beings. It must be safe – beautiful, versatile, and permanent – existing forever without change and decay.

Notice, *please*, that in utter contradiction to a consensus among many twentieth-century authors that Plotinus consistently devalues sensible things and living beings in relation to "higher realities," Plotinus says that the existence of sensible objects is necessary and natural. The One gives because it must: "Since it was perfect it had to generate, and not be without offspring when it was so great a power" (5.1.7). In various passages in the *Enneads* Plotinus argues that the "higher realities" are needed to ground, maintain, and guarantee the reality of human experience. Moreover, those universal realities, Plotinus's three hypostases – the One, Intellect, and Soul – are not "out there"; "they are present in ourselves." They are the features of ourselves that form, maintain, and transcend biology. When we know who we are, the three hypostases are us!

Plotinus again articulates the injunction that prompted his earlier discussion of soul, namely, advocacy of "fleeing the body" in order to identify with soul. Once more he advises:

> This higher part of the soul is naturally separated, [but we should not] incline to the body – if by any chance one could make the remaining part of the soul ascend and *take along with us to the heights* that of it which is established here below, which alone is the craftsman and modeller of the body and is actively concerned with it. (5.1.10)

What would happen to body if the "remaining part of soul" could actually be detached from body? Bereft of soul's life, body would die. His statement is hyperbole, however, for the "upper" soul cannot be "separated" from the part of the soul that cares for body. His point is that the anxious fear with which soul clings to body is unnecessary. Soul cannot desert body until, at death, body deserts soul (1.9.1).

"These statements of ours are not new," Plotinus tells his readers, invoking their respect for ancient thought, especially that of Plato. He reiterates the necessity of concentration, effort, and exercise for grasping things "not immediately perceptible." The turn is metaphorically expressed as a turn to the *in*side of the universe, the inside of human being, and a different kind and quality of attention is required. Plotinus concludes, "It is as if someone was expecting to hear a voice which he wanted to hear and withdrew from other sounds and roused his power of hearing to catch what, when it comes, is the best of all sounds which can be heard" (5.1.12). In his metaphysical discussion of the three hypostases, Plotinus has inadvertently reverted to a more pressing agenda, namely, stimulating his reader to turn to the source.

Plotinus realized that his agenda had changed in the process of writing from metaphysical description to homiletics. The beginning of his next treatise (5.2) finds him worried about whether, in his preoccupation with demonstrating the connectedness of the universe, he has given short shrift to the One's transcendence. Yet this very short treatise does little to rectify the problem, for once again Plotinus stresses the continuity of the One with the entities it generates and supports. To the question of how the One can give what it does not have, namely multiplicity, Plotinus says that it is precisely *because* there is nothing in the One that all things come from it:

> it is the principle of all things. The One is not being, but the generator of being . . . The One, perfect because it seeks nothing, has nothing, needs nothing, overflows, so to speak, and in its superabundance makes something other than itself. Nothing is separated or cut off from that which is before it. All these things are the One and not the One. (5.2.1)

In this passage Plotinus says that the One's formative power reaches as far as plants. He uses a metaphor he has not thus far used to describe the relationship of the One to the many forms of life it creates:

> It is like a long life stretched out at length; each part is different from that which comes next in order, but the whole is continuous with itself, but with one part differentiated from another, and the earlier does not perish in the later. (5.2.2)

Soul's Life

At the mid-point of his writing career Plotinus returned to considering some "Difficulties About the Soul" (*Ennead* 4.3–5). These treatises have been called the heart of the *Enneads*. Like his early treatises, they explore soul as hinge or pivot of the universe and, among the hypostases, the object of Plotinus's primary philosophical interest. Soul "gives us knowledge in both directions" (4.3.1). Although there is redundance and repetition in these later treatises, Plotinus thinks the investigation of soul always worthwhile: "What could one more reasonably spend time in discussing and investigating extensively than this?" The ancient "command to know ourselves" is obeyed when we have a thorough understanding of soul. In what follows I focus on Plotinus's extension and nuancing of his earlier thought.

He describes more economically and decisively than formerly how soul can be spoken of as in "parts," when in fact soul is one thing everywhere. With a spiritual substance, he says, "that which is called a part will be the same as the whole, not a part of the whole" (4.3.3). He again emphasizes the contiguity of the hypostases, picturing souls as "fastened [to the One] by their edges on the upper side" (4.3.4).

Plotinus provides a new framework for his exploration of soul, emphasizing that the universe is "a single mighty living being" within which a dynamic life circulates (4.4.11–12). This framework helps him understand soul's descent more accurately and generously than in the earlier treatises. In a universe pictured as "a single mighty living being" – a phrase he repeats several times – soul's descent can be understood as spontaneous and natural. Each soul:

> comes down to a body made ready for it according to its resemblance to the soul's disposition . . . A natural principle compels each to go in its proper order to that to which it individually tends . . . There is no need of someone to send it or bring it into body at a particular time, or into this or that particular body, but when its moment comes to it it descends and enters where it must of its own accord. (4.3.12–13)

Souls descend, then,

> neither willingly nor because they are sent, nor is the voluntary element in their going like deliberate choice, but like a natural spontaneous jumping or a passionate natural desire of sexual union. (4.3.13)

Plotinus suggests several images of soul's relationship with body: he pictures soul as a gardener "concerned about the maggots in [a] plant and anxiously caring for it." Alternatively, soul could be thought of as like "a healthy person who is at the service of his neighbours, while a sick person is at the service of his body" (4.3.4).

Differences between the early treatises on soul and these of his mid-career are subtle but important. One has already been mentioned. Body is cast much less as a trap for soul and soul's care for body is more prominent. Soul reflects the universe in its identity and individuation:

"each soul remains one and all are one together" (4.3.5). Souls "sing . . . with one voice and are never out of tune" (4.3.12). As in the early treatises, a "community of feeling" among people happens because "all souls derive from the same from which the soul of the whole derives too," but now Plotinus has a different explanation of differences between people. Having said earlier that different bodies cause these differences, he now says that differences are caused by the fact that "different souls look at different things and are and become what they look at."[14]

Moreover, in his mid-career treatises, he emphasizes soul and body's mutual predilection for one another and benefit to each other:

> There never was a time when this universe did not have a soul, or when body existed in the absence of soul, or when matter was not set in order; *but in discussing these things one can consider them apart from each other* . . . If body did not exist, soul would not go forth, since there is no place other than body where it is natural for it to be. (4.3.9)

Plotinus's image of the union of soul and body is a house:

> There came into being something like a beautiful and richly various house which was not cut off from its builder, but he did not give it a share in himself either; he considered it all, everywhere, worth a care . . . The universe lies in soul which bears it up, and nothing is without a share of soul. (4.3.9)

"Universe extends as far as soul goes," and "wherever body extends, there soul is." Plotinus's universe is intimate: "nothing is a long way off from anything else"; any distance is "a matter of difference and not being mixed" (4.3.11).

In this volatile universe, individual souls are rather tenuously invested in bodies. As life, soul migrates from body to body, and "responsibility lies with the souls which have come down for coming down in such a way that some are put in this place and others find themselves in that." Different souls adopt different relations with destiny. Some "become subject," while others are "self-possessed" and able to choose a "life lived more in the intelligible" (4.3.14–15).

Plotinus examines the common understanding of soul as "in body." Because body makes soul (as life) visible, people imagine that body contains soul. But really, body is in soul, "the unimportant in the more important, what is held together in that which holds it together" (4.3.20). How, then, is soul present to body? Plotinus examines multi-

flapping /
flapping in the
wind, my soul

ple metaphors, none of them perfectly satisfying – the architect and the house, the steersman in the ship, and fire in air. The problem of finding an apposite metaphor is that soul's independence from body must not be elided, for there is a "part of the soul in which body is and part in which there is no body" (4.3.22).

Plotinus also rethinks soul's powers; he does not eliminate any of the powers he had discussed previously, but adds several not mentioned in his earlier treatises. Soul has multiple powers which it dispenses as appropriate: for example, soul circulates nutrition throughout the body and manages body's growth, but even more importantly, soul remembers. "Body's nature, moving and flowing, must be a cause of forgetfulness; remembering belongs to soul, as sweetness in a mixture of wine and honey belongs to honey" (4.3.26). Soul has two different kinds of memories, those which reach soul through body and those experiences occurring within soul. Soul's memories can be either images or words. After death, soul is at first filled with memories of its former life. Gradually, however, soul's individuality is diluted by memories of other lives, and then soul either is drawn by its desires to another body, or it exists "alone," that is, without a body, in the soul of the All.

Plotinus urges detachment from present "human concerns" so that "human memories" do not impede soul's progress. The "higher" soul's memories are more valuable than those of the "lower" soul whose task is care for body and who feels emotional engagement. But it is not a matter of repressing memories of family, desires, and the familiar haunts of one's life, but of gathering this "multiplicity into one." The soul has "a unified intuition of all its objects and can think them all together. The particulars are included in knowledge of the whole" (4.4.8).

In speaking of intellect it is not quite right to think in terms of memory, for "each and every thing is present there" – not remembered, but immediate, accessible. Intellect matches the diversity and mutiplicity of human experience: "The All is full of the richest variety: all rational forming principles are present in it, and an unbounded store of varied powers" (4.4.36). Soul is defined by its memories: it "is and becomes what it remembers" (4.4.3). But memory does not need to be conscious to affect soul; quite the opposite. Plotinus anticipates Freud's theory of the unconscious in his remarks:

> Even when one is not conscious that one has something, one holds it to oneself more strongly than if one knew ... perhaps if one knew, one

would have it as something else, being different oneself, but if one does
not know that one has it one is liable to be what one has; and this is
certainly the experience which makes the soul sink lower. (4.4.4)

The implications of this passage are worth further reflection. In failing
to distinguish itself from its physical and emotional experiences in body,
soul self-identifies with body and is tied to temporality, forgetting the
"place" of timeless unity. Plotinus's examples of "sinking into the body"
are revealing; he does not cite such passions as lust or avarice, but
illness, weakness, and old age – situations in which bodily concerns
and care require disproportionate attention. The tendency of "composite" life is to swing from one extreme to the other, from engrossment
in body to "longing for communion" (4.4.18). Plotinus defines pain
as the withdrawal of soul from body; pleasure consists of "soul again
fitting itself back in the body" (4.4.19).

To translate the awareness of timeless unity into daily life is to see
the universe as a "single mighty living being" not externally administered, but "working from inside, from the principle of its life" (4.4.11).

> This one universe is all bound together in shared experience and is like
> one living creature, and that which is far is really near . . . and since it is
> a living thing and all belongs to a unity nothing is so distant in space
> that it is not close enough to the nature of the one living thing to share
> experience. (4.4.32)

The movement of the "one living creature" is "a single ballet in a rich
variety of dance movements" (4.4.33). It is "absolutely necessary"
that this "single living thing" have "an internal self-communication of
its experiences" (4.4.35), but most people cut themselves off from that
communication by "not considering the whole of ourselves to belong
to it" (4.4.34). Plotinus states his often repeated belief in the trustworthiness and safety of the universe: "nothing that belongs to the All can
be discarded by it." In this richly varied living being, we "encounter
the extraordinary with astonishment, though we should be astonished
at these ordinary things too if we were unfamiliar with them and someone presented a detailed account of them to us and explained their
powers" (4.4.37).

Once one has understood this picture of the universe, it becomes
obvious that prayer cannot function as a plea for special attention.
Petitions, like magic, do often seem to produce what one needs but
that is because of "sympathetic connections within the universe."

Things happen, not by the deliberate choices of the gods, but by "natural necessity." As Plotinus had explained in earlier treatises, the function of prayer is a reorientation of consciousness by which the person praying turns deliberately toward the Good. "We must not assume that the All can be affected" by prayers (4.4.42). "The life of the universe does not serve the purposes of one individual but of the whole" (4.4.39). *Providence is of the whole* (4.4.45).

problem

Plotinus concludes by considering "enchantment," the most obvious, but perhaps not the most significant, form of which is magical spells. Himself the object of magical attacks in which he felt his "limbs squeezed together and his body contracted 'like a money-bag pulled tight'," Plotinus did not doubt the efficacy of magic. In fact, Porphyry says that Plotinus himself practiced magic to the extent of making the attacks against him recoil on the attacker (*Life* 10). Magic works, Plotinus explains, because powers already circulating in the universe can be harnessed to affect another part of the same universe. If anyone "put a magician outside the All," he would be powerless. There are also milder enchantments, like music.

But there is also a more pervasive form of enchantment by which everyone is affected: "everything which is directed to something else is enchanted by something else . . . all practical action is under enchantment, and the whole life of the practical man: for he is moved to that which charms him" (4.4.43). "Contemplation alone remains incapable of enchantment because no one who is self-directed is subject to enchantment." Clearly, Plotinus uses words like "enchantment" and "fascination" to refer to activities that, at least to a degree, lack freedom and choice. He equates practical life with irrational impulse; a person reacts according to his socialization, social location, and other factors that create one's particular perspective. The appearance of choice is illusory. Enchantment is unavoidable in large arenas of life: we need to survive, and we are concerned about, and often responsible for, others' survival. But we should not delude ourselves that activities addressed to these purposes are self-directed. Only in contemplation can one be completely self-directed in the sense that "he is one, and that which he contemplates is himself, and his reason is not deluded, but he makes what he ought and makes his own life and work" (4.4.44).

In the context of his social and intellectual culture, Plotinus steered a course among alternative views of the relationship of soul and body in mid-third-century Rome. He did not define the body either as worthless or as the site for practicing "techniques of the self," but his teaching on soul supplies an alternative to his society's massive attention to bodies.[15] Body is to be attentively and tenderly cared for, not because one *is* one's body, but precisely because body is needy and dependent on soul's ministrations. In chapter 5 I discuss Plotinus's teaching on life after death, teachings which represent an implicit criticism of the Christian belief in resurrection of the body. Chapter 4 examines Plotinus's teachings on body in the context of mid-third-century Roman society.

4
Body in Third-century Rome

We encounter the extraordinary with astonishment, though we should be astonished at these ordinary things too.

Ennead 4.4.37

One of the most challenging tasks historians can undertake is to attempt to reconstruct the physical experience of another age. Some facts about diet, medical procedures, and social arrangements are usually available, but physical experience differs so markedly even within one's own society that speculations about other societies are at best impressionistic and crude. Moreover, class, age, and gender, among other variables, affect physical experience so intimately and constantly that it can seem fruitless to try to reconstruct others' experience in the absence of descriptions written by the people themselves.

Clearly, suggestions about distinctive features of the physical, emotional, and intellectual experience of people of a particular society must finally be speculative. But to attempt such reconstruction is, nevertheless, both fascinating and helpful for setting an author's ideas in their original context. In this chapter I examine Plotinus's description of body in the context of several prominent features of his society's interest in bodies. I will focus on two public sites which help to localize these interests in third-century Rome. In concentrating on games at the Roman colosseum and public baths, however, I touch on only the most distinctive characteristics of Roman public culture, omitting other important variables such as work, diet, disease, and living conditions.

An even more significant omission relates to Roman women. Women usually come into focus in Roman literary sources when they participate in the male world of public life – when they are Christian martyrs like Perpetua and Felicitas, when they occasionally appear in the arena as gladiators, or as prostitutes. In the public life discussed here, women appear only as spectators confined to the top tiers of the colosseum or as participants at the public baths.[1] Their invisibility reflects – and results from – their society's expectation that women's place was primarily in the private sector, the home. There is much more ample evidence of men's lives, but expectations of masculinity in third-century Rome were at least as stringent as expectations for femininity: "to be a man was to run risks, to stand up to danger, . . . and violence was part of that culture's normal behavior."[2]

Colosseum games and public baths were the two main sites of Roman leisure. Both focused on bodies either, in the case of the games, as the focus of a spectator sport, or, at the baths, on bodies – one's own and others' – as sites/sights of pleasure. Both colosseum and baths were public places with free admission in which the class distinctions of a rigidly stratified society were blurred, contested, and temporarily reconfigured.

The Colosseum

A good deal of fascinating scholarly work has been done in the last decade or so on the culture of the Roman colosseum. My purpose is not to repeat or summarize that work, but rather to engage it in order to demonstrate a cultural preoccupation that crossed class lines, required the expenditure of huge sums of money, time, and energy, and was a preoccupation of the visual arts and literature of the time. The colosseum in Rome, built under Vespasian toward the end of the first century CE, seated about 50,000. In the mid-third century (248 CE) while Plotinus was teaching in Rome, one of the largest spectacles of the Roman world, the thousandth anniversary of the founding of Rome, took place in the colosseum.

Gladiatorial combats were celebrated in the Roman republic in connection with important funerals, but in the empire the games diversified. The calendar of Furius Dionysius Philocalus (354 CE) set aside 176 days of the year for spectacles, of which 10 were specifically for gladiatorial and wild beast shows.[3] A close link between the military culture of the Roman empire and the "murderous games" of the colosseum is evident. Violence was "an unambiguous statement of the power . . . [of] the Empire itself."[4] Emperors gained popularity through lavish spending on shows featuring hundreds of gladiators, rare animals, and inventive stage sets. In the morning, *venationes*, wild beast "hunts," occurred, a euphemism for the slaughter of animals brought

from all parts of the empire at huge expense. At noon, many spectators took a break while criminals and prisoners were executed.[5] In the
afternoon, *munera gladiatoria* occurred, in which pairs of gladiators
fought to the death. The excitement surrounding the games permeated
Roman society. It is attested by the many murals and mosaics, some of
exceptionally high quality – depicting gladiators and exotic animals in
Roman homes.[6] Keith Hopkins writes, "To capture the experience [of
an afternoon at the colosseum] we would have to blend sight, sound,
and smell."[7]

The games had several practical aims: Romans considered punishment a deterrent and they punished offenders spectacularly. In a society with no adequate police force, the games dramatized the emperor's
power to organize society and prevent crime. Moreover, the games
focused and broadcast the emperor's agency and wealth, Rome's power
over the natural world, and its ability to crush the enemies of Roman
order whether criminal, religious, or political.[8] The games also provided entertainment, proclaimed public prosperity, and permitted
everyone to share the fruits of empire. But these aims do not adequately
explain the predilection of a whole society for "extraordinary violence, publicly consumed."[9] Nor do they account for the massive "in-
vestment of time, wealth, and emotion" across social classes.[10]

Can one "get there from here" in imagination? American values at
the start of the twenty-first century are, in some ways, a poor starting
place from which to consider the games of the Roman colosseum.
Accustomed to being entertained by screen violence, we may be startled by the fact that the violent deaths of the Roman colosseum were
actual, not simulated. Nevertheless, there are some similarities between
contemporary North American media culture and third-century
Rome.[11] Roman society seems to have been the first entertainment
culture, the first society to use entertainment to stimulate, reward, and
pacify a whole population. American society uses entertainment similarly. A combination of entertainment and consumer goods keep Americans getting up and going to work in the morning. More subtle
similarities with Roman society can also be identified. For example,
we are accustomed to watching violent acts while empathizing with
the hero's power rather than with the victim's pain.[12] Similarly, stadium crowds were desensitized by the routine violence they witnessed.
As entertainment, victims were dehumanized, their bodies served as
spectacles for audiences' insatiable thirst for the distractions of "bread
and circuses."[13]

How did Roman audiences rationalize their pleasure at the sights, sounds, and smells of the colosseum? Historians, attempting to avoid cultural imperialism, give several explanations: First, in order to support the empire's regular military bloodshed, it was necessary to accustom the whole population to violence. Second, the crowd context of entertainment violence minimized individual feelings of responsibility. Third, in the "steep stratification" of Roman society, those who were destroyed were considered worthless.[14] As Coleman has pointed out, the class stratifications of Roman society rationalized cruelty against lower-class people: "When the upper classes are equated with true humanity, the lower classes are sub-human and therefore legitimately liable to cruel treatment."[15] Fourth, the ritual humiliation – by dress, torture, or mutilation – of those punished in the arena further enforced a distance between spectator and victim, making it less possible for the onlooker to sympathize with the victim's suffering.[16] Although spectators are occasionally described in Roman sources as feeling sympathy for animals, they apparently did not feel a similar sympathy with humans.[17] Finally, the fascination of sheer horror should not be overlooked.

There are also subtle cultural and psychological reasons for the games' popularity. The games represented "a Roman male reading of the Roman male experience."[18] In order to understand the games as Romans did, we must recognize that gladiatorial games were regarded as sports. The games' violence, though fascinating to modern historians, was not the point. The point was skill, self-control, and style: "to master oneself and one's body," and to know how to die.[19] According to J.P. Toner, a colosseum crowd was not a "bloodthirsty mob but the most urbane sophisticates in the world."[20] They recognized, appreciated, and rewarded courage and skill, not merely brute strength.

Paradoxically, even though gladiators were thought of as sub-human, they were also admired, even idolized. In Rome, it was not enough to have a male body, a man had to also be virile, and virility was a quality that always needed to be demonstrated or proved.[21] Gladiators modeled manliness, "austere, masculine, [and] inflexible," exhibiting the male body as a "symbol of controlled style."[22] Gladiators' pictures were painted on placards and buildings. Pliny said that "the portraiture of gladiators has been the highest interest in art for many generations now."[23]

Although in theory gladiators fought "to the death," it was not always the case that one of the combatants died. Wiedemann points out that gladiatorial combat was also an "opportunity for a condemned man to regain his physical and social life."[24] Spectators frequently gave the "thumbs up" gesture to a defeated gladiator who had acted courageously and skillfully in the fight. In fact, Potter estimates that gladiatorial combats ended in the death of one of the combatants approximately one time in ten.[25] Wiedemann also suggests that gladiators' chances of dying in a match should not be compared with those of players in modern sporting events, but with ancient life expectancies. The Roman world was one in which "three persons out of five would die before they reached their twenties."[26]

In antiquity, the objections raised by moralists like Cicero and Christians like Tertullian were not based on the games' cruelty to victims but rather on the damage to spectators caused by witnessing routine bloodshed. The games "mobilized emotions" and clouded reason, making people less rational and thus "less properly human."[27] Seneca wrote:

> Nothing is so damaging to good character than the habit of wasting time at the games; for then it is that vice steals secretly upon you through the avenue of pleasure . . . I come home more greedy, more ambitious, more voluptuous, even more cruel and more inhumane, because I have been among other human beings.[28]

Yet the longevity of the games attests to their crucial social functions. In the West, gladiatorial combats that began in the republic were finally suppressed in 407 CE; wild beast fights were outlawed in 523 CE.

In Roman society leisure was thought of differently than it is in our own society. Even if many or most Americans do not achieve this ideal, Americans, living in a society influenced by the Protestant work ethic, expect work to be meaningful. It seemed obvious to most Romans, however, that leisure (*otium*) was to be valued more highly than work. What was contested was what should be done with one's leisure. Michel Foucault's books, *The Care of the Self* and *The Use of Pleasure*, describe an elite male culture in the first centuries CE that prized *otium* for creating and cultivating a self defined by ascetic self-control and philosophical study. At the end of the fourth century, this ideal was still compelling. Augustine, as a new convert to Christianity, withdrew from social life with a few close friends to pursue a Christian version of Roman philosophical *otium*.

In the Roman empire, however, leisure was not the sole prerogative of the elite classes. Urban plebs, who were feared by emperors and the elite classes as potential sources of insurrection, also enjoyed leisure, but the empire's wealth created a social problem. Leisure was a contested site in the century of our interest, the third century. What should be done with it? The wealth of the empire created a social problem. The elite classes did not want the plebs to become accustomed to luxurious food, drink, and possessions so they consumed this wealth themselves, thus weakening traditional moral sensibilities. Moreover, the upper classes participated in a "gentrification of popular culture" that gradually dissolved the stern virtues of the Roman republic.[29]

All social classes organized their leisure around the games. The colosseum represented an area of equalization in a sharply stratified society.[30] Although seating was strictly by rank – *ordo* meant both rows of seats and social rank – all shared the same sensory thrills.[31] The games were "specialized highlights of Roman culture which came to represent . . . Rome itself."[32]

The Baths

The second aspect of Roman life explicitly focused on bodies was the public baths. Unlike games that occurred approximately once a month, baths were an "integral part of daily life." Like the games, the baths were provided by the emperor for the people. Roman baths were among the architecturally grandest of public buildings. Some, like the Baths of Diocletian, still stand. Every effort was made to render them luxurious. They were complex recreational facilities, including hot and cold baths, food, massage, beauty salon services, and prostitution. The baths of Caracalla, completed in 217 CE, featured mosaic floors, walls of marble, stucco reliefs, gilt bronze doors, and large sculptures. Three large bath chambers, the frigidarium (cold room), the calidarium (hot room), and the tepidarium (warm room), were enhanced by a steam room and swimming pools as well as by rooms for exercise and massage.

At the baths, social tensions were enacted as class lines were asserted by the pomp with which the wealthy and their retinues arrived, and subverted as they disrobed. When dress with its clear markings of social status was discarded, status became difficult to detect except by "body, voice, conduct, and attitude."[33] Social status was reassigned according to physical status; visible beauty replaced visible wealth. Cleanliness was not the primary purpose of the baths. Literary accounts emphasize that what Romans enjoyed about the baths was the leisure, relaxation, and pleasures rather than cleanliness. As a youth, the fourth-century Roman North African, Augustine of Hippo (one of few men of his time who revealed such intimate details), was observed to have an erection on the occasion of a visit to the baths with his father.[34] Quasi-medical regimes were also practiced at the baths. Baths were part of a "concern with total health rather than [with] cures and remedies, . . . a way of living."[35] Relief from stress and psychological comfort was also a benefit of the baths. Later in life, Augustine went to the baths when his mother died to seek the soothing physical comfort that could "drive sadness from [his] mind."[36] Romans expected psychic healing as well as physical relaxation at the baths.

In baths and at the colosseum, Roman bodies were on display. Both pleasures and pains were enjoyed by spectators. It was in this social context that Plotinus thought about body.

Plotinus on Body

Porphyry began his *Life of Plotinus* with the declaration: "Plotinus, the philosopher of our times, seemed ashamed of being in the body." In what follows, I examine Porphyry's statement from several different perspectives, the most important of which is Plotinus's own discussions of body. A philosopher's ideas of body, like those of all human beings, reveal not only his philosophical commitments and allegiances, but also his intimate experience and familiar cultural associations.

Few philosophers identify the personal and cultural experiences that shape their thinking. Few authors in our time or in Plotinus's time, reveal intimate influences, partly because they are often unconscious, and partly because the philosopher is too engrossed in communicating his insights. Similarly, authors seldom say what it is they fear, resist, or contest in the conversations immediately surrounding them. They simply state their position as coherently and forcefully as possible.

Since it is difficult to identify subtle but important influences on an author who lived many centuries earlier, historians tend to name only the most evident intellectual influences. Yet our own experience teaches that beneath our intellectual allegiances lie numerous experiences that have attracted us to particular proposals and not to others equally available and accessible. Historians are faced with a quandary: if we remain in the relatively safe territory of intellectual influences, we risk misunderstanding fundamental features of the historical author's thinking; if we suggest that certain personal, social, and cultural experi-

ences influenced the author's work, we risk becoming unprofession-
ally speculative.

The key to this dilemma is timing and geographical setting. If certain social and cultural practices can be located in the author's immediate vicinity, I assume that he was not unaware of these practices
even if he does not refer to or discuss them. If there is independent
evidence such as, for example, a contemporary biography, we may get
some further information about the author's affinities and aversions.
However, a biographer's interpretation of his teacher, even if it is informed by daily contact, is still an interpretation. If the biographer's
own philosophical writings are extant, the contemporary historian can
be helped to see how the biographer's intellectual commitments influence his interpretation.[37] In short, although history is more an art than
a science, suggestions often can be documented. Sometimes they cannot.

I refer, of course, to Plotinus and Porphyry. What are we to make of
Porphyry's strange revelation that Plotinus habitually sucked from his
wet-nurse's breast until he was eight years old, giving up the habit
only when he was teased for it?[38] Is Porphyry's reader intended to
infer that Plotinus's childhood embarrassment informed his more negative statements about body and pleasure? Why did he tell Porphyry
about this in the first place? – it seems very unlikely that Porphyry
could have heard it from anyone else since Plotinus was born and
raised in Egypt and Porphyry met him only after he came, in adult-
hood, to Rome. Finally, we cannot know. It is even unlikely that
Plotinus himself could have described the incident's significance in relation to his philosophy. Minimally, what Porphyry's information offers is a reminder that philosophers, like other people, think with and
through a rich collection of experiences and that their philosophical
proposals rely on these experiences in ways that cannot always be
identified and articulated.

Long after Plotinus's death when he wrote the *Life*, Porphyry remembered Plotinus's description of his shame over a bodily pleasure.
But childhood shame should not be related too hastily to the philosophical disdain Porphyry claimed that Plotinus felt for body. Shame
is a feeling; "disdain" is a philosophical stance. Porphyry wanted his
readers to connect this biographical information with the interpretation with which he began his account: "Plotinus seemed ashamed of
being in a body." If Plotinus's own writings sometimes convey a distinctively philosophical disdain, a preference for over-looking – looking over – body rather than the "shame" Porphyry claims, must we

not question Porphyry's interpretation? If, in addition, Porphyry's other writings reveal considerably more pessimism about body than do Plotinus's own writings, should we not challenge Porphyry's interpretation of Plotinus's "shame" in the light of Plotinus's own explicit denial – the only time he used the word "shame" in the *Enneads* – that there is anything to be ashamed of in embodiment?[39] To feel shame over embodiment, Plotinus says, is fundamentally to misunderstand the nature of the universe, for human bodies are a natural and necessary part of a whole.

> It is not proper for anyone to speak ill of even this universe as not being beautiful or the best of all things which have body ... there will be nothing to be ashamed of in its product; for it produced a whole, all beautiful and self-sufficient and friends with itself and with its parts, both the more important and the lesser, which are all equally well adapted to it. (3.2.3)

Indeed, Porphyry's own philosophical stance was much more pessimistic about body than that of Plotinus.[40] Porphyry's admiring description of Plotinus's negativity about his own body contradicts Plotinus's own statement.[41] Porphyry says, in further demonstration of his statement, that Plotinus "could never bear to talk about his race or his parents or his native country." Moreover, according to Porphyry, Plotinus refused to have his portrait painted, objecting, "Why really, is it not enough to have to carry the image in which nature has encased us, without your requesting me to agree to leave behind me a longer-lasting image of the image, as if it was something genuinely worth looking at?"[42]

As we have already seen, other interpretations of Plotinus's words are both possible and plausible. He may, for example, have simply disliked attention of this kind, preferring to keep his students' mind on his teachings rather than on himself as an individual.[43] Or maybe Plotinus's statement should simply be classified as the sort of jest people sometimes make when they are asked to stand still and smile for a camera.[44]

According to Porphyry, Plotinus did not go to the baths – he does not indicate why. He gives this information admiringly as further demonstration of Plotinus's reluctance to indulge his body. He does, however, report that Plotinus had himself massaged every day at home, information that undermines Porphyry's intention of demonstrating Plotinus's indifference, if not aversion, to caring for his body. Moreover, Porphyry understood Plotinus's massages as part of a regime of health care, a prophylactic measure against disease. When the plague of the 250s broke out and his masseurs died, Plotinus contracted the "acute diphtheria" from which he eventually died.[45] Yet Porphyry's famous statement that Plotinus was "ashamed of being in a body" directs most readings of the *Enneads*.

Because Plotinus's philosophy is frequently criticized for its alleged disparagement of nature, body, and matter, it is especially important to examine carefully what he actually said about body and sense objects. But it is equally important to explore his philosophy in relation to the culture and society in which he lived. In this chapter's conclusion I will suggest some reasons for Plotinus's confusing comments on body.

Plotinus treated body as a subject for sustained reflection, focusing several important treatises on body. It would not be a distortion to say that Plotinus was preoccupied with how to establish a secure place for body, despite its continuous shape-shifting and obvious lack of permanence. He was especially struck by the simultaneous fragility and preciousness of body and he wanted to find the best way to think of body in relation to reality.

Plotinus discussed body in two distinct rhetorical contexts. The first context is metaphysical. His intent in this context is to describe body in a way that emphasizes its integration in the spiritual universe. Here the metaphor of "image" governs his representation of body and the sensible world. And he counted all sensible things, including soil and rock as bodies – formed matter, matter given substance by soul. Bodies, with their notorious vulnerability and transience, are images of the human which is, in turn, an image of permanently existing intellectual form. Plotinus distinguished between kinds of images on the basis of whether or not they assume and require the presence of their prototype. For example, portraits do not assume the presence of the person whose painting it is. Indeed, they are usually done to preserve memory of the person in her/his absence. They stand for, or represent, the missing original. On the other hand, images in mirrors, pools of water, and even shadows require the presence of the original. If the original vanishes, so does the image.

Plotinus valued these two kinds of image very differently. Body is image on the model of a mirror or pool; its prototype is present: "We breathe and are preserved because that Good has not given its gifts and then gone away but is always bestowing them as long as it is what it is" (6.9.9). The model emphasizes the continuing *presence* of intellect in the sensible world. If informing intellect were to draw apart from the sensible, all order would dissolve into blankness or chaos. Plotinus found the image that represents its original in its absence of very little worth. He denied that a portrait could be "genuinely worth looking at."[46]

The second context in which Plotinus considered body is practical, namely, he sought to motivate his hearers and readers to practice contemplation. When these concerns were uppermost in his mind his treatment of body was different from – and less positive than – his metaphysical descriptions. A passage in *Ennead* 6.7.31 is a good example:

> The soul which has its love ready to hand does not wait for a reminder from the beauties here, but because it has its love, even if it does not know that it has it, it is always searching and in its wish to be borne away to that Good has a contempt for the things here, and when it sees the beauties of this world it distrusts them, because it sees that they are in bodies of flesh and polluted by their present dwelling and disintegrated by multitudes and are not the true beautiful things themselves; for those, being as they are, would never bring themselves to enter the mud of bodies and dirty themselves and disappear. But when it sees the beauties here flowing past it, it already knows completely that they have the light which plays on them from elsewhere. And then it is borne away, skilled in finding what it loves, and not leaving off till it catches it. (6.7.31)

These different evaluations of the meaning and value of body are not, as we will see, necessarily contradictory or inconsistent. But they are confusing. I will first treat Plotinus's metaphysical discussion of body.

Matter

Plotinus's first treatment of the conceptual problem of body occurs in *Ennead* 2.4. Porphyry titled the treatise "On Matter," declaring Plotinus's intention of getting to the bottom of the issue of the status of body. In treatises written earlier he had written of body either as foil for the greater beauty and value of soul, or he had insisted on body's inclusion in an unbroken, intimately connected universal circulation of life. Neither of these approaches to body, however, investigates body for its own sake. Neither examines its simultaneous fragility and vulnerability together with the experience we have of the preciousness of our own and others' bodies. What *is* body? What comes with or is entailed by embodiedness? Is body part of *who we are*? How should we conduct our embodied and located lives?

Ennead 2.4 ("On Matter") takes up these questions. It is an unusually long treatise, but it is only part of Plotinus's extended treatment of body and matter. His other major discussion, a bit later in his authorship, occurs in the context of his polemic writing against Gnostics and other dualists who said that the universe is the evil product of an evil creator. Porphyry divided Plotinus's polemic against dualists into four *Enneads* – in order, 3.8; 5.8; 5.5; and 2.9. I consider first his earlier treatise, *Ennead* 2.4, and then come to the arguments of his middle period, his treatises against Gnostics. The earlier treatise approaches the question of body and matter from the perspective of Plotinus's own philosophical concerns, while the latter treatises converse with philosophical and religious opponents. Together these treatises provide us with a picture of the range and flexibility of Plotinus's ideas about body.

Ennead 2.4 begins by asking whether matter is a "substrate" (Aristotle's suggestion), or a "receptacle" (Plato's term). Knowing Plotinus's philosophical loyalties, it will not be a surprise that he prefers the latter. But he presents Plato's understanding in a distinctively Plotinian way. He accepted Plato's authority but recognized that Plato did not make every facet of his philosophy crystal clear. Like a good disciple, he appropriated Plato critically, imaginatively, and creatively, bringing Plato's insights to the questions and issues of his own time, as well as allowing these to interpret Plato's thoughts.

Is matter "some sort of substrate?" Plotinus dismisses this proposal rapidly. He considers it unfruitful and does not wish to dwell on it. Well, then, is there a kind of matter that is incorporeal and that preexists bodies of any sort? Is there matter in intellect? For Plotinus, the answer to this question will be decisive, since existence in intellect is the required condition of reality. He answers that there is "intelligible matter," but that it differs dramatically from "matter here." We will need to examine this peculiar assertion that matter exists in intellect. Plotinus may have been compelled to affirm the existence of matter in intellect in order to account for the existence of "matter here."

By itself, matter is "undefined and shapeless," but Plotinus says that matter should not be "despised," for this undefined shapelessness is precisely why matter is valuable to the rational forming principles. Matter is necessary: "there is need of matter for beings that come into existence and are made into one thing after another" (2.4.2). In fact, neither matter in intellect nor "matter here" is ever truly shapeless; intelligible matter *is* the forming principles, and matter here is always formed. It is body, a composite of matter and form. The difference between them is that intelligible matter is "all things at once," and "always the same," while matter here is "all things in turn and only one thing at each particular time" (2.4.3).

In order to identify what matter is, Plotinus must isolate it from form, a separation which does not exist in actuality but which can be achieved conceptually. Forms, he says, have both common features and uniqueness in the "shape which belongs to each." His argument thickens, revealing its importance to Plotinus's central commitments: "If there is an intelligible universal order, and this universe is an imitation of it, and this is composite, and composed of matter, then there must be matter There too" (2.4.5). There could be no "universal order" unless there were something on which form was actually inscribed. Plotinus describes an intimate interdependence between intellect and the sensible; he ignores, for the moment, "higher" and "lower": "If intelligible reality is at once many and partless, then the many existing in one are in matter which is that one, and they are its shapes: conceive this unity as varied and of many shapes" (2.4.4).

Plotinus reminds his readers that what he is suggesting here is a *conceptual* analysis of what are, in fact, unities: "conceive this unity" ... [then] "take away in your mind." In *reality*, that is, in intellect, as well as in actuality – here, matter is "never without shape but is always a complete body, but all the same a composite one." Intellect pitches, matter catches: "As long as it can [intellect] advances into the depth of body. And the depth of each individual thing is matter; so all matter is dark, because the light [in each thing] is the rational forming principle" (2.4.5).

Plotinus acknowledges that this conceptual activity can be misunderstood; it can come to be thought of as a description of actuality. He quotes Plato as saying that matter was apprehended by a "spurious reasoning." What Plato meant, Plotinus says, was that "the mental representation of it will be spurious and not genuine" in the sense that it is "imaginary representation," not a description of reality. What exists in intellect is stable and permanent. What exists here is informed matter, shifting and transient.

Plotinus returns to the two alternatives he sketched at the beginning of the treatise: is matter substrate or receptacle? Perhaps, he says, his abrupt dismissal of matter as substrate was premature. He is now ready to accept certain interpretations of both views. If it is intelligible matter that is proposed as substrate, this will be acceptable, for in intellect, shape is true shape. If, by "receptacle," Plato meant to point out that "there must be something underlying bodies which is different from the bodies themselves," it accords with Plotinus's analysis of composites. Bodies do not exist when form alone is present: "they must be composed of matter and form: form is in relation to their quality and shape, and matter to their substrate, which is [necessarily] undefined because it is not form" (2.4.6).

Having discussed these difficulties, Plotinus now tries to say what matter *is*. His assertions, however, are necessarily denials. It is *not* body, for no qualities can be attributed to it. It is not composite, but "simple and one thing, destitute of all qualities." How is one to conceive of, to *visualize*, sizelessness in matter? Plotinus asks. The exercise he proposes illustrates something about the nature of thought itself:

> What will you conceive anything whatever without quality to be? What is the act of thought, and how do you apply your mind to it? By indefiniteness; for if like is known by like, the indefinite is known by the indefinite. The concept, then, of the indefinite may be defined, but the application of the mind to it is indefinite . . . that which wants to be a thought about it will not be a thought but a sort of thoughtlessness. (2.4.10)

Can indefiniteness be thought with precision? What is the vision of the unfocused (mental) eye? Indefiniteness. The descriptions Plotinus offers complicate rather than clarify the obscurity: it is "like sight in darkness," like seeing "absence of shape and absence of colour and something lightless, and without size as well." "If indefiniteness is not seen in this way, it will already be giving matter a form." So then, is this an exercise in thinking nothing? No, for when the soul thinks nothing, "it is not affected at all." When it tries to think matter, on the other hand, it receives a strangely affecting "impression of shapelessness."

What will be "left over" (in thought) when all form is removed is thinking of "a dim thing dimly and a dark thing darkly." So far so good, but Plotinus adds that reason must also "think it without thinking." He admits that the exercise will not be a pleasant and reassuring experience, for soul is "distressed by matter's indefiniteness" (2.4.10). The exercise might even be dangerous, for the attention and concentration it requires brings soul into matter's orbit: "having nothing to delimit, [soul] spills itself into indefiniteness" (2.4.11).

Since matter resists definition, it is "carried about here and there into every form, and since it is altogether adaptable [it] becomes many by being brought into everything and becoming everything." This, however, means that matter "makes the greatest contribution to the formation of bodies." Matter "is necessary both to quality and to size, and therefore to bodies; it is not an empty name but is something underlying, even if it is invisible and sizeless" (2.4.12).

As we will see in chapter 6, Plotinus follows roughly the same procedure for identifying matter that he uses for describing the One. Positive affirmations carry his argument only so far before he resorts to apophatic declaration:

> It is not by the senses that [matter] is apprehended: not by the eyes, for it is without colour; not by the hearing, since it makes no noise; nor has it taste or smell, so it is not nostrils or tongue that perceive it. Is it touch, then? No, because it is not a body, for touch apprehends body, because it apprehends density and rarity, hardness and softness, wetness and dryness; and none of these apply to matter. It is apprehended *by a process of reasoning*, which does not come from mind but *works emptily*. (2.4.12)

Some of Plotinus's most tortured prose occurs in his treatment of matter.[47] He says, for example, that matter is non-existent, but then quickly adds that it "has a certain kind of existence." It is defined by "its relationship to other things, its being other than they." Form imposes limit; matter is the unlimited. Paradoxically, the One is matter's source; although "unlimitedness is not in the One, the One produces it." Limit and the unlimited need each other. Limit brings unlimitedness to "actuality and perfection." Plotinus's examples are the sown field and the pregnant woman. Before fertilization, both had potential for productivity; sowing and conception render each "more what it is" (2.4.13).

Plotinus concludes with one of his most puzzling and misunderstood assertions. Matter, he says, is evil. He explains: "that which has nothing because it is in want, or rather *is* want, must necessarily be evil." Matter lacks thought, virtue, beauty, strength, shape, form, and quality: "Must it not then be ugly? Must it not be utterly vile, utterly evil?" But these categories, with (to modern ears) their moral overtones, do not fit the phenomenon Plotinus seeks to describe. "Utterly vile," "ugly," and "utterly evil" are quite useless expressions for an entity that is always and only *other* than the phenomena to which these evaluative judgments are adapted. The point is that without soul's mediation of intelligible form, matter is invisible and dead. Lacking form, matter is "not real; it is something other, *over and above the beauty of real being*" (2.4.16).

Plotinus on Gnostics

Gnosticism was "an understanding of existence, an answer to the human dilemma, [and] an attitude toward society that is worthy of being taken seriously by anyone willing and able to grapple with serious issues."[48] Christian Gnosticism was loyal to a faith that emerged with nascent Christianity itself, namely, belief in God's transcendence in relation to the world of human experience. Gnostics' strong instinct was to protect God's purity from entanglement and contamination in the world of the senses. Because they denied another crucial Christian belief – the Incarnation of Jesus Christ, with its strong statement about the meaning and value of human bodies – Gnostics were excluded as heretics from Christian churches from the early second century forward.

But Plotinus was not concerned with Gnostics' relationship to Christianity. He addressed Gnostics as Platonist heretics. Realizing that many Gnostics based their teachings on parts of Plato, Plotinus nevertheless deplored the fact that they ignored the full context of Plato's teaching, emphasizing his most dualist and body-hating statements at the expense of his comprehensive and integrative worldview. Codex IV of *The Nag Hammadi Library* contains a Coptic translation of a section from Plato's *Republic* that substantiates Plotinus's allegation that Gnostics used Platonic doctrine. Plotinus taught "Against the Gnostics" (*Ennead* 2.9) in the 265–6 academic year.

What Gnostic literature did Plotinus know? James M. Robinson, editor of *The Nag Hammadi Library*, suggests that he had read *Zostianos*, *Allogenes*, *Three Steles of Seth*, and the *Trimorphic Protennoia*.[49] Porphyry's *Life* also mentions several authors Plotinus knew.[50] It has been suggested that Gnostics against whom Plotinus wrote were probably Sethians, "a sect whose teaching stood very close to the Christian heretic Valentinus."[51] Porphyry simply calls them Christians.

What Plotinus primarily deplored about Gnostic teachings was their non-negotiable condemnation of body and the sensible world. These Gnostic themes are evident if not prominent in the Nag Hammadi treatises Plotinus is thought to have read. A strong female gendering of the sensible world male gendering of the intelligible world is evident. The *Three Steles of Seth* makes no mention of body or the sensible world but instructs: "Flee from the madness and bondage of femininity, and choose for yourself the salvation of masculinity."[52] In third-century Roman culture, these gendered images were frequently used literary tropes; they identified qualities accessible to both women and men.[53]

Plotinus says that some of his best friends accepted Gnostic teachings – he does not know how they manage to do so! He addresses his argument to them rather than to Gnostics "for we could make no further progress towards convincing them" (2.9.10). The issues addressed by Plotinus's four treatises against Gnostics are at the heart of his philosophical interests. The first three treatises resume some metaphysical questions surrounding the practice of contemplation, but his focused polemic against Gnostic teachings occurs in *Ennead* 2.9.

Gnostics differed from one another in details but they shared a worldview, and it was to this worldview that Plotinus objected. Although it does not do Gnostic teachings justice to consider them only from the perspective of an antagonist, I will nevertheless need to focus on Plotinus's objections to Gnostics for what is conveyed about Plotinus's philosophy. Some Gnostic teachers were capable of the same level of subtle nuance as Plotinus, and it is clear from their contemporaries that Plotinus and certain Gnostics could rather easily be mistaken for the other. An element of sibling rivalry is evident in Plotinus's tone, despite his strenuous efforts to demonstrate that his own position and Gnostics' beliefs have little in common.[54]

Plotinus objected to Gnostics' claim that the sensible world is the evil creation of an evil demiurge. Even before we examine his treatment of the issue in 2.9, it is evident from that Plotinus will find this construction of reality deeply repugnant. For him, the universe and everything in it is the good creation of a single and simple source called, for purposes of reference only, the One or the Good. The universe informed and sustained by the One exhibits goodness and beauty throughout; some entities have more, some less according to their spiritual proximity to the One.

The source can be called a number of names: the Good, the First, the One, the Self-sufficient, Father, and God, but it is impossible to go behind the One to any other starting principle or origin. The One, intellect, and soul account for all the phenomena of the universe; he warns against positing more principles – or fewer. Intellect is closest to the One, "unchangeably the same, without any sort of decline, imitating the Father as far as is possible to it." At the next distance, soul circles intellect. Although it is essentially indivisible, soul has "parts," one of which is "directed to the intelligible realities, one to the things of this world, and one is in the middle between these." Soul manages body "with a wonderful power by its contemplation of that which is before it." Insofar as soul directs its contemplation to its source, it is beautiful and powerful, receiving from its source, and giving to body, it is "illuminated as it illuminates" (2.9.2).

Each metaphysical sphere "of necessity must give of its own to something else as well, or the Good will not be the Good, or Intellect Intellect, or the soul this that it is ... Of necessity, all things must exist forever in ordered dependence upon each other." The Platonic doctrine of the eternality of the universe supports Plotinus's contention that nothing can be dissolved except those entities which have something into which they can be dissolved. Matter, he says, is eternal, for there is nothing into which it can be dissolved. Moreover, "if matter is going to remain alone, the divine principles will not be everywhere but in a particular limited place; they will be, so to speak, walled off from matter; but if this is impossible [as Plotinus clearly holds], matter will be illuminated by them" (2.9.3).

Gnostics use a Platonic allegory to explain the evil creation of the universe. They say that soul created the world after soul had shed its wings, i.e. in a fallen and diminished state. Plotinus replies that the shedding of wings does not apply to the soul of the All. The Soul of the All made the world by contemplating the higher realities, not by "a declination."

Plotinus also objects to Gnostics' claim that the pesky and painful things in the world testify to its evil origin. There *are* many painful and unpleasant things, he acknowledges, but to judge it evil for that reason neglects both the wider utility of those unpleasant things and the fact that the sensible world, the world of immediate human experience, is not, and cannot be, a perfect world. It is an *image* of the intelligible world and it should be valued in its own niche, for:

> What other more beautiful image of the intelligible world could there be? For what other fire could be a better image of the intelligible fire than this fire here? Or what other earth could be better than this, after the intelligible earth? And what sphere could be more exact or more dignified or better ordered in its circuit after the self-enclosed circle there of the intelligible universe? And what other sun could there be which ranked after the intelligible sun and before this visible sun here? (2.9.4)

"But really!" Plotinus exclaims. He is indignant at Gnostics who, presumably, have all the normal human limitations but nevertheless claim extraordinary insight. Are they not, like ourselves, "only just come to birth and hindered by so many things that cheat us from coming to the truth?" He criticizes the anthropomorphism of the claim that human wisdom is the ultimate wisdom of the universe. These people, he says, claim to be able to grasp the universal order, and the excellence of form and arrangement, yet they are "particularly addicted to complaining about the disorder here around the earth!" In their complaints,

> they do not honour this creation or this earth, but say that a new earth has come into existence for them, to which, say they, they will go away from this one: and that this is the rational form of the universe. And yet why do they feel the need to be there in the archetype of the universe which they hate? (2.9.5)

Plotinus also had some more pedestrian complaints: "These are the terms of people inventing a new jargon to recommend their school." He especially resented their use of Plato, complaining that their interpretation "falsifies Plato's account . . . [and] degrades the great man's teachings." However, he grudgingly admitted that praiseworthy aspects of their teachings are borrowed from Plato: immortality of soul, the intelligible universe, the first god, the necessity for the soul to distinguish itself from body, and the ascent from becoming to being. But according to Plotinus, Plato said it better. Gnostics "introduce all sorts of coming into being and passings away, and disapprove of this universe, and blame the soul for its association with the body, and censure the director of this universe" (2.9.6).

Plotinus endeavored to sort Platonic from Gnostic teachings on body. He did so primarily by distinguishing individual souls from the All-soul, which is not bound by bodies as are individual souls, but maintains bodies effortlessly. In relation to bodies, he says mildly, "we are not their masters." The All-soul "runs over the surface, ordering things to stay in their places." Within individuals, however, the parts "are bound by a second bond" – body. Thus soul does not need to "press upon them from outside" to keep them together.

The parts of the universe move according to their nature. But some parts suffer or are destroyed "because they are not able to endure the order of the whole." Plotinus gives a touching example:

> as if when a great company of dancers was moving in order a tortoise was caught in the middle of its advance and trampled because it was not able to get out of the way of the ordered movement of the dancers: yet if it had ranged itself with that movement, even it would have taken no harm from them. (2.9.7)

The appropriate attitude toward the universe, Plotinus says, is "reverent care." "It is not right to disapprove of the management of the All," whose life is not disjointed, but "coherent and clear and great and everywhere life, manifesting infinite wisdom."

The universe is, in short, an image of the intelligible world.

> If, being an image, it is not that intelligible world, this is precisely what is natural to it; if it was the intelligible world, it would not be an image of it. But it is false to say that the image is unlike the original; for nothing has been left out which it is possible for a fine natural image to have ... If there is another universe better than this one, then what is this one? But if there must be a universe which preserves the image of the intelligible world, and there is no other, then this is that universe. (2.9.8)

The archetype is not to be blamed for the faults of the image. "The causes are not present there which make people bad here below, and there is no badness of body, disturbed and disturbing" (2.9.8).

However souls have come into bodies, Plotinus says, the task is to live in the universe in accord with the principles of the higher world. If, for any reason, that is not possible, the universe gives you permission to take your leave. Plotinus's injunction is to love it or leave it! (2.9.8).

Similarly, unjust social and political conditions do not constitute evidence that the world is evil. The good and wise person does not expect equality in wealth. Nor does he expect that those with wealth have an advantage over those who are impoverished. He pictures two kinds of people, those who are good and wise, and "the mass of men." The "common crowd is here to do manual work to provide for the necessities of the better sort." The world is like a stadium in which "some win and others lose" (2.9.9).

Did Plotinus participate in the colosseum culture of his time? If so, he does not mention it, but he repeats here the attitude of a spectator who takes no responsibility for the suffering of the victim of a poorly matched fight. His description is harsh, but we should ask how it corresponds to Porphyry's account of Plotinus's daily care for the widows and orphans he brought into the household of his own benefactor. According to Porphyry, Plotinus had a generous ethical practice, but his philosophical ethic did not acknowledge his practice.[55]

If we bring together what Plotinus did not reconcile in his philosophy, namely, his worldview and his actions, his attitude seems to be that, having done whatever one can do to alleviate suffering, one should accept with equanimity the inequality of life. Ultimately the task is to attend to oneself, becoming as good as possible, yet without thinking that one is the only good person in sight. Plotinus recommends "an absence of boorish arrogance," recognizing that "there is room for the others at God's side" (2.9.9).

The universe exists through the goodness of a perfectly good God and the human soul can become godlike by directing its attention and affection to intellect. "But to set oneself above intellect is immediately to fall outside it." Arrogance precludes a person from advancing, and encourages him to think himself better than others. Still addressing Gnostics who claimed to have a privileged position because of their esoteric knowledge, Plotinus asks, "If you think that God in his providence cares for you, why does he neglect the whole universe in which you yourselves are?" Those who have real knowledge of the universe understand that providence is of the whole and do not claim special favors. "For one must not look at what is agreeable to the individual but at the All" (2.9.9).[56]

Because Gnostics do not understand the organization of the universe, they censure it. Recognition of what is "first, second, and third," precludes blaming entities who are occupying their natural place and exercising their natural attributes. "One should rather calmly and gently accept the nature of all things, and hurry on oneself to the first." Each is "essential to the completeness of the All" (2.9.13).

Human beings have not been placed in the universe for "tyrannical rule, but as the givers of beauty and order." Yet, it is fruitless to hope that all people should be good, since this is impossible. Moreover, trying to manipulate the universe by exercising magical skills is unworthy of one who accepts the universe's movements in the context of the goodness of the whole. To practice magic, or to pray for special exemption from pain and suffering, is disrespectful. It assumes that the universe is at the mercy of "any one of us who is skilled in the art of saying precisely the right things in the right way." If the higher powers could be influenced by human skills they would not be the powerful and majestic entities they in fact are. Rather than praying for cures, one should correct the excesses that cause disease (2.9.14).

Practical Effects

Plotinus now considers the *effects* of Gnostic teachings rather than their accuracy. He is concerned that Gnostic arguments persuade people to despise the universe and the beings in it. By analogy, he considers Epicureans' focus on pleasure as the ultimate goal of human life, and says that the effect of the teaching is to make them egoistic and hedonistic.[57] Gnostics who claim to possess secret and salvific knowledge – have a better start than Epicureans in disregarding bodily pleasures. By failing to rightly value the universal order, however, they have no basis for ethical behavior; "nothing here is of value for them." They write no treatises on virtue, for, in a valueless world, behavior is indifferent.

Plotinus is impatient with religious instructions that say "Look to God," but do not specify how this is to be done in practical terms. He insists that virtue is the indispensable access to any knowledge of God: "It is virtue which goes before us to the goal and, when it comes to exist in the soul along with wisdom, shows God; but God, if you talk about him without true virtue, is only a name" (2.9.15).

The heart of Plotinus's objection to Gnostics is that their contempt for the universe and everything in it does not result in making a person good. If such a person reveres the gods, for example, he must do so in a curiously unfeeling way, for "anyone who feels affection for anything at all shows kindness to all that is akin to the object of his affection . . . every soul is a child of the Father." Plotinus points out that loving the higher world (as Gnostics say they do) entails loving this world, for "how could this universe exist if it were cut off from that other world?"

Plotinus returns to an earlier issue, apparently a sore point with him, namely Gnostics' claim that God cares for them, and for them alone. Plotinus refutes this childish favoritism by saying that God cares for the universe; he is "present to all, . . . so that the universe will participate in him." "Providential care is much more of wholes than of parts." Far from possessing esoteric knowledge of the intelligible universe as they claim, Plotinus says,

> [Gnostics] do not even see this one here. For how could there be a musician who sees the melody in the intelligible world and will not be stirred when he hears the melody in sensible sounds? Or how could there be anyone skilled in geometry and numbers who will not be pleased when he sees right relation and proportion, and order with his eyes? For indeed, even in pictures those who look at the works of art do not see the same things in the same way, but when they recognize an imitation on the level of sense of someone who has a place in their thought they feel a kind of disturbance and come to a recollection of the truth. This is the experience from which passionate loves arise. (2.9.16)

Can anyone who is transported by the beauty of a face, or any of the other beauties in the world of sense, be "so sluggish in mind and so immovable" that she will not ask, "What wonders, and from what a source?" (2.9.16).

Plotinus accuses Gnostics of literalism. They have heard Plato "reproaching the body for the kind of hindrances it puts in the way of the soul," but instead of hating body, they should have responded by "stripping off this bodily nature *in their thought*" – the only place it *can* be eliminated, short of death. Had they done so, they would have seen "an intelligible sphere, embracing the form imposed upon the universe." They would notice, and be awed by the power of the intelligible world, which is its greatness. They would see that body, "not beautiful in itself," nevertheless shares in the great beauty that forms and orders the universe.

> But perhaps they may say that they are not moved, and do not look any differently at ugly or beautiful bodies; but if this is so, they do not look any differently at ugly or beautiful ways of life, or beautiful subjects of study; they have no contemplation, then, and hence no God. For the beauties here exist because of the first beauties . . . But one should notice that they would not give themselves airs if they despised something ugly; they do so because they despise something which they begin by calling beautiful: and what sort of a way of managing is that? . . . There are such beauties in things perceived by the sense . . . that one admires their maker, and believes that they come from the higher world, and *judging from them*, says that the beauty there is overwhelming; one does not cling to them, but goes on from them to the beauties of the higher world, but without insulting these beauties here. (2.9.17)

Misrepresentations of Plotinus as body-denying and world-despising should be finally laid to rest by this passage which summarizes Plotinus's respect for the beauty of the sensible world. His interest in minute details of *how beauty works* in attentive experience demonstrates his loving eye as much as do his metaphysical statements about the meaning and value of body. He considers, for example, "whether it is really possible for anything to be beautiful outwardly but ugly inwardly." He has noticed that "those who are called beautiful and are ugly within have an outward beauty, too, which is not genuine."

> But if anyone is going to say that he has seen people who are really beautiful but are ugly within, I think that he has not really seen them, but thinks that beautiful people are other than who they are. But if he

has really seen them, then their ugliness was something superadded, not really belonging to people who were beautiful by nature: for there are many hindrances here below to arriving at perfection. (2.9.17)

Plotinus's eye, practiced at seeing informing beauty in sensible beauty, actually takes surface beauty as a trustworthy sign that in fact there *is* beauty within, that the ugliness of disposition or meanness of character are not intrinsic to the beautiful person's nature! Far from finding surface beauty illusory and deceptive, Plotinus assumes that "really seeing" a beautiful body entails seeing the *person* as beautiful. He even makes excuses for the beautiful body/person accused of inner ugliness: "there are many hindrances here below to arriving at perfection" (2.9.17).

But perhaps, Plotinus writes, returning to his larger argument, Gnostics talk the way they do about the body in order to urge people to distance themselves from the needs and pleasures of body and to seek identity with soul. Sympathetic as he is with the project, he has two questions about this strategy: Does it accurately reflect reality?, and does it work? He has argued throughout his writings that such a view of the universe is inaccurate, and moreover that it entails serious moral consequences. He condenses his philosophical argument into a parable:

This would be like two people living in the same fine house, one of whom reviles the structure and the builder, but stays there none the less, while the other does not revile, but says the builder has built it with the utmost skill, and waits for the time to come in which he will go away, when he will not need a house any longer: the first might think he was wiser and readier to depart because he knows how to say that the walls are built of soulless stones and timber and are far inferior to the true dwelling place, not knowing that he is only distinguished by not bearing what he must – unless he affirms that he is discontented while having a secret affection for the beauty of the stones. While we have bodies we must stay in our houses, which have been built for us by a good sister soul which has great power to work without any toil or trouble. (2.9.17)

The wise person lives in her body as does soul in the All, that is, "not clashing with, nor yielding to the pleasures or sights that hurl themselves upon us from outside, and not being disturbed by any hardship." Humans are placed in an arena of chance and choice. Exercising choice, we can "repel the strokes of fortune by virtue," turning a painful situation into a learning experience. We can "make some of them less by greatness of mind and [we can make] others not even troubles because of our strength." We can "know what is better and pursue it, and not show ill feeling against others who can and do always pursue it, as if they did not" (2.9.18).

What is needed for achieving this perspective is self-discipline that refuses to see one's own struggles and suffering as unique and declines to claim (by prayer or by magic) special protection or special privilege. A disciplined exercise of loving and detailed attention is key, a "seeing" without ostentation and without weakness.[58] Beyond these attitudinal requirements, whatever there is to be learned about human life in the universe can be learned from committed attention to a beautiful object. Or, as Plato said, one can learn from beautiful mathematical propositions, or ways of life, or fields of learning. The important thing is not to be distracted by fears, angers, and fruitless longings.

The World We See

How is our vision of trees and stones and people affected by an adequate understanding of the universe? Is our appreciation for individual objects likely to be dwarfed by our sense of the All to which they belong? Plotinus replies by insisting that individual things and beings retain their identity and significance. They stand in their own light, for, after all, they exist because they are necessary. "What a thing is is the reason why it is." But he goes on to say that nothing exists in isolation, for all things "jointly establish cause and are caused together in relation to each other" (6.7.2). "All things are . . . for each other, and the whole is perfect and complete . . . the substance and the essential nature and the reason why are one" (6.7.3). The fact that we have senses proves that we "came into birth" by divine foresight, for what use would senses have been to disembodied minds? "Why then eyes? That there shall be everything. And why eyebrows? That there shall be everything" (6.7.3).

Who are we *really*? A human being, he says, is a soul with a particular kind of rational forming principles that is *disposed to* (but not necessarily joined with) a body of a particular kind. We are double; we are, simultaneously, a soul using a body, and a distinguishable (but not separable) person that "belongs to a soul already more divine which has a better man and clearer senses." The second person (actually the first person!) never leaves intellect, but its body double is attached to it, "mixing itself in, forming principle to forming principle" (6.7.5). The person is real because of the life that flows to it from that other person, that bright inhabitant of intellect. We *are*, then, what soul makes of us.

Every quality existing in intellect is matched in sense: "sense-perceptions here are dim intellections, but the intellections there are clear sense-perceptions" (6.7.7). There is loss in the translation of intellect into sensible, but even in the best of all possible worlds, bodies would still be necessary. In fact, this *is* the best of all possible worlds, an icon of divine beauty. But the important point to keep in mind is that intellect is not limited to bodily conditions; it exists simultaneously "there" in inexhaustible energy and brilliance. *And it is who we are.* Here senses fatigue; boredom dulls vision; we constantly seek some wonderful new stimulus to freshen our lives. We fall in love; we seek entertainment; we forget to look at one another, and, above all, we forget ourselves – our real selves and the amazing glory of the life we share with a "richly varied" company of living beings – the hands, fins, flippers, and paws we hold.[59] Plotinus urges his reader to do the daily, disciplined, and rewarding work of remembering who we are.

Our task is to find intellect in the world of the senses. Even what we call "irrational" is part of intellect, a weaker form of rationality. "It is not thoughtless but a particular kind of intellect: for it is a particular kind of life" (6.7.9).

In short, intellect has everything that is in our world. In his enthusiasm to show this, Plotinus almost says what he could never say, namely that "there" exists because "here" requires it. Intellect exists because living beings require a common source. My life, *as* life, is not different from your life or the life of a horse or an ant. Unity and diversity entail each other; they are mutually referential terms.

> And certainly if [the perfect life] is composed of many, it must on the other hand be one; now it is not possible for it to be composed of many and all of them the same: if it was, it would be a self-sufficient one. It must then be composed of things differing again and again in form, like every composite being, and each individual must be preserved, as their shapes and forming principles are. For the shapes also, of human beings, for instance, are composed of so many different elements, though that over all is one. And they are better and worse than each other, eye and finger, but they belong to one; and the whole is not worse, but because it is so, it is better. (6.7.10)

Everything we see has its origin in intellect: fire, water, plants, earth, stones, and mountains.

An ensouled forming principle is working within them and giving them form. Certainly the sky there must be a living being, and so a sky not bare of stars ... But obviously there is earth there also, not barren, but much more full of life, and all animals are in it, all that walk on and belong to the land here below, and, obviously, plants rooted in life; and sea is there, and all water in abiding flow and life, and all the living beings in water, and the nature of air is part of the universe there, and aerial living things are there just as the air itself is ... all things are filled full of life, and, we may say, boiling with life. (6.7.12)

Intellect never departs from its creation; "its substances run along with its wanderings." Sameness and otherness are essential to intellect; they are the stuff with which the rich variety is created. If the universe were not varied, it would stand still and, if it stood still, "it would not think ... [or] even exist." "But all its journeying is through life, and [it is all] through living beings ... The life is the same, but because it is always other, not the same." "There is no thing which does not make its contribution to the totality of things, ... by being other it may make this contribution" (6.7.13). In short, intellect is "this one varied thing" (6.7.14).

Plotinus uses the example of a face for the unified diversity of intellect. A face is one entity, but it is not a lump: it "has both nostrils and eyes; and the nose is not one thing, but there is one part and again another of it, if it is going to be a nose; for if it was simply and solely one thing it would be a lump." Divisions in intellect are not confusions, but different things making up a whole or unity. This, he says, "is what is called the love [*philia*] in the All"; we love things that are separate, "but the true love is all things being one and never separated" (6.7.15).

Unfortunately, like many other authors who want to praise something, he does so by contrasting it with something else.[60]

This life then, multiple and universal and primary and one – who is there when he sees it does not delight to be in it, despising every other life? For the other lives, the lives below, are darkness and little and dim and cheap; they are not pure and pollute the pure lives. (6.7.15)

The question is how to attain and, even more importantly, to maintain a vision of the larger life of intellect. Imagination, in the best sense of the word, is essential. One must imagine the real, finding the images and the exercises that make the larger life vivid.

If one likens [intellect] to a living richly varied sphere, or imagines it as a thing all faces, shining with living faces, or as all the pure souls running together into the same place, with no deficiencies but having all that is their own, and universal intellect seated on their summits so that the region is illuminated by intellectual light – if one imagined it like this one would be seeing it somehow as one sees another from outside; *but one must become that, and make oneself the contemplation.* (6.7.15)[61]

We should not overlook the fact that it was Plotinus's defense of body against those who believed it to be the evil creation of an evil creator that prompted him to these exhortations to contemplation. His rhapsodic account of the beauty of the visible world can also be read as a demonstration of contemplation. He enumerates sensible things, recalling their permanent and perfectly beautiful prototypes in intellect. In chapter 6 my discussion of the close relationship of sensible objects and contemplation continues.

Conclusion

In this chapter I have explored Plotinus's construction of his own position on the meaning and value of body as an alternative to several proposals offered by his society. Paradoxically, the torn and bleeding bodies with which Romans were so fascinated at the colosseum had high entertainment value but little human worth. On the other hand, the Gnostics against whom Plotinus wrote expressed a philosophical disdain for body. Plotinus called the bluff of their anti-body rhetoric when he looked behind their words to their assumption that they must denigrate body verbally precisely *because* of its beauty and potential for pleasure. Neither entertainment society nor Gnostics, in Plotinus's view, got body right. He endeavors to understand body more accurately. For Plotinus, body is an image, the perfect reflection of its continuing source of life.

I turn next to an issue raised in chapter 3 that is strongly related to body, namely Plotinus's denial that there is a personal deity who protects and cares for individuals. What are the consequences of his insistence that "providence is of the whole?"

5
Providence: Does the One Care for Us?

The universe lies in safety.   *Ennead* 3.4.4[1]

The One does not give and pass, but gives on forever.
                                                      Ennead 6.9.9

Among the most vivid questions of the first centuries of the common era were those concerning the support and care humans can reasonably expect from the universe. Do the gods care for us? If so, how is their concern revealed? What do we need to do to elicit it? What is our responsibility for other living beings? What good does philosophy do in our lives? These are perennial questions but the urgency with which they are asked and answered varies with the circumstances in which individuals and societies find themselves.

In the third century a number of circumstances made questions about providence and its role in human life pressing. For Christians, the Decian persecution of the 250s, a persecution initiated by an emperor, empire-wide, and unprecedented in its harshness, was such a circumstance.[2] But other features of the mid-third century were closer to Plotinus. The 250s also brought an extremely contagious plague of great severity, probably bubonic plague, but carrying with it a "synchronous prevalence of many diseases."[3] Said to have originated in Ethiopia and spread to Europe through Egypt, the plague can be traced for nearly twenty years; it began in 251 and was still active in 268.[4] Two masseurs who ministered to Plotinus daily in his home died in the plague.[5] Dio Cassius reports 2,000 deaths a day in Rome.[6] In North Africa Cyprian, Christian bishop of Carthage, described the plague:

> The bowels, relaxed into a constant flux, use up the strength of the body. A fire, conceived in the marrow, ferments into wounds in the jaw. The intestines are shaken with continual vomiting. The eyes burn

with blood. Sometimes the feet or other parts of the limbs are cut off
because of the infection of disease, causing putrefaction.[7]

The plague's social effects were as devastating as its physical effects.
People "crowded into the larger cities; only the nearest fields were cultivated; the more distant ones became overgrown, and were used as
hunting preserves; farm land had no value because the population had
so diminished that enough grain to feed them could be grown on the
limited cultivated areas." In Italy "the human race was all but destroyed
and the earth was returned to a state of deserts and forests."[8] In such
circumstances queries about providence were especially urgent.

By the mid-third century a relatively new social service, remarked
on by several contemporary authors, was established in the Roman
empire. Christian churches, under the administration of bishops, became charitable institutions.[9] A letter written by Pope Cornelius in
250 CE states that more than fifteen hundred widows and persons in
distress were cared for by the church in Rome. Moreover, the church
"acted as trustee for widows and was responsible for maintaining orphans, as had long been the case in Jewish synagogues."[10] Bishops
often cared for orphans and widows in their own households.[11]

Porphyry's description of Plotinus's role in caring for widows and
orphans is remarkably similar to that of a Christian bishop.

> Many men and women of the highest rank, on the approach of death,
> brought him their children, both boys and girls, and entrusted them to
> him along with all their property, considering that he would be a holy
> and god-like guardian. So his house was full of young boys and girls . . .
> He patiently attended to the accounts of their property . . . and took
> care that they should be accurate.[12]

Plotinus also "gave serious thought" to the education of these children. Porphyry says that he listened to them again and again as they
recited their lessons. Similarly, bishops administered the education of
orphans.[13]

Although they discharged the same duties in relation to needy people, Plotinus and Christian bishops rationalized these roles differently.
Christian churches were explicitly instructed in scripture to care for
widows and orphans. In so doing, they imitated the personal providence in which they believed. Plotinus held a very different worldview,
a worldview that is not easy to relate to his own ethical actions, but
which, nevertheless, led him to concern and responsibility very similar
to that of Christian bishops.

One of Plotinus's latest treatises, divided into two by Porphyry, *Ennead* 3.2–3, discusses providence. Porphyry reports that Plotinus sent him these treatises in the first year of the reign of Claudius II (268 CE); he probably wrote them, then, within two or three years of his own death in 270 CE and while he was suffering from the disease from which he died. Porphyry names this disease as diphtheria, but most historians agree that it was a form of leprosy. For some time before his death, Plotinus's symptoms were evident to himself and his friends: "his voice lost its sonority as his throat grew worse, and his sight became blurred and his hands and feet ulcerated." He left Rome to retire to a friend's country estate because "his friends avoided meeting him."[14] It seems, then, that Plotinus had his own urgent reasons for articulating a comforting and realistic understanding of providence. In this treatise, which Armstrong calls "the finest of all Greek contributions to theodicy," Plotinus is "thinking aloud."[15]

How Providence Works

Plotinus begins his description of the role and activity of providence by reminding his readers about the nature of the universe in which providence works. It is not proper, he says, for anyone to speak ill of the universe. The universe is "whole, all beautiful and self-sufficient and friends with itself and with its parts" (3.2.3). In this universe, "each part is not cut off from the whole"; nor is any part separated from any other part, "even if they are opposites." All are "parts of a single universal eternal living being" (3.2.1).

Intellect originates the universe, but Plotinus reminds his reader that intellect does not create by careful planning or by "one thing acting on another," but spontaneously and effortlessly.[16] Intellect generates its sensible image as the natural and necessary consequence of its power and beauty. In intellect, forming principles exist in harmony, without internal competition. But when "something comes to be in bulk," it is easy to see that "parts are in different places, and then one could really get in another's way and even consume it." For this All of ours is not intellect and rational principle, but *participates* in intellect and rational principle" (3.2.2). Conflict and strife occur naturally in this richly varied universe.

Plotinus imagines that if the universe could speak it would soliloquize thus:

> A god made me, and I came from him perfect above all living things, and complete in myself and self-sufficient, lacking nothing, because all things are in me, plants and animals and the nature of all things that have come into being, and many gods, and populations of spirits, and good souls and people who are happy in their virtue . . . Everything in me seeks after the Good, but each attains it in proportion to its own power; for the whole heaven depends on it, and the whole of my soul, and the gods in my parts, and all animals and plants and whatever there is in me (if there is anything) which is thought to be without life. And some things appear to participate only in being, others in life, others more fully in life in that they have sense-perception, others at the next stage have reason, and others the fullness of life. One must not demand equal gifts in things that are not equal. (3.2.3)

The parts of this vivid, colorful, dynamic living being are not sedentary or self-contained. Life is a kaleidoscope.

> Souls, changing their bodies, appear now in one form and now in another, . . . for life is in motion here, but unmoved there . . . like a life breathing and stirring which is the respiration of that life at rest. The attacks of living beings on each other, and their destruction of each other, are necessary; they did not come into existence to live forever. (3.2.4)

Within this lively and energetic universe, many of the circumstances we might tend to ascribe to providence are actually the result of choices made by living beings. Even when chance intervenes – "men must fall sick if they have bodies" – choice exists:

> This belongs to the greatest power, to be able to use even the evil nobly and to be strong enough to use things that have become shapeless for making other shapes . . . As for people getting what they do not deserve . . . it is correct to say that nothing is bad for the good man and nothing, correspondingly, good for the bad one. Providence ought to reach everything, and its task ought to be just this, to leave nothing neglected. (3.2.5)

A person is never a helpless victim of whatever happens. She also shapes her experience.

Two principles guide Plotinus's understanding of providence: First, he assumes an "excellently disposed" universe. Since the All depends on Intellect, we must assume and seek to demonstrate "in what way each [part] is excellently disposed." The second principle depends on the first: "Providence ought not to be blamed for the doings of souls." His task, then, is to show "in what way these lower parts are excellently disposed" (3.2.7). He will do so, but first he must clear away some underbrush. He seeks some sphere of human responsibility between the exaggerated claims of religion and magic to manipulate the universal powers, and humans' frequently overriding sense of helpless victimization.[17]

Sorting his way through several contemporary suggestions about the role of providence, Plotinus searches for a path that at once reveres and honors the universe and preserves human responsibility. "Providence ought not to exist in such a way as to make us nothing" (3.2.9). His problem is how to define something between inexorable fate and a completely random universe. Humans must have room for integrity, meaningful action, and responsibility. He gives a panegyric on "man" that might be envied by the most enthusiastic Renaissance author: "man is a noble creation, and being woven into the All, has a part which is better than that of other living things, of all that live on the earth" (3.2.10).

We live, Plotinus says, in a universe in which everything is exactly as it must be. Yet there is human freedom and agency. These two postulates need further examination. Consider first the evidence of our eyes. Universal order extends to everything, "even to the smallest." We recognize universal order by

> the beauty of appearance which extends to the fruits and even the leaves of plants, their beautiful flowers which appear so effortlessly, and their delicacy and variety. Moreover, all this has not been made once and come to an end, but is always being made as the universal powers move in different ways in this world. (3.2.13)

Creation is "without rational planning," but nevertheless the origin is "the rational principle" (3.2.15). "Matter does not come along and dominate [the rational principle], but was brought along so that things should be in this state." Later Plotinus insists that rational form is the agent, "so that matter will not be dominant and the formation come second" (3.3.4). But matter must be woven into the rational principle if they are to be complete. If matter were separated from rational principle, both would suffer: "If matter is going to remain alone, the divine principles will not be everywhere but in a particular limited place; they will be . . . walled off from matter; but if this is impossible [as Plotinus thinks it is], matter will be illuminated by them" (2.9.3).

Having said this, however, it is important to remember that matter is never perceivable in experience – only in concept. Plotinus defines matter as inert and lifeless, lacking a forming principle. But he immediately adds that "there are no corporeal things that are inert and lifeless . . . nothing in physical reality *is* inert and lifeless" (6.7.2).[18]

Human beings are part of "a manifold life [that] exists in the All." In order to make this clear and concrete, Plotinus says that in this vibrant universe, death "is a changing of body, like changing of clothes on the stage," or, sometimes (when we are ready), "a putting off of body, like in the theatre the final exit." As if sensing the dismay of his opponents, or even of his students, Plotinus adds, "What would be so terrible about a change of this kind, of living beings into each other?" Even those who die prematurely simply "go away and come back quicker" (3.2.15).

But the question, "How can there still be wickedness?" in a perfectly ordered universe is worrying. Plotinus would like his audience to agree with him that, within the whole, everything makes perfect sense and evils are only apparent. Perhaps it will help if he describes the "rational forming principle of our universe" again, demonstrating that "it is reasonable for it to be like this." The rational forming principle of our universe is "a sort of outshining of intellect and soul, *a life* that quietly contains a rationality." Since life is activity, what sort of activity is the life of the universe? An artistic activity. Thus, "the plot of the play is one though it contains in itself many battles." Plotinus can only insist that virtue is the norm, while evil actions are still "linked up with the good ones" within a single providence. Evil actions are consequences that follow *necessarily* from our failure to act virtuously.

> [Evil deeds] come from us, and we are not compelled by providence but we connect them, of our own accord, with the works of providence or works derived from providence, but are not able to link up what follows according to the will of providence but do so according to the will of the people who act or according to something else in the universe, which itself is acting or producing some effect in us not according to the will of providence. (3.3.5)

Within the universal order, opposites play a unique and pivotal role. As he has said earlier, the so-called opposites are "parts of a single universal living being." And thus, "all opposites are entwined together, form and matter, for instance" (3.3.6). The whole "agrees with itself," though the parts are frequently, inevitably, and necessarily in conflict. In fact, it is opposition (*enantia*) that generates the diversity of the whole; in this universe, opposites are merely "extreme distinctions." Actually opposites work together as do the "opposable" thumb and the fingers. The universe perceived by the senses looks less like a unity than it really is. To a human gaze, the differences stand out and the struggle of each against all seems paramount. But seen from a larger perspective, these individual struggles are simply the "urgent straining of the part towards the whole" (3.2.17).

This would seem to imply, Plotinus acknowledges, that we should sympathize with wicked men who play a necessary and important role in the whole by providing a contrast by which we learn what is good. But Plotinus says that it is the rational forming principle we must admire, not specifically the bad men. A bad man has still chosen to go to "the place that suits him and holds the position he has chosen." Indeed, bad men are to be blamed because they have made choices within a combination of necessity and freedom (3.3.4).

Plotinus uses the ancient metaphor of sound throughout his treatise on providence. "There is fitness and beauty in the whole only if each individual is stationed where he ought to be . . . each, by contributing his own sound, helps towards the perfection of the melody." "All the notes of the pipe are unequal, but the melody is complete, made up of all." If the parts of the universe, he says, are "struck in a particular way," each responds either with silence or with its own tone (3.3.5). From the mix of all the tones and the silences comes "a kind of single voice of the living creature." Providence creates the exquisite harmony of the parts.

Plotinus's metaphor almost obscures his doctrine of the inequality of souls. "Some [inequality is] from other causes," he says, and some is "from the beginning." What are the effects of this belief in inequality among souls? Does it explain phenomena accurately and generously? If we believe that souls are equal, for example, we may expect that all people will exhibit similar personal achievement. If, however, we believe as Plotinus did that souls are not all equal, might we be more inclined to generosity in accepting dissimilar achievements?

Plotinus concludes the first part of the treatise with a rush of questions about soul's relation to rationality. He begins the second part, *Ennead* 3.3, with the question of opposites and their different appearances that depend on whether one looks at them from the perspective of the whole, or whether one focuses attention on the individuals themselves. As he has stated earlier, not only are opposites integrated into the whole, but a unity is produced from opposites. Because opposites come from a single unity, even though they "grow out different," they are drawn into a single common order. The "generalship of providence" orders all. Is our attention to be on the individuals or on the whole? A different evaluation of inequality follows from our choice of perspective.

One can arrive at an awareness of interconnection inductively by first picturing species, going on to picture genera, and going right on up to "that which makes being possible." Having accomplished that exercise, one can proceed from the top downwards, "dividing and seeing the one dispersed." These exercises, basically the same exercise from different starting points, are exercises in imagining the real (3.3.1).

What part does an individual play in the whole going-on? She chooses from among roles provided by the universal order. "Each kind of [person] then goes according to nature and the rational principle to the place that suits him, and holds the position he has chosen" (3.2.17). Yet, while her choices are not infinite, she "is not a mere casual interlude in the All but [she is] counted in as just the person [she is]" (3.3.3). Nevertheless, individuals are living creatures, not disembodied souls, and thus they stand at a distance from their origin, a distance that, for Plotinus, always represents a "fading away." Strikingly however, his attention is not on how faded living creatures are, but on how vivid, how colorful they *still* are: "See how far what has come into being stands from its origin, and yet, it is a wonder!"

The question of the hierarchy of soul over the composite living creature, so distressing to many late-twentieth-century people, is not important to Plotinus. He acknowledges the issue only to dismiss it: "one ought not to inquire whether one thing is less than another but whether it is as itself sufficient; for all things ought not to have been equal" (3.3.3). Soul is self-sufficient but body is not, requiring soul's animation before it becomes living creature. Similarly, because the rational principle is not equally divided, individuals do not have equal portions. Plotinus must finally invoke former lives to explain evident and otherwise inexplicable inequalities. Yet the whole is providential, pure provision. In "its descent from above it reaches from the beginning to the end" (3.3.5).[19]

A developed art of intentional attentiveness to the sensible world is necessary if one is to see the nature of the universe. "One who in any way contemplates the form and the rational principle also contemplates the formed thing." He might have said, as Plato did, and as his meditation in this treatise has instructed, that one *begins* with the "formed thing," then analyzes in concept what is never isolated in experience, namely, rational forming principle and material object.

Always contemplating "things which are mixed and continually go on being mixed," the contemplator must look more deeply into (not above or beyond) "formed things":

> these things here below are carried along with those things in heaven, and those in heaven with these on earth, and both together contribute to the consistency and everlastingness of the universe . . . For it would not have been right for all things to be cut off from each other. (3.3.6)

Plotinus reaches the conclusion that better and worse, being relative terms, require each other if either is to have meaning. "Those who make the demand to abolish evil in the All are abolishing providence itself" (3.3.7). "All things exist together in ordered dependence on one another" (2.9.1).

Why Me, Lord?

How does an individual fare in the kind of universe Plotinus described? In *Ennead* 2.9.5, discussed in chapter 4, he takes up this question in relation to Gnostic views. Can individuals align themselves with universal gifts in such a way as to avoid pain and reap benefit? What should an individual's attitude be toward the whole of which he is a part? Plotinus rails against the self-centeredness of Gnostics' claim that they alone among "living creatures" have a special relationship with intellect. They say, he reports, "that *their* soul is immortal and divine but that the whole heaven and the stars have no share in the immortal soul." Moreover, believing themselves to enjoy a privileged perspective – a god's-eye-view – of the divine order of the universe, they complain about the universe's multiple imperfections, dishonoring the beauty and integrity of the sensible. This prideful misconstruction of the universe's provisions has pervasive and profoundly damaging effects, Plotinus says, even causing Gnostics to ignore the most immediate and accessible evidence of the universe's nature. They deny its beauty.

As we saw in chapter 4, "despising the universe and the beings in it" produces an attitude of moral indifference (2.9.15). Both an exaggerated estimate of the value of body and the sensible world, and rating it too low have consequences.[20] Gnostics' rhetoric of disparagement masks the fact that they actually rate it too highly; that is, they expect it to function, not as image, but as the intellect itself. If one expects the sensible world to be permanent and flawless, the "many unpleasant things in it" pop into the eye, things difficult to explain and accept, given Gnostics' assumptions. If, however, one accepts body and the sensible as *image*, the transient and poignant beauty of our surroundings becomes vivid: "But if there must be a universe which maintains the image of the intelligible world, and there is no other [universe but the one we know], then *this is that universe*" (2.9.8). Indeed,

> what other fairer image of the intelligible world could there be? For what other fire could be a better image of the intelligible fire than the fire here? Or what other earth could be better than this, after the intelligible earth? And what sphere could be more exact or more dignified or better ordered in its circuit after the self-enclosed circle there of the intelligible universe? And what other sun could there be which ranked after the intelligible sun and before this visible sun here? (2.9.4)

Gnostics "censure the nature of the universe" because they do not understand "the order of succession," or what we might call "the hierarchy." If one thinks of the sensible as what-there-is period, then the apparent imperfections of the sensible are glaring. Understanding simultaneously the hierarchy and the interconnection of intellect and the sensible world precludes blaming the "lower entities": "Things that are less than the first should not be reviled; one should, rather, calmly and gently accept the nature of all things, and hurry on oneself to the first" (2.9.13).

Plotinus's metaphor (quoted in chapter 4) of the tortoise who is trampled underfoot because it does not align its movements with the universal dance raises the issue of injustice (2.9.7). Plotinus does not question whether the tortoise is *capable* of dancing. The tortoise, a creature that necessarily moves very slowly, may be physically unable to move both in the pattern and at the pace of the dancers. He must, then, be sacrificed to their movement, a casualty to the beautiful dance.

All living beings endeavor to manage coordination with the dance but myriad human and non-human beings like the tortoise because of age, illness, size and shape, or other particularities, cannot discern the pattern and/or cannot keep up. Nothing personal. For some, however, it is possible temporarily to bring thinking and actions into alignment with the movement and pattern of the whole. In doing so, they participate in, and contribute to, the circulation of the universe's strong energy (2.9.13). And this is humans' task and role: to help to bring beauty and order to the whole.

This brings us to the difficult conclusion of Plotinus's examination of how the universe works. "Providential care," he says, "is much more of wholes than of parts." Plotinus acknowledges that some of his students and friends think that God cares for them uniquely, and it is to them that he addresses his alternative picture of how providence operates (2.9.10). God cares for the universe, not for individual tortoises. The severe mercy of the universe is its demand that its participants accept the way things are and attune themselves to it. When they do so, God "will be present to all and will be in this universe . . . so that the universe will participate in him" (2.9.16).

God cares for individuals only as parts of the whole. Individuals should not endeavor to bend the universe to themselves, but rather to bring themselves into alignment with the way the world works. He objects to magic and astrology on these grounds. Magic sometimes works, he says, due to the universal sympathy, but to resort to magic is to attempt to claim special attention. It assumes that the universe is at the mercy of "any one of us who is well skilled at saying precisely the right things in the right way." Persuasive speech, like magical powers, can, at best, explain, enable understanding, and provide perspective; it cannot change the choreography of the dance. "Those who are dear to God know this, and take kindly what comes to them from the universe, if any unavoidable necessity befalls them from the movement of all things" (2.9.9).

Is there more to say about providence? Yes, Plotinus's sense of the "perfect safety" of the universe must contribute to our picture of providence.[21] "The universe lies in safety" (3.4.4; 6.4.5). For Plotinus, the universe is trustworthy in some profound but ultimately ineffable way. How does this doctrine relate to his insistence that providence does not care for the parts in isolation from the whole? There can be "perfect safety" only if I accept (utterly and to the core) the possibility that I might, at any moment, be chewed up and spit out in a "benignly indifferent" universe.[22]

But, Plotinus says, this *is* what there is, isn't it? So why don't we acknowledge and accept it? Why all this "special pleading," this me, me, me? Why continue to seek reasons why someone gets cancer – they did not eat right, got no exercise, were unhappy, old, etc. – so that I can feel that I am not vulnerable to similar suffering? The most strenuous spiritual discipline of all, according to Plotinus, is to recognize that I am not singled out for special treatment no matter what I believe or how virtuously I act, or – for that matter – how carefully I eat and exercise. I will get, by chance, whatever circulates to me through the universal exigency. Those who understand the nature of the universe and their situation in it will enjoy and/or bear what is provided uncomplainingly.[23]

In his treatises on providence Plotinus emphasizes the unity and integrity of the whole universe and God's care for it. The well-being of individual "parts," even intelligent parts, is inevitably fragile and incidental. The universe does not punish, except by what Augustine, stealing a page from Plotinus's book, would later call "wholly necessary connections."[24] Punishment is no more personal than the gifts of the universe are. Plotinus says that the gods do not punish by "deliberate choice"; rather, "all that comes from above happens by natural necessity, as actions of parts on parts, and as consequences of the life of the one universe" (4.4.39). Moreover, "we ourselves contribute much to what happens" to us. Our choices have necessary and irreversible effects. "All things go their quiet way according to a justice which nobody can escape" (4.4.45). What is left to human beings is to learn to turn toward the light, seeking and welcoming its gifts. Or we can, to some limited extent, hide and barricade ourselves against the indiscriminate and rich variety of benefits and pains. But to open oneself to one is to open oneself to the other.

Finally, however, we should not take personally a very broad range of the things that occur and that impinge on our lives, for "the life of the universe does not serve the purposes of each individual but of the whole" (4.4.39; 45; 3.3). The point is the health of the whole and "the All is healthy when every part is disposed where it should be." Providence is of the whole.[25]

Should We Care for Each Other?

If the universe does not care for needy individuals, why should we care for one another? Was Plotinus's ethical practice consonant with his philosophy? These questions arise when we consider the apparent discrepancy between Porphyry's description of Plotinus's self-sacrificing concern for the orphaned children for whom he cared and his discussion, in *Ennead* 2.9.9, of "winners and losers." Shouldn't those who for various reasons cannot fall into step with the universal dance simply be considered losers and left, like the tortoise, to perish? Wouldn't that attitude most adequately reflect a realistic understanding of the universe?

Although Plotinus did not discuss the reason for his altruism, his practices seem to belie his philosophical stance. Porphyry reports that Plotinus "did not approve of eating the flesh even of domestic animals"; he also refused medicines concocted out of wild beasts' flesh (*Life* 2). Did he do so for principled reasons? Porphyry's choice of words – "did not approve" – seems to suggest so. His sexual ethic seems to have been similarly ascetic. His relationships with both men and women were emotionally intimate on a daily basis. Women were "devoted to him" and to philosophy, and he shared a home with Gemina and her daughter. His male friends and his students do not appear to have been distinguished in his mind; he interacted with both as friends. Yet he seems not to have been sexually engaged either with women or men.[26] In practice, Plotinus seems to have lived a traditional "philosophic life" of sexual abstinence and dietary restriction, a life characterized by "getting rid of passion."

What does it mean to get rid of passion? By Plotinus's time, this was a conventional phrase employed to refer, not to passionate engagement with ideas, but to careful management of bodily and emotional excesses of any sort. What was thought to be problematic about "passion" was that it often leads to compulsive actions. It lacks self-direction, diminishing a person's freedom. Passions are to be ordered by establishing alternative habits and exercises (6.8.6). But to focus on "passions" is to make practices centered on body the center of one's spiritual discipline. Management of food and sex, however, get one only half-way to the goal, removing impediments but creating no positive practices. By contrast, living as continuously as possible in intellect was, for Plotinus, the point of spiritual discipline.

Porphyry explains Plotinus's mild asceticism as the casual by-product of his intense interest in intellect: "Though he shielded so many from the worries and cares of ordinary life, he never, while awake, relaxed his intent concentration upon the intellect" (*Life* 9). Porphyry implies that the social services Plotinus practiced did not distract him from his habitual concentration. "Being at the disposal of all who had any sort of acquaintance with him," acting as an arbitrator in legal disputes, and managing a "houseful" of children seems to have been utterly consonant with his intellectual commitments. Yet his philosophical discussion of social and economic inequality states blandly that life is full of "winners and losers," neither of which the right-thinking person will notice or assist. Indeed, his treatise "On Virtue" (1.2) states that the point of virtue is to "escape from here" by "being made like god." It does not provide an ethic that encourages generous caretaking of needy others.[27]

I suggest that Plotinus, like many other philosophers and theologians, knew more than his philosophy told. It is likely that his calm acceptance that "the world is like a sports-ground where some win and some lose" (2.9.9) was a metaphor derived from his social experience. In the colosseum both winners and losers had precise roles to play. Romans thought of the colosseum as a "level playing field," a blend of "competition and chance," in which there were winners and losers.[28] Plotinus's description of the inequalities of life mirrored an entertainment culture that dehumanized its victims and identified with winners. Just as the "purpose of elite philosophy was to inculcate *virtus* [root: *vir*, manliness], so the games were to act as a mass philosophy."[29] Indeed, Plotinus's injunctions to his pupils against whining in misfortune or pain might have been taken directly from the "philosophy" of the colosseum. "One must not behave like someone untrained, but stand up to the blows of fortune like a great trained fighter" (1.4.8).

But this interpretation of colosseum culture's influence on Plotinus's philosophical ethics, if read in isolation from his practice and his picture of the universe, is reductive. His unwavering commitment, even in the face of his own death, to the life of the whole must be central to an evaluation of his ethics. And for this, the critical context for his remarks on winners and losers is that Plotinus did not merely speak carelessly of the lives of others; he included himself among the sometime winners and losers. He accepted, without recorded complaint, his own disease and death, and he sought, to the end of his life, to increase his awareness of the universal context in which his dying words make sense: "Try to bring back the divine in you to the divine in the universe."[30] His descriptions, throughout his writings, of the universal life to which he owes personal allegiance is generously inclusive, even though his remarks on winners and losers seem to assent to injustice.

The Good Life

What is "provided" for living beings? *Ennead* 1.4 ("On Well Being") discusses the community of the good life. It would be absurd, he remarks, to deny that non-human living things – like plants – enjoy "the good life." Yet there seem to be reasons to identify the good life with rational beings since only these can make judgments about life's goodness. Significantly, Plotinus decides against most of the Greek philosophical tradition by insisting that well-being "is to be found simply in *life*." Life, the substance of soul, *not rational life*, is the fundamental good on which well-being depends.

Well-being, then, is a property of soul: "the common life of body and soul cannot possibly be the life of well-being" (1.4.16). Soul is the source of "the best among realities . . . being really alive, perfect life" (1.4.3). Our condition is not that of *having*, but of *being* life; "everything else is just something [we] wear" (1.4.4).

Evil

Evil cannot occur to the good person, the person who identifies with soul. The "common life" of the human composite may bring pain, but the good person does not fear it, knowing that "he must give to this bodily life as much as it needs and he can, but he is himself other than it and free to abandon it, and he will abandon it in nature's good time and has the right to decide about this for himself." The good person regards her body as does "a musician . . . his lyre," that is, she will care for and bear with it for the instrument was given "for good reason" (1.4.16).

Pain and sickness can occur without damaging the person's possession of the true good. Thus, a suffering person is not to be pitied: "His light burns within." If the pain becomes too great so that one is not able to live well, "the way lies open to depart" (1.4.7). Because of this, Plotinus suggests, to sympathize with others who are in pain is "a weakness in our soul" (1.4.8). Consistent with his assertion of life, not rational life, as the basis of well-being, Plotinus says that even unconsciousness does not remove well-being. Although we may not be consciously engaged in intellectual activity, "we *are* the activity of the intellect . . . when that is active, we are active" (1.4.9). Indeed, he reflects, consciousness is an ambiguous good. When we are absorbed in an activity, we are usually not self-conscious. Plotinus's example is reading: "conscious awareness, in fact, is likely to enfeeble the very activities of which there is consciousness" (1.4.10).

Plotinus's description of the good person owes much to ancient prototypes of the sage. What is pleasant in a life that may be marbled with misfortune is that "the good [person] is present to himself; his pleasure and happiness are at rest ... [he is] always happy. His state is tranquil and undisturbed" (1.4.12).

In one of his last treatises, *Ennead* 1.8, Plotinus collects his thoughts, scattered throughout the *Enneads*, on evil. While himself experiencing a physical evil – the disease which ultimately brought him death – he explored "What evil is and what is its nature; where it came from; and whether it really exists." Evil cannot be a form, he says, but is actually a "privation of form." He would even prefer not to investigate evil, for how can something non-existent be investigated?, but to focus on good, "on which everything else depends" (1.8.1–2). He nevertheless restrains himself, postponing his examination of "The Primal Good," *Ennead* 1.7, to the final treatise of his life.

The first and most difficult thing to understand about evil is that it is necessary. "There must be something which is unbounded in itself and absolutely formless and has all the other attributes of evil" in order for form to have something on which to print its designs. That something is matter. Paradoxically, matter, which "exists by necessity," does not have being. Yet "the All would not exist at all if matter did not exist" (1.8.7). Plotinus associated evil with untrustworthy, slippery matter, insubordinate matter that constantly slides away from form, causing the multiple distresses he presently experienced. Because they are mixed with matter, bodies "evade reality in their continual flow."

Read hastily, these statements give the impression of a dualism Plotinus was at pains to deny in other passages. Does matter exist, or doesn't it? If it is evil, why is it necessary? If it exists in intellect, can it be all bad? The confusion and even contradiction of his statements about matter require the reader to supply the "*hoion*" (so to speak) for which Plotinus pled and with which, he said, all language must be taken (6.8.13; 3.9.6). His whole philosophy and its reiterated goals must provide the lens through which we understand matter. Habits of thinking carried over from our experience of sensible objects that either are or are not, here more than elsewhere in Plotinus's philosophy, distort. For matter, as we have seen, both is and is not.

Anyone who has suffered injury, disease, or old age, knows that bodies do not provide trustworthy identities. Bodies are vulnerable to a relentless undertow of change, growth, diminishment, and ultimately, corruption in death. Plotinus blames matter for every violation of the beauty of form. Illness is "defect and excess of material bodies"; ugliness is "matter not mastered by form"; poverty is deprivation of things needed "because of the matter with which we are coupled." Yet when Plotinus considers Plato's instruction to "take flight from here," he says that Plato did not mean that we should go away from bodies and the earth, but "he means that we must fly from wickedness" (1.8.6). To "separate oneself from the body," similarly does not mean committing suicide, but self-identifying with the unambiguous life of soul.

What is matter, the culprit? Plotinus suggests a thought experiment to help his reader comprehend matter. The meditation he proposes is a *via negativa*, and his method of understanding matter is strikingly parallel to the method he proposed for apprehending good. One reaches an understanding of the Good or the One by abstraction, by taking away material concreteness, particularity, and attribution. Similarly, what matter is can be grasped by taking away all form, just as vice can be grasped by conceptually removing virtue. "We do not see absolute wickedness, because it is unbounded; we know it by removal" (1.8.9).

We may think of this exercise as an unthreatening armchair exercise, but Plotinus warns that it can be deeply frightening. "In the process of taking away all form, we apprehend formlessness *in ourselves*" (1.8.9). This is the "exercise" children perform lying awake at night in a sweaty bed, imagining that they might not have existed. Plotinus's description is worth quoting at length. Try to stay with it.

> This which sees matter is another intellect which is not intellect, since it presumes to see what is not its own. As an eye withdraws itself from the light so that it may see the darkness and not see it – leaving the light is so that it may see the darkness, since with the light it cannot see it; but without something it cannot see but only not see – that it may be able to see in the way it is possible to see darkness; so intellect, leaving its own light [form] in itself and as it were going outside itself and coming to what is not its own by not bringing its own light with it experiences something contrary to itself, that it may see its own contrary. So that is how this is. (1.8.9–10)

There is a reason why this exercise is so frightening. If you were to remain with this picture of formless matter, allowing it to become your reality, it would be the death of your soul, "to sink in matter and be filled with it" (1.8.13). Plotinus pictures matter as a needy and complaining creature that "begs" and "bothers" soul, wanting it "to come right inside."[31] If soul succumbs, it forgets its "separate place" and becomes too weak to summon its own power to explore and strengthen its connection with intellect.

We should not forget that Plotinus's purpose in this passage is to goad his reader to identify with soul. He speaks differently in other contexts, emphasizing matter's critical importance: "If matter did not exist [in a manner of speaking], nothing would come into existence, and there would be no image if a mirror or something of the sort did not exist [for] this is the nature of an image, being in something else" (3.6.14). Similarly, he writes in the treatise chronologically following "On Evils," that if evils did not exist, "the All would be imperfect." Nor does he limit this view to physical evils, for he says explicitly that even moral evil can be productive, rousing us "to serious thought about our way of living, not allowing us to slumber complacently" (2.3.18).

Good

Plotinus's last treatise is a synopsis of his philosophy.[32] His approaching death led him to present in this short treatise, as clearly and simply as possible, the concepts by which he had lived and would die.

That which is sought by all beings and toward which all beings struggle is the Good. The Good "stays quiet," circulating goodness by its "very abiding." Plotinus suggests metaphors for the Good: a circle with radii, or the sun with rays. All things without exception share in the Good, even "soulless things;" even though one can identify things that lack soul's life – a portrait, perhaps? – they still share intellect's form.[33] Human beings, having both soul's life and intellect's form, have "a twofold approach to the Good" (1.7.2).

Life, Plotinus says, is good, but every living being does not share equally in life: "in the bad, life limps; it is like an eye that does not see clearly; it is not doing its proper work" (1.7.3). If life is a good, must we not think of death as an evil? Plotinus asks the question rhetorically. His philosophical commitments, as well as his existential situation, will not permit him to entertain the question for long. If, as he has argued in earlier treatises, life and soul "go on" after an individual's death, then death must be a good. It permits soul to pursue its proper activities without the demanding and frequently insubordinate body. It can even, if it does not go on to incarnation in another body, become part of the universal soul that directs the All effortlessly. Life is good (for the good), he concludes, but "death is an [even] greater good." Plotinus's struggle to accept his own death by understanding death as good, yet without violating his own philosophical affirmation of life, leads to these puzzling and misleading musings. To ask oneself, can I imagine a situation in which I might want to talk as Plotinus does here, is to acknowledge that philosophy is never detached from the concrete circumstances of a philosopher's life. His tortuous reflections in the last treatise he wrote should alert the careful reader to the relevance of Plotinus's imminent death and thus to the inadequacy of interpretation that does not take into account Plotinus's struggle simultaneously to reassure himself and to affirm life.

Moreover, his last written words reveal his lifelong frustration with language as a medium of communication. "One is forced to say" that life in the body, though "an evil in itself," can be made good by soul's virtue, that is, by distinguishing itself from body during life. He paraphrases Plato's definition of philosophy as "practice for dying." Death is part of what is "provided," but humans can choose how to greet it. Like vanquished gladiators we can adopt the heroic pose of the conquered awaiting the mortal blow. Like Socrates we can pay our debts and be off without fuss. Meanwhile, what is "in our power" is to choose life in a universe filled with chance, to accept the universe's exuberant provisions and to create with this haphazard mixture of benefit and suffering, a good life. Finally, the provision is beauty. That is why the one who attains the vision of the "inconceivable beauty" is happy, and the one who fails to attain it has "failed utterly" (1.6.7).

Seen from the individual's perspective, the provision is ambiguous – evil and good, pain and gift. There is, however, a perspective from which one can see the whole provision as dazzling and trustworthy beauty, as "perfect safety in the universe." And Plotinus has some advice on the most effective way to achieve that vision. In chapter 6 I discuss his instructions for contemplation.

6
"Go On Up": the One and Contemplation[1]

> Life is too short to devote much of it to activities that are not at the heart of what it is to be human.[2]

How should we live? In the third century, this was not understood as primarily an ethical question, but a question about what activities and lifestyle was best suited to generating and maintaining "more life." What are the practices by which one can best sustain a "sharp quick sense of life"?[3] On what basis can an individual build a life characterized simultaneously by vivid experience and integrity? What conception of the universe can be found that is both accurate and orienting?

Mainstream and Gnostic Christians, philosophers, and popular Roman culture all had answers to this cluster of questions, though their answers differed greatly from one another. All agreed that orienting and strengthening soul was the goal, but their methods differed. I begin by discussing a third-century consensus among Christians and philosophers (other than Plotinus) that body is the most direct and trustworthy access to soul. Practices or exercises engaging body were seen as the most dependable methods for soul-building. In the context of these proposals, Plotinus advocated what he thought was a more direct and reliable method of strengthening soul, the source of life. That method was contemplation.

Life and the Good Life

By the mid-third century, Roman Christians were numerous and diverse. Before fourth-century controversies established doctrinal orthodoxy, multiple groups identified themselves as Christian. Their secular neighbors did not usually bother to distinguish among them. As we have seen, Plotinus probably confused Christians who believed in the creation of the world by God, the incarnation of Jesus Christ in fully human flesh, and the resurrection of the body, with Gnostics who held that the sensible world was created by an evil power and was thus a constant source of evil and difficulty for soul.[4]

Christianity, Judaism, and Platonism coexisted in the same social, intellectual, and religious environment in the early centuries CE. This environment was characterized by a syncretism that was not always intentional or even conscious. For example, later theologians have seen a vast barrier between Jewish and Christian monotheism and Greco-Roman polytheism, but even that division was not absolute in the third century. Plotinus's universe, animated by the One, could easily accommodate multiple deities. Despite his absolute commitment to the One as source of all that exists, he wrote: "It is not contracting the divine into one, but showing it in that multiplicity in which God himself has shown it, which is proper to those who know the power of God, inasmuch as, abiding who he is, he makes many gods, all depending on himself and existing through him and from him" (2.9.9).[5] Third-century polemics, far from indicating to modern readers that the positions of various philosophers, Christians, and Gnostics were miles apart, should instead alert us to efforts to clarify blurred positions and fine points of difference.

Plotinus did not mention Christianity, but it is likely that he understood Gnostics – as some of them understood themselves – simply as Christians.[6] But he could hardly have been unaware of the Christian movement, for parts of the *Enneads* were written during the first empire-wide persecution of Christians.[7] It would have been difficult for Decius's campaign against Christianity to escape the attention of anyone living in Rome at the time. Decius ordered that all citizens perform a ritual sacrifice to Jupiter on January 3, 250; by January 20, 250, Fabian, the bishop of Rome had been arrested, tried before the emperor, and executed. Subsequent Roman bishops also died in the persecution: Cornelius in 253 CE; Lucius in 254 CE; and Stephen some time between 254 and 257. Though the persecution did not result in great numbers of martyrs, Christian churches throughout the empire "practically collapsed," as many "Christians joined their pagan neighbors in a rush to sacrifice."[8]

Differences that seemed profound to their adherents looked trivial to onlookers. From Plotinus's perspective, as from that of government officials, the finer points of belief escaped attention, as Marcionites,

Gnostics, and Christians were burned alive together. Apparently, only the Gnostic strains of Christianity seemed to Plotinus sufficiently threatening to be worth detailed refutation. A generation later, Porphyry would understand that Christianity represented a considerable danger to Platonic thought and would become a committed anti-Christian apologist.

Christian interest in body's role in religious subjectivity was shaped by several doctrinal and practical concerns. According to the doctrines of creation, the incarnation of Jesus Christ, and the posthumous resurrection of body, Christians valued body highly. Christians' interpretation of doctrine, however, was also shaped by their debates, their experience of persecution, and their religious practices.

In fact, Plotinus and contemporary Christian authors were allies in anti-Gnostic polemic. Resisting Gnostics' teaching that redemption referred only to the human soul or spirit presently trapped in the physical world, Tertullian wrote: "And since [Gnostics] assume it as a main tenet, that Christ came forth not to deliver the flesh, but only our soul, how absurd it is, in the first place, that he made it into just that sort of bodily substance which he had no intention of saving."[9] He cites Christian practices as proving the importance of body in religious life:

> To such a degree is the flesh the pivot of salvation, that since by it the soul becomes linked with God, it is the flesh which makes possible the soul's election by God. For example, the flesh is washed that the soul may be made spotless: the flesh is anointed that the soul may be consecrated: the flesh is signed that the soul too may be protected: the flesh is overshadowed by the imposition of the hand that the soul may be illuminated by the Spirit: the flesh feeds on the body and blood of Christ so that the soul may be replete with God.[10]

Plotinus would surely have found this rhetoric excessive, and indeed, Tertullian was not entirely characteristic of Christian authors in his focus on the physical basis of religious practices. Neither was he entirely idiosyncratic, however. Irenaeus, a much less dramatic Greek writer, similarly insists, against his Gnostic opponents, on the centrality of Christ's incarnation and its intimate and profound meaning for the Christian. Like Tertullian he cited Christian practices of baptism and eucharistic celebration as evidence of the importance of the physical within Christianity:

> How can they say that flesh passes to corruption and does not share in life, seeing that flesh is nourished by the body and blood of the Lord?
> ... As the bread which comes from the earth, receives the invocation of

God, and then it is no longer common bread, but Eucharist, but consists of two things, an earthly and a heavenly; so our bodies, after partaking of the Eucharist, are no longer corruptible, having the hope of the eternal resurrection.[11]

Plotinus's Greek contemporary, Origen, also shared Tertullian's strong affirmation of a resurrection of the human body after death:

Our flesh indeed is considered by the uneducated and by unbelievers to perish so completely after death that nothing whatever of its substance is left. We, however, who believe in its resurrection, know that death only causes a change in it and that its substance certainly persists and is restored to life again at a definite time by the will of its creator and once more undergoes a transformation; so that what was at first flesh . . . and was then dissolved through death and again made "dust and ashes" . . . is raised again from the earth and afterwards, as the merits of the indwelling soul shall demand, advances to the glory of a spiritual body.[12]

Origen was interested no less than Plotinus in how a person's connection with life could be strengthened. Origen's proposal, however, differs from Plotinus's. Origen advocates Christian faith, intentionally chosen and deliberately practiced.

Let us therefore take up eternal life. Let us take up that Which depends upon our decision. God does not give it to us. He sets it before us. "Behold, I have set life before thy face." It is in our power to stretch out our hand, to do good works, and to lay hold on life and deposit it in our soul. This life is the Christ who said, "I am the life." This life is that which now is present in shadow but then will be face to face . . . What sort of life shall we live when we are no longer living under the shadow of life but are in life itself? . . . Let us hasten toward this life.[13]

Origen's only practical suggestion in this passage is "good works." He echoes Stoic moralists who insisted that humans exist in a mixed condition of choice and chance and urged that only what lies within the possibility of choice should be considered important.

Neither Plotinus nor Christians valued body for its own sake, but because of its visible association with life.[14] Both Plotinus and Christians were eager to demonstrate, however, that body is not the source of life, but that life is given to body by God through the medium of soul. As we saw in chapter 3, Plotinus insisted that soul is the source of body's life, both pre-existing body and, when body weakens, going on to animate other bodies. Christians' interest in life was intensified by the constant threat and frequent reality of persecution, but even Christians who did not experience persecution were reminded in hymns, sermons and liturgies that the point of their religious commitment was more life: "true life comes from partaking in God."[15] A fourth-century eucharist prayer by Serapion of Thmuis in Egypt reads "We beg you, make us truly alive." Origen, who died from prison injuries during the Decian persecution, wrote: "All who wish to follow [Christ] can do so, though overcome by death, since death has now no strength against them: for no one who is with Jesus can be seized by death."[16]

For Plotinus, as for Christians, the question was how to achieve the greatest access to the source of life. Perhaps (to digress for a moment), this is the ultimate question for everyone, then and now, prompting the most diverse proposals – from "sex, drugs, and rock'n'roll" to prayer. The question "How should we live?" integrates issues of ethics and morality with the question of which lifestyle and activities produce the richest sense of life.

There is no doubt that Plotinus was a late participant in a philosophical lifestyle organized by what Michel Foucault called a "hermeneutics of the self."[17] In the early centuries of the common era, elite men cultivated certain "arts of existence" focused on

> those intentional and voluntary actions by which men not only set themselves rules of conduct, but also seek to transform themselves, to change themselves in their singular being, and to make their life into an *oeuvre* that carries certain aesthetic values and meets certain stylistic criteria.[18]

Care of the self took the form of "an attitude, a mode of behavior; it became instilled in ways of living; it evolved into procedures, practices, and formulas that people reflected on, developed, perfected, and taught."[19] These exercises were also a social practice, informing and intensifying relationships and requiring the help and support of others. Moreover, religious, psychological, and medical considerations entered choices of a regime for self-construction. Implicit in these exercises of sexual and dietary restriction was "a particular and intense form of attention to the body."[20]

The primary tool of these "arts of existence" was the careful management of the most intense human pleasures, food and sex. By austere regimes of diet and sexual abstinence, men discovered "how easy it was . . . to dispense with everything to which habit, opinion, education, attention to reputation, and taste for ostentation have attached us."[21] Indeed, they trained themselves in an erotics of ascesis, that is, to find pleasure in no pleasure.[22] Diogenes Laertius wrote:

> For even the despising of pleasure is itself most pleasurable, when we are habituated to it; and just as those accustomed to a life of pleasure feel disgust when they pass over to the opposite experience, so those whose training has been of the opposite kind derive more pleasure from despising pleasure than from the pleasures themselves."[23]

Yet another group of third-century people explicitly sought "more life," a life free from the deadening effects of habit and socialization. These were Christian ascetics who adapted and extended the elite philosophical methods of "care of the self." In the fourth century, Christian asceticism would constitute an alternative to an imperially favored church, but it developed in the third-century atmosphere of persecution and martyrdom.

Asceticism focused scrutiny on body and its capacity to reveal the condition of the soul: "For those who have attained to purity of heart *by means of the body* and who in some measure have applied themselves to the contemplation of created things know the grace of the Creator in giving them a body."[24] The ascetics of the Egyptian desert believed that minute observation of physical symptoms revealed the state of one's soul more accurately than introspection. Palladius wrote:

> There are many things which testify concerning spiritual excellence, such as the colour of the face which blossoms with ascetic labours, and the manner in which the apparel is put on, and a peaceable manner, and a mode of speech which is not inflated, and modesty of countenance, and a discourse which is not crooked, and cheerfulness of the mind, and an understanding which is full of knowledge.[25]

Spiritual health is revealed in "the colour of the face," but spiritual malaise is similarly replete with physical symptoms:

> The most fierce passion is anger ... It constantly irritates the soul and above all at the time of prayer it seizes the mind and flashes the picture of the offensive person before one's eyes. Then there comes a time when it persists longer, and is transformed into indignation, and stirs up alarming experiences at night. This is succeeded by a general debility of the body, malnutrition with its attendant pallor, and the illusion of being attacked by poisonous wild beasts.[26]

The "demons" against which ascetics struggled were labeled variously by different authors: anger, lust, jealousy, boredom, to name only a few. What the demons had in common was that they effectively deadened the life of prayer, creating lassitude and inertia. Deadness was repeatedly named as the enemy of Christian life, not only by ascetics, but by many other authors who endeavored to name the essence of Christian experience. "God takes away the deadness in us," Origen said.[27] Irenaeus said, "True life comes from participating in God."[28] And, at the end of the fourth century, Augustine wrote: "Only they can think of God without absurdity who think of God as life itself."[29]

Third-century proposals for how to achieve the state of being fully alive were amazingly diverse, from the excitement of secular entertainment at the colosseum to Christian rituals – "we beg you, make us truly alive" – to philosophical and Christian asceticism. Yet despite great differences in metaphysics and methods, all agreed that some form of observation and management of one's own body was key to the success of a spiritual discipline. In the context of this consensus, Plotinus's proposal was unique. He did not even find in Plato the suggestion he makes, namely, that the most immediate and direct connection to the source, power, and vividness of life can be achieved through contemplative practice. Knowing by experience that contemplation is not easy, Plotinus supplied both instructions and thought experiments designed to help his students conduct this practice. He also sought to attract his reader to contemplation by describing its glories and fruits. But his most compelling argument was that contemplation produces *more life*. Intellect, he says in two different contexts, is "boiling with life" (6.7.12). For Plotinus, the goal of the spiritual discipline of contemplation is a "vision" – he will criticize and ultimately jettison the term – of the One source of life.

The One: *Via Positiva*

Plotinus considers "The Good, or the One" in several treatises and parts of treatises throughout his writing career. The One is impossible to define and notoriously difficult to characterize. Plotinus speaks of it in terms of a *via positiva* and a *via negativa*. Like Plato before him, he sought images with which to picture what he wanted to communicate.[30] He also cited ancient precedent as his authority: "These statements of ours are not new; they do not belong to the present time, but were made long ago, not explicitly, and what we have said in this discussion has been an interpretation of them, relying on Plato's own writings for evidence that these views are ancient" (5.1.8). The One exists before all things but is not synonymous with all things. The "origin is not divided into the All." It is pure productive power; "if it did not exist, neither would all things." "What is above life is the cause of life." Think of a spring, Plotinus says, or think of the life of a huge plant whose origin is in its root, but which spreads over the whole, the "origin of a multiple life." Plotinus says, "It is a wonder how the multiplicity of life came from what is not multiplicity."

> We go back everywhere to one. And in each and every thing there is some one to which you will trace it back, and this in every case to the one before it, which is not simply one until we come to the simply one; but this cannot be traced back to something else. (3.8.10)

Ennead 6.9 begins with the premise: "It is by the one that all beings are beings." But, Plotinus asks, what does this mean? He suggests several different kinds of oneness: an army, a chorus, a flock, a house, and a ship. Each of these, he says, fails to be an adequate model because each is, in different ways, a composite. But nevertheless each demonstrates, in a rough and ready way, the quality of oneness. Less tangible entities also rely on unity: health is the order and unity of body; beauty is a unified arrangement of parts; virtue is a unification of desires and values. It is also possible to participate in unity to a greater or lesser degree. Entities having separate and free-standing parts – like a chorus – exhibit the least unity; bodies have more, while soul has the greatest. Even though it is not the source of its own unity, it contains the power to unify other things.

Plotinus reminds his reader of one of his fundamental axioms, namely, that being and substance are one. The awareness of being, he says, is sufficient to make a person recognize its oneness. Both universal being and personal being rely on oneness; but from a human perspective, being is evident as life, and is at its most intense in intellect. The source of being, however, is not identical with all things; thus, "it cannot be intellect, for in this way it would be all things since intellect is all things; and it cannot be being, for being is all things" (6.9.2). Being is the gift of the One, Plotinus says elsewhere, but since the One is beyond being, it gives what it does not have.

How did soul "slide" away from identity with being, "the Formless?" Here, focusing on the One, he presents a much more pessimistic picture than he had given in *Ennead* 4.8.[31] Soul lacks capacity for comprehending the One, so it "slides away and is afraid that it may [end up with] nothing at all . . . [I]t gets tired and gladly comes down and falls away from all this, till it comes to the perceptible and rests there *as if on solid ground*." What can break soul's fall? Plotinus doesn't say in this passage, but he is clear in other contexts that only soul's conscious and voluntary choice can reverse the slide. It is anything but automatic: "one must lift oneself up . . . ascend . . . become one . . . haste to the Good"; "one must become Intellect and entrust one's soul to and set it firmly under Intellect, that it may be awake to receive what it sees, and *may by the Intellect behold the One*" (6.9.3).

The One can be "beheld" – or, more accurately, "touched," but description is approximate at best and distorting at worst. Even to say that it is "one" or "the cause" only says something about ourselves, because "we have something from it." All we can do is to "run round it outside . . . and want to explain our own experiences of it, sometimes near it and sometimes falling away in our perplexities about it" (6.9.3).

Perplexities are inevitable, for human consciousness of the One is not the result of reasoning "but by way of a presence superior to knowledge." Reasoned knowledge, usually humans' best method, represents a falling away from presence, a painfully laborious effort. "One must therefore run up above knowledge, . . . [departing from] things known and from every other . . . object of vision" (6.9.4).[32]

This description sounds rather daunting. Can you get there from here? Teaching, Plotinus says, "goes as far as the road and the traveling, but the vision is the task of one who has already determined to see" (6.9.4). Since Plotinus devoted his life to teaching, however, he must have thought that providing a road map and the means of transport counted for something. But he is also realistically aware of teaching as a relationship in which the intentions and qualifications of the student play a decisive role in the student's ability to learn.

Moreover, teeth-gritting determination is not sufficient. It can, in fact, keep the person who seeks to ascend distracted from the vision by the effort required. What is needed is passion (*eros*). The kind of eros that is useful, however, is "like that of a lover resting in the beloved," not anxious desire, but confident contentment. Instead of coming to a dramatic encounter with a separate other, the student will only be able to "grasp" and "touch" the One *by her likeness*, "by the power in [her] akin to that which comes from the One," namely her unity (6.9.4). A final requirement is the ability to persist in pursuit of an experience that, even when achieved, does not feel like the satisfactions or gratifications to which we are accustomed.

> But when the soul wants to see by itself, seeing only by being with it and being one with it, it does not think it yet has what it seeks, because *it is not different from what is being thought.* But all the same this is what one must do if one is going to think about the One. (6.9.7)

This is indeed a terse description of "naked" seeing. It would certainly serve to dissuade thrill-seekers from pursuit of the vision!

Why should the One be sought? The Good is everywhere and no-where. Nervous about the validity of his discussion, Plotinus introduces it in *Ennead* 6.8 with a disclaimer, "now we must depart a little from correct thinking in our discourse *for the sake of persuasion*" (6.8.13). After describing the One as a circle around which everything moves, he reiterates his hesitation: "This is how one has to speak of him since one is unable to speak of him as one should" (6.8.18). The point of description, however, is not to characterize the One, but to inspire others to seek the One: "Raised up, then, towards that by what has been said one should take hold of that itself." Once one knows how to see the One, one can look anywhere and "it appears everywhere to him as if before the eyes of his soul and, wherever he fixes his gaze, he is looking at him, unless he leaves the God and fixes his gaze elsewhere and thinks no more about him" (6.8.19).

Up to a limit, reasoning is useful for the pursuit of the One. Reasoning is possible in the first place because the universe is orderly. Plotinus dismisses the view that reality is governed by chance and accident. He does not direct his teaching to people who think like this, he says, but to those "who posit another nature than bodies and have gone up as far as soul" (6.9.5). These can readily understand that soul derives from intellect, the source of rational principles. "After this," they must understand that intellect contains reasoning and that intellect holds "all things in itself" and *is* all things, "multiplicity which is undivided and yet again divided." Intellect lies closest to the One; it is "not dispersed in itself but is in reality all together with itself and its nearness to the One has kept it from dividing itself" (6.8.17). "This marvel of the One" doesn't exist as an object in relation to other objects, but as generating intellect which is the substance of all things. At best the name, "the One," indicates "an invisible idea" and names a natural human desire for a unified soul. The fluidity and dynamism Plotinus describes as a property of the One must finally be the method by which the One is sought.

The One: *Via Negativa*

> The One is the end of philosophical inquiry: We must go away in silence and inquire no longer, aware in our minds that there is no way out. For why should one even inquire when one has nothing to go on to, since every inquiry goes to a principle and stands still in it? And besides, one must consider that every inquiry is about either what something is, or of what kind it is, or why it is or if it is. Now being . . . [is known] from what comes after it. And the question "why?" seeks another principle; but there is no principle of the universal principle. (6.8.11)

The *via negativa* is finally the only appropriate method for apprehending (insofar as this is possible) the One; "it" is not being, not substance, not life.

> But if you grasp it by taking away from it, you will be filled with wonder. And throwing yourself upon it, and coming to rest within it, understand it more and more intimately, knowing it by intuition and seeing its greatness by the things which exist after it and through it. (3.8.10)

Plotinus puts it another way: in vision, there are usually two distinguishable entities, a viewer and an object. Dissolve the doubleness into a unity of seeing and seen, and you will have a sense of the relationship of intellect and the One. The One is not separate but continuously and intimately informs visible phenomena, and its beauty, flowing through intellect, reaches the sensible world:

> Intellect is, certainly, beautiful, and the most beautiful of all; its place is in pure light and pure radiance and it includes the nature of real beings; this beautiful universe of ours is a shadow and image of it; and it has its place in all glory, because there is nothing unintelligent or dark or unmeasured in it, and it lives a blessed life; so wonder would possess the one who saw this too, and, as he should, entered it and became one with it. (3.8.11)

Plotinus says of the One, "Now he is not as he is because he cannot be otherwise, but because being what he is is the best" (6.8.10). By asking "what is it?" it becomes clear that the answer is not a definition, but "grasping it, if possible, in our minds by learning that it is not right to add anything to it."[33] "One must remove the cause of the difficulties by excluding from our concentrated gaze upon it all place" (6.8.11).

A curious passage considers how the One can be "fit into our thought." At issue seems to be whether it is more effective to think of the One in abstract or personalized terms. Plotinus begins this discussion using impersonal abstract language: "it is the greatest of all things, not in size but in power." He suddenly shifts to gendered personal language: "but when you think of him as Intellect or God, he is more, . . . " but then shifts back: "there must be something supremely self-sufficient [and] it must be the One, which is the only thing of such a kind as not to be in need." He is forced to negative statements: the One does not wish for anything, does not think, and must not even be called good (6.9.6).

These rather opaque and difficult instructions boggle the mind. Good. At that point, "stand fast . . . and contemplate." But contemplate "without casting your thought outward"; what you seek is something that is "always present to anyone who is able to touch it."

> Just as with other things it is not possible to think anything when one is thinking something else and has one's mind on something else, but one must add nothing to what is being thought about, that it may really be it which is being thought about, so here one must know that it is not possible when one has the impression of something else in one's soul to think that One. (6.9.7)

The soul must "let go of all outward things and turn altogether to what is within, . . . even ignoring itself" (6.9.7).

Suppose that one manages to achieve a vision of the One. How does such an experience affect one's life? Plotinus recognizes two different paths, both informed by such a vision: life in the world and perpetual contemplation. He refers to Minos, the protagonist of a pseudo-Platonic dialogue, who came away from contemplation "filled full of law giving by the divine touch" so that he "laid down laws in its image." In this passage, Plotinus does not praise one of the two paths over the other; each has its own validity. Whether a person is occupied with civic affairs or a life of contemplation, "the One is not outside anything but is in company with all without their knowing."[34]

Contemplation

> Plotinus's goal was to be united to, to approach the God who is over all things. Four times while I was with him he attained that goal, in an unspeakable actuality and not in potential only. (*Life* 23)

Porphyry reports that these episodes were the result of Plotinus's "eager longing for the One." Plotinus did not discuss them in detail, but perhaps alludes to them when he mourns the inability of language to describe the "absolutely simple." Intellect can come into contact with the One: "but when it has done so, while the contact lasts, it is absolutely impossible, nor has it time, to speak . . . One must believe one has seen when the soul suddenly takes light" (5.3.17).

Plotinus mentions briefly a frequent occurrence in which he experienced "identity with the divine." It is not clear that the events Porphyry recalled are identical with those to which Plotinus referred. Scholars differ about whether Plotinus experienced contact with intellect or with the One, but since the One is the active foundation of all unity, the point is moot.[35] Plotinus's description, quoted in an earlier chapter, is worth quoting again:

> Often I have woken up out of the body to my self and have entered into myself, going out from all other things; I have seen a beauty wonderfully great and felt assurance that then most of all I belonged to the better part; I have actually lived the best life and come into identity with the divine; and set firm in it I have come to that supreme actuality, setting myself above all else in the realm of Intellect. Then after that rest in the divine, when I have come down from Intellect to discursive reasoning, I am puzzled how I ever came down, and how my soul has come to be in the body when it is what it has shown itself to be by itself, even when it is in the body. (4.8.1)

Plotinus is less concerned with defining his experience than with the strong conviction it brought. Yet the power of those experiences compelled him to keep attempting to communicate their consummate value to others, frustrating as the search for adequate expression was.

The soul's movement in contemplation, Plotinus says, is not, like body's movement, in a straight line. Its natural movement is "a circle around something, something not outside but a centre, and the centre is that from which the circle derives, and it will move around this from which it is and will depend on this." Failure to distinguish between the linear motion of body and the circular motion of soul keeps soul swimming in body, but soul can also remember and exercise its own "natural movement." Part – but not all – of soul's energy must be spent on maintenance of body. That "part" of soul is "held by" body, "as if someone had his feet in water, but the rest of his body was above it." In Plotinus's metaphor, "we lift ourselves up by the part that is not submerged in body and by this join ourselves at our own centres to something like the centre of all things . . . and we are at rest" (6.9.8).

Plotinus turns to personal language as he pictures soul's desire for the One:

> We are always around it but do not always look to it; it is like a choral dance: in the order of its singing the choir keeps round the conductor but may sometimes turn away, so that he is out of their sight, but when it turns back to him it sings beautifully and is truly with him; so we too are always around him – and if we were not, we should be totally dissolved and no longer exist – but not always turned to him; but when we do look to him, then we are at our goal and at rest and do not sing out of tune as we truly dance our god-inspired dance around him. (6.9.8)

Contemplation also reveals the nature of the bond between living beings. Soul is one, so separation and alienation must result from embodiment. "Bodies are hindered from communion with each other by bodies." We cannot feel another's physical pain as we can (with generosity) feel one another's emotional pain. Contemplation, by which the oneness of life and being become experiential, renders vivid the actual connectedness of living beings (6.9.8).

The passages at the end of *Ennead* 6.9 contain some of Plotinus's richest prose. He reminds his readers that the possibility of participating in the "god-inspired dance" is not imaginary, but firmly rooted in the reality of the universe:

> We are not cut off from him and separate, even if the nature of body has intruded and drawn us to itself, but we breathe and are preserved because that Good has not given its gifts and then gone away but is always bestowing them as long as it is what it is. But we exist more when we are turned to him and our well-being is there, but being far from him is nothing else than existing less. (6.9.9)

More life, for Plotinus, is the result of strengthened participation in the "active actuality of Intellect." Lest we think that this is an abstract goal, however, the most immediate results of more life are practical –

righteousness and virtues. This process is not one of adding anything
to oneself; rather, it is the soul "becoming itself, . . . for since the soul
is other than God but comes from him it is necessarily in love with
him." Plotinus compares "heavenly love" with the loves we experience "here below," and with "what it is like to attain what one is most
in love with." But earthly loves are "loves only of images," and therefore of a lesser intensity. In this passage he does not suggest that our
present loves are anything but contrasts with heavenly love. He does
not, for example, suggest that they prepare us for, or participate in,
love of the One. Rather, "true life" is to be attained *at the expense of
earthly loves*:

> We must put away other things and take our stand only in this, and
> become this alone, cutting away all the other things in which we are
> encased; so we must be eager to go out from here and be impatient at
> being bound to the other things, that we may embrace him with the
> whole of ourselves and have no part with which we do not touch God.
> (6.9.9)

The reward for rejecting other things is the vision. But the vision is
one's true self. The One is not another, but One, single and simple:

> There one can see both him and oneself as it is right to see: the self
> glorified, full of intelligible light – but rather itself pure light – weight-
> less, floating free, having become – but rather, being – a god; set on fire
> then, but the fire seems to go out if one is weighed down again. (6.9.9)[36]

Why doesn't everyone remain in this state? Because soul is limited by
its care for body. "There will be a time when the vision is continuous," but at the considerable expense of leaving body, the aspect of
the human that separates it from the whole. "Joined, as it were, centre
to centre," soul "does not see and does not distinguish and does not
imagine two" (6.9.10). Plotinus finishes the treatise, aware he has not
adequately expressed an inexpressible experience: "The vision is hard
to put into words . . . that Good is not disclosable, it prohibits the
declaration of the divine to another who has not himself had the good
fortune to see" (6.9.11).

Plotinus is painfully aware of the strong limitations of communication and teaching. If one has had the experience, however, she retains
in memory the experience of knowing herself to be *image*. This understanding is more like a relaxation of anxious attention than like straining
every nerve.[37] Plotinus evokes what he means by phrases such as "quiet

solitude," "state of calm," "not busy about himself," and "altogether at rest."

These expressions merely approximate an experience that should not even be called "contemplation," but simply "another kind of seeing," "a being out of oneself," "simplifying," "giving oneself over and pressing toward contact" (6.9.11). Perhaps Plotinus questions "contemplation" because it still implies preoccupation with one's own activity. His second set of expressions are more passive and receptive. He implies that both kinds of expressions are necessary, both need to be held in tension to evoke the experience.

The circularity of the process is indicated by the fact that the starting point, as well as the consummation, is perceiving oneself *as image*. Then, one can "go on from oneself as [from] image to original." "This is the life of gods and of godlike and blessed, deliverance from the things of this world, flight in solitude to the solitary" (6.9.11).

Ennead 3.8 (titled by Porphyry "On Nature and Contemplation and the One"), explores contemplation in a different context. Plotinus begins the argument with deceptive casualness:

> Suppose we said, playing at first before we set out to be serious, that all things aspire to contemplation, and direct their gaze to this end – not only rational but irrational living things, and the power of growth in plants, and the earth which brings them forth – and that all attain to it as far as possible for them in their natural state . . . could anyone endure the oddity of this line of thought? (3.8.1)

This is precisely what Plotinus *will* claim. To begin with, however, he says that since the discussion is "among ourselves," the topic can be discussed "playfully" without risk of misunderstanding. Contemplation may seem an odd topic to discuss playfully, but Plotinus adopts rhetorical disingenuousness in order to attract and engage his reader.

"Every action is a serious effort towards contemplation," he states (3.8.1). However, some actions are more "contemplative" than others. It is voluntary action, action that is chosen and intended, that contributes to contemplation. Often human beings cannot be said to act intentionally; rather, we are dragged toward "the outer" by either compulsory (externally compelled) or compulsive (psychologically driven) action. But we are already ahead of ourselves. What about entities that cannot be said to act, much less to act intentionally? What about earth, trees, and plants? What is their contemplation?

Clearly, Plotinus says, matter is needed for nature (a form) to work on. But nature does not produce analogously to human creation, that is, with hands, tools, or conscious intention. Nature creates while remaining concentrated on intellect and the One. "If it stays unmoved as it makes, and stays in itself, and is a forming principle, it must itself be contemplation" (3.8.3). Action, however, entails a rational component, distinguished from the action but prompting and shaping it. Thus, action is a spontaneous practical form of contemplation. "Making, for [nature], means being what it is, and its making power is coextensive with what it is. But it is contemplation ... for it is a rational principle" (3.8.3). Plotinus imagines nature responding indignantly to the question of why it makes:

> Don't ask! Understand in silence, you, too, just as I am silent, and not in the habit of talking. Understand what, then? That what comes into being is what I see in my silence, an object of contemplation that comes to be naturally, and that I, originating from this sort of contemplation have a contemplative nature. (3.8.4)

Interpreting nature's speech, Plotinus says that it means that nature is

> the offspring of a prior soul with a stronger life; that it quietly holds contemplation in itself ... in its own repose and a kind of self-perception, and in this consciousness and self-perception it sees what comes after it, as far as it can, and seeks no longer, but has accomplished a vision of splendour and delight ... Nature is at rest in contemplation of the vision of itself, a vision which comes to it from its abiding in and with itself and being itself a vision; and its contemplation is silent but somewhat blurred. (3.8.4)

Plotinus explains that nature's contemplation is weaker than that of intellect, its original; thus its productions are weaker. Similarly, human beings whose vision is weak are "carried into action, so as to see what they cannot see with their intellect ... Everywhere we shall find that making and action are either a weakening or a consequence of contemplation" (3.8.4).

So much for nature's contemplation. What about soul? How is soul's contemplation productive? All soul's activity is contemplation, but at different levels of strength. Soul has a dual nature – a part "above and always filled and illuminated by the reality above," and a part that "goes forth always, life from life." "All goes on noiselessly," contemplation, and action that "bends back again to contemplation." Noiselessness is, for Plotinus, the mark of confident contemplation: "in proportion as the confidence is clearer, the contemplation is quieter, in that it unifies more, and what knows, insofar as it knows – *we must be serious now* – comes into unity with what is known" (3.8.6).

Plotinus casts playfulness aside and becomes serious because he has a new agenda. He is no longer descriptive, speculating according to his philosophical principles on the natural world's contemplation, but "serious," in advocating that his hearer/readers accept the discipline of conscious and intentional contemplation. Speculation is play, but life is serious.

Contemplation does not require discursive reasoning, which implicitly admits deficiency even in seeking to overcome deficiency. The contemplator "has already finished reasoning, . . . but in relation to himself he is vision. For he is already turned to what is one, and to the quiet which is not only of things outside but in relation to himself, and all is within him" (3.8.6). The best of human creativity is, in this (limited) way, similar to the One's creativity. It emerges spontaneously from "the rational principles within," that is, from a contemplative activity (3.8.7).

Life is the natural product of the universe's contemplation, but the individual soul takes the shape of its habitual object(s) of contemplation; this is "living contemplation." All lives are thoughts, since all include a rational principle, but "one is dimmer than another" (3.8.8).

> If, then, the truest life is life by thought, and is the same thing as the truest thought, then the truest thought lives, and contemplation, and the object of contemplation at this level, is living and life, and the two together are one. (3.8.8)

This is the crux of Plotinus's proposal for "more life." Soul, the giver of life is also the individual's connection with intellect. And intellect, the origin of thought, "is not the intellect of one individual, but is universal; and being universal, is the Intellect of all things." Intellect, in turn, comes from the One. Our access to intellect and the One is "by the likeness in ourselves." Since "there is nowhere where it is not, there is something of it in us too . . . Just as if there were a voice filling an empty space, . . . and by setting yourself to listen at any point in the empty space, you will receive the whole voice, and yet not the whole" (3.8.9).

To say that intellect seeks the One is misleading, for intellect "must return, so to speak, backwards, and give itself up, in a way, to what

lies behind it." Plotinus's expression is awkward, uneasy, full of quali-
fication and hesitancy. He is anxious not to leave false instruction; in
short, his tone is anything but the playful mode in which he began the
discussion.

Intellect

Plotinus's most vivid and detailed account of the contemplative ascent
to the One is given in *Ennead* 6.7. This treatise of his middle period is
concerned to show that the very possibility of the ascent depends upon
the fact that the sensible world and intellect are not in actuality two
worlds, but one world "apprehended in different ways on different
levels."[38]

After a discussion of the role of the sensible world and the body in
the dual human being ("part" adapted to the sensible world and "part"
remaining in intellect), Plotinus comes to his favorite topic, contemplation. Again, his tone alters as his task changes, that is, when he
seeks, not to describe the universe, but to provoke commitment to a
spiritual vision. We must, he says, "go on still darting upwards" from
earth's manifold beauties. Where does the common being and life of
all phenomena come from? From intellect, of course, but even beyond
intellect, from the Good. The Good is itself shapeless and formless,
but Intellect, by "living towards it," was satiated and full and became
all things: "intellect came to be by being filled" (6.7.16). Intellect's
life, however, was "a trace of that Good and not his life." Intellect is
"life, [already] defined and limited" (6.7.17).

Ennead 5.8, "On the Intelligible Beauty," focuses the issue of "how
it is possible for anyone to contemplate the beauty of Intellect and of
that higher world." Plotinus begins with an illustration that at first
seems remote from his topic: "Let us suppose a couple of great lumps
of stone lying side by side." One is shapeless (well, not actually, but it
has not been shaped to any recognizable form); the other has been
chiseled and carved by a master artist. The art which has created the
sculpted stone is greater, Plotinus says, than the art that can be seen *in*
the sculpture, because it is more remote from matter. His principle is
that "everything extended departs from itself." Thus, "every original
maker must be in itself stronger than what it makes" (5.8.1).

Plotinus's strongest argument for the value of artistic creation occurs in this passage. To anyone (like Aristotle, for example) who says

that art works simply imitate nature, Plotinus responds that "the arts do not simply imitate what they see, but they *run back up to the forming principles* from which nature derives; then also they do a great deal by themselves, and, since they possess beauty, they make up what is defective in things" (5.8.1).

He moves his consideration from works of art to "things that come into existence naturally as beauties." What is the source of their beauty? Certainly, Plotinus says, it is not "the blood and the menstrual fluid" (in the case of mammals), but the form supplied by intellect.[39] Recalling Helen of Troy and Aphrodite, he asks:

> Is not this beauty everywhere form, which comes from the maker upon that which he has brought into being, as in the arts it was said to come from the arts upon their works? Well, then, are the things made and the forming principle in matter beautiful, but the forming principle which is not in matter but in the maker, the first immaterial one, is that not beauty? (5.8.2)

Plotinus's theory of vision supports this point: "we do not yet see a thing when it is outside us, but when it comes within, it influences us. But it comes in through the eyes as form alone: or how could it get through anything so small [as the pupil of the eye]?" (5.8.2). The maker must be more beautiful than his creation, for he stands closer to the source of beauty than does the object he makes.

Intellect's activity is wisdom, but, as he has said numerous times, wisdom does not create by "contemplating propositions." Rather, intellect's forms are "beautiful images in that world . . . images not painted but real" (5.8.5). The arts can – but do not always – refer to intellect's wisdom. Plotinus gives an example: the wise men of Egypt drew images in their temples – "one particular image of each particular thing" – in order to demonstrate the non-discursiveness of the intelligible world. By formulating religious understanding in images rather than in propositions, they showed that "every image is a kind of knowledge and wisdom" (5.8.6). Like some works of art, sensible objects are articulations of intellect's wisdom. Thus, anyone "who knows how to admire" the sensible world is able to see intellect's wisdom inherent in it.

The world we see did not come into existence by careful planning – "planning of this sort is quite impossible!" Rather, "all things exist in something else," and because there is "nothing between" sensible objects and intellect, "something like an imprint or an image of that other suddenly appears." This making, Plotinus insists several times, is done without "noise and fuss," without "toil and trouble."

> All that is here below comes from there, and exists in greater beauty there . . . All this universe is held fast by forms from beginning to end: matter first of all by the forms of the elements, and then other forms upon these, and then again, others; so that it is difficult to find the matter hidden under so many forms. Then matter, too, is a sort of ultimate form. (5.8.7)

Notice Plotinus's "insistence on the immediate and intimate relationship of the intelligible and the sensible" and "the relative unimportance of the mediation of soul. Soul never has a world of its own intermediate between the intelligible and sensible worlds; it belongs to both worlds and is . . . thought of as linking them."[40] Having minimized the role of soul in bonding intellect and the sensible, however, Plotinus can also adopt a perspective from which soul is pivotal and essential. "Soul is not in the universe, but the universe is in soul: for body is not the soul's place, but Soul is in Intellect and body in Soul, and Intellect in something else."

> [Intellect] has not, then, gone away from other things, nor is God himself in them, nor is there anything which possesses the First, but it possess everything. Therefore it is in this way also the Good of everything, because all things have their being directed towards it and depend upon it, each in a different way. Therefore, some things are better than others, because some things have more existence than others. (5.5.9)

The relationship of the sensible world to intellect is that of mirror image – "remove the archetype and the image will perish" (3.6.13).[41] The value of "image" must be understood within the context of Plotinus's discussion of the intimate contiguity of intellect and the sensible world. *There is nothing in between, and no distance separating them.* Moreover, "whenever someone admires a thing modelled on something else, he directs his admiration to that on which the thing is modelled." But we often forget, or even do not know, that our beautiful world is an image of intellect. One can, however, infer from the beauty of our world, the transcendent and overwhelming beauty of that which forms it (5.8.8).

> Because things there are disposed as they are, the things here are beautifully disposed; . . . [the world order] is not the result of following out a train of logical consequences and purposive thought: it is before con-

sequential and purposeful thinking; for all this comes later, reasoning, and demonstration, and the confidence [produced by them]. (5.8.7)

Plotinus offers a thought experiment for seeing the sensible as image. He instructs his reader to gather in imagination the elements of the visible universe: the heavens, sun, and the other heavenly bodies, earth, sea, and all the living creatures. Picture these inside a transparent sphere. Keeping this picture in mind, imagine another sphere by subtracting its mass from the first sphere. Plotinus passes rapidly over the difficulty of this feat, for the next step is even more difficult. Here "outside" help is needed. Plotinus advocates prayer to the god who made the universe that he may come (in a manner of speaking), bringing with him all the gods (who are really one).[42] The god's power, that of intellect, is indescribably great. It is undiminished by "a petty power of body," which (from this perspective) would dilute and weaken it. Intellect's power

> has nothing but its being and its being beautiful. For where would its beauty be if it was deprived of its being? And where would its reality be if it was stripped of its being beautiful? For in deficiency of beauty it would be defective also in reality. For this reason *being is longed for because it is the same as beauty*, and beauty is lovable because it is being . . . both are one nature. (5.8.9)

What has happened to Plotinus's exercise? No longer discursive, it seems to have collapsed into immediacy, sustained by the magnificent energy of the gods. The mark of reality is beauty. In intellect, "the colour which blooms on the surface is beauty, or rather, all is colour and beauty to its innermost part: for its beauty is not something different from itself, like a surface bloom." Prayer, which turns the person's attention to the One, is the necessary route to this unqualified beauty. The vision is the penetration of the whole soul by beauty. "There is no longer one thing outside and another outside which is looking at it, but the keen-sighted has what is seen within . . . One must transport what one sees into oneself, and look at it as one, and look at it as oneself" (5.8.10).

As Plotinus said in an earlier treatise, once a person has attained this unitive vision, the final step, like the first step, is to see *herself* as image, and then "to dismiss the image, beautiful though it is, and come to unity with herself, making no more separation," one with the god. The trick of the stereoscope – seeing two pictures as one – can oscillate with seeing the one (reality) as two (the sensible world and intellect):

To begin with he sees himself, while he is different from the god; then he hastens inward and has everything, and leaves perception behind in his fear of being different, and is one in that higher world; and if he wants to see by being different, he puts himself outside . . . If he sees it as different, he is not yet in beauty, but he is in it most perfectly when he becomes it. (5.8.11)

To further characterize the experience, Plotinus compares it with health. Illness has a more violent impact on consciousness than the "quiet companionship of health," which "comes and sits by us as something which belongs to us and is united to us." Illness, Plotinus says, does not produce self-knowledge because "it is alien, not our own." Similarly, "when our knowledge is most perfectly conformed to Intellect, we think we know nothing because we are waiting for the experience of sense-perception, which says it has not yet seen, and never will see things like these" (5.8.11).

"We have explained how [a person] can do this as another, and how as himself," Plotinus concludes his discussion of method. It's all done with mirrors; if the trick works the image catches the original, overcomes its otherness, and holds simultaneously oneself and one's source. The sensible is necessary if the intelligible is to be revealed:

for it is *utterly unlawful* that there should be no beautiful image of beauty and reality. This image imitates its archetype in every way: for it has life as what belongs to reality as a representation of it should, and it has its being beauty since it comes from that higher beauty; and it has everlastingness in the way proper to an image . . . for as long as that higher reality gives its light, the rest of things can never fail: they are there as long as it is there; but it always was and will be. (5.8.12)

Like health, this beauty is neither alien nor distant; it is our own. *For this reason it is difficult to isolate it for purposes of identification*, and we think that we have not seen it when we have arrived at a sense of its vast and naked intimacy. Yet,

when we ourselves are beautiful, it is by belonging to ourselves, but we are ugly when we change to another nature: when we know ourselves we are beautiful, but ugly when we are ignorant of ourselves. Beauty therefore is in that higher world and comes from there. (5.8.13)

Not satisfied that he has provided the necessary instruction, Plotinus tries again in *Ennead* 5.5, "That the Intelligibles are Not Outside the Intellect, and On the Good." He begins with some questions about knowing. "From where will [soul] acquire the confidence that things are so?" he asks. Sense perception has the advantage of being near at hand, but how do we know that it provides trustworthy information about intellect? The objects of sense perception and intellect are different: sense perception is adapted to perceiving images of things, while intellect grasps the essence of things in themselves. Yet intellect embodies a peculiar kind of truth, not propositional truth which would be a statement about something outside ("we must not look for the intelligibles outside"), but the identity of knower and object, "one nature, Intellect, all realities and truth" (5.5.3).

Theories of knowledge that assume a knower and a known must be discarded if we are to grasp Plotinus's point. Intellect *is* what it knows: "if there is anything before it, Intellect knows clearly that this is what it derives from, and if there is anything after it, it knows clearly that this is itself." "All this" that we see in the sensible is also there in the intellect, "and really there. So that the real truth is also there, which does not agree with something else, but with itself, and says nothing other than itself, but it is what it says, and it says what it is" (5.5.2). Sense perception must be considered "opinion" in relation to the essential knowledge of intellect.

Plotinus pictures the connections but immediately confronts a difficulty; intellect "hangs from" the One but is also its pedestal: "The First [One] is enthroned above and set firm on high on Intellect in this its beauty, like a pedestal, and the pedestal, Intellect hangs from it" (5.5.3). The apparent difficulty, however, is with the awkwardness of the picture based, as it is, on sense perception. The point is that the universe is not built up from sensible world to soul, from soul to intellect, and from intellect to the First, but each sphere depends on, or hangs from, the one above it.

Plotinus's spheres, supported from above, lie immediately adjacent to one another – touching, overlapping, intimate. The sensible world, which is the most immediate, is, in fact, the "least real" (5.5.11). The seeking soul must ascend through and beyond the familiar world of objects and bodies, must "go on up" to a less familiar, but actually even more intimate world. Her sense experience is of the many; she must *intentionally* seek "the one thing." She must seek the One distinct from the phenomena informed by it, the "pure, real One, unrelated to anything else." Plotinus returns to inquiring about human access to the One.

> Reverse your way of thinking or you will be left deprived of God, like the people at festivals who by their gluttony stuff themselves with things which it is not lawful for those going in to the gods to take, thinking that these are more obviously real than the vision of the god for whom they ought to be celebrating the festival. (5.5.11)
>
> You must rush to one, and not any longer add anything to it, but stand absolutely still in fear of departing from it, and not progress the least little way towards two. (5.5.4)

Plotinus has said that the sensible does not provide trustworthy knowledge of the unity of all things, but he acknowledges that there is another sense in which, seen through the right lenses, it does. We know, for example, that the sensible reveals something about its source. "That which came to exist, substance and being, has the image of the One since it flows from its power" (5.5.5). The One is formless, the *principle* of all particulars, not a particular itself. Thus it is beyond being, "not this." The one who wants to contemplate "what is beyond the intelligible will contemplate it when he has let all the intelligible go; he will learn that it is by means of the intelligible, but what it is like by letting the intelligible go" (5.5.6).

Plotinus laments the difficulty of expressing the ascent: "But we in our travail do not know what we ought to say, and are speaking of what cannot be spoken, and give it a name because we want to indicate it to ourselves as best we can. But perhaps this name 'One' contains only a denial of multiplicity" (5.5.6). He returns to a metaphor he often finds useful, namely, actual seeing. Seeing, he says, is double; the eye cannot see itself, it requires both an object and a medium (light, air) through which the object can be perceived (5.5.6). But if the eye wants to see, not an object, but the medium, "it looks at light and the source of light." By a further step in the analogy, the eye can see "its own light," by lowering the eyelid and pressing on it. Then "by not seeing, it sees most of all: for it sees light."

> Just so Intellect, veiling itself from other things and drawing itself inward, when it is not looking at anything will see a light, not a distinct light in something distinct from itself, but suddenly appearing, alone by itself in independent purity. (5.5.7)

This light does not, strictly speaking, come from anywhere.

> It appears or does not appear. So one must not chase after it, but wait quietly till it appears, preparing oneself to contemplate it, as the eye

awaits the rising of the sun; and the sun rising over the horizon . . . gives itself to the eyes to see. (5.5.8)

Just as the eye's own light is always present but can be seen only when the eyelid is pressed, so the One is always present, but is seen only when one has made the considerable effort of ascent. The One is seen, "not as having come, but as being there before all things." It is the entities that come after which come and go. "It is really a wonder how he is present without having come, and how, though he is nowhere, there is nowhere where he is not" (5.5.8). *What you (can) see is what you get* – either broken shards, transient and isolated, or the unity of "richly varied" entities, oneself among them, in the All, circling the One.

Most people, Plotinus says, have "forgotten that which from the beginning until now they want and long for. For all things reach out to that and long for it by necessity of nature, as if divining by instinct that they cannot exist without it." Remembering one's most central and intimate longings is the necessary condition of satisfaction.

> The grasp of the beautiful and the wonder and the waking of love for it come to those who, in a way, already know it and are awake to it. But the Good, since it was there long before to arouse an innate desire, is present even to those asleep and does not astonish those who at any time see it, because it is always there and there is never recollection of it; but *people do not see it because it is present to them in their sleep.* (5.5.12)

Desire for the Good is even "more ancient" than the desire for beauty. Everyone who has attained the Good feels ultimate satisfaction. Beauty is more elusive. "Not all see beauty, and when it has come into existence they think it is beautiful for itself and not for them . . . beauty here belongs to the one who has it."

> The Good is gentle and kindly and gracious, and present to anyone when he wishes. Beauty brings wonder and shock and pleasure mingled with pain. It even draws those who do not know what is happening away from the Good, as the beloved draws a child away from its father; for Beauty is younger. But the Good is older, not in time but in truth, and has the prior power: for it has all power. (5.5.12)

The Good is both interior to and beyond the phenomena we see in the sensible world.

More Life

> When [Plotinus] was on the point of death ... he said, "Try to give
> back the god in you to the divine in the All!" and, as a snake crept
> under the bed in which he was lying and disappeared into a hole in the
> wall, he breathed his last. (*Life* 2)

Plotinus's teachings on contemplation are the necessary context for
these last words. A teacher to the end, Plotinus advised his disciple
Eustochius to *begin now*, in the midst of life, to practice placing oneself within the All. By trained and regularly exercised contemplation
one can practice identification with the strongest part of one's self,
which Plotinus calls "the god in you."

According to Plotinus, the practice and the benefits of contemplation
coincide. Contemplation is partly conceptual, a cultivated awareness of
oneness, and partly emotional, a practice of releasing the jealousies,
addictions, and resentments that cumulatively create a vitiation of the
vividness and energy of one's life. Porphyry did *not* say, as one translation indicates, that as he lay on his deathbed *Plotinus* was endeavoring
to transfer his own self-identity to the divine. At the point of death it
would have been too late to achieve this unless it were by then well
practiced, second nature, or more accurately, *first* nature. So, with his
dying breath, he urged his disciple to begin practicing *now*. Without
this training, death represents the loss of the only world one knows, the
sensible world and its closest representative, one's own body.

Life is called good for two reasons, because it originates from the
Good, and because "everything that has life desires the Good; life is the
activity of the Good." Life defines soul's intimate kinship with Good:

> When anyone ... sees this light, then truly he is also moved to the Forms,
> and longs for the light which plays upon them and delights in it, just as
> with the bodies here below our desire is not for the underlying material
> things but for the beauty imaged upon them. For each is what it is by
> itself; but it becomes desirable when the Good colours it, giving a kind
> of grace to them and passionate love to the desirers. (6.7.22)

This passionate love is the energy needed for the ascent. Paraphrasing
Plato's myth of the charioteer (*Phaedrus* 246A), Plotinus writes:

> But when a kind of warmth from thence comes upon [soul], it gains
> strength and wakes and is truly winged; and though it is moved by

passion for that which lies closest to it, yet all the same it rises higher, to something greater which it seems to remember. And as long as there is anything higher than that which is present to it, it naturally goes on upwards, lifted by the giver of its love. (6.7.22)

Soul's effort to ascend is matched by the Good, which "lifts" it by attraction. As long as soul remains at the level of intellect, it will not feel the "rush;" it is as if it were "in the presence of a face which is certainly beautiful, but cannot catch the eye because it has no grace playing upon its beauty." Plotinus compares the situation to the difference between looking at a beautiful dead face and a living face.

And is not an uglier living man more beautiful than the beautiful man in a statue? Yes, because the living is more desirable; and this is because it has soul; and this is because it has more the form of good; and this means that it is somehow coloured by the light of the Good, and being so coloured wakes and rises up and lifts up that which belongs to it. (6.7.22)

The Good makes intellect, and from intellect comes souls' life and everything else that "has a share in reason or intellect or life." The Good's creative activity, however, is not confined to one point in time. It continues to make, not only holding the things it has made in being, but also making "the thinking things think, and the living things live, inspiring thought, inspiring life and, if something cannot live, existence" (6.7.23). Plotinus's emphasis is not on an order of making that privileges those living beings capable of rational thought, but on the fundamental community of living beings, each participating as it can in the gifts of the Good.

The Good is not only a general good; it is also the particular good of each living being. The Good is not "the feeling one has when one attains it," but something that gives to each one "what is appropriate to it." Plotinus states that although form (intellect) is "akin" to soul (life), the ultimate good must be sought not in what is kin, but in "what is better than the thing itself." "If these conclusions are correct," he says,

the movement upwards grasps the good present in a particular nature, and it is not the desire which makes the good but there is desire because there is a good, and something comes to those who possess it, and also pleasure in the possession. (6.7.27)

Although pleasure may not be the appropriate motivation for seeking the Good above intellect, its attainment is certainly pleasurable.

So Intellect was raised to that height and stayed there, happy in being around that Good; but the soul also which was able turned to it and, when it knew and saw, rejoiced in the vision and, in so far as it was able to see, was utterly amazed. It saw, as if in utter amazement, and, since it held something of it in itself, it had an intimate awareness of it and came into a state of longing, like those who are moved by an image of the loved one to wish to see that same beloved. (6.7.31)

Plotinus imagines opponents. Someone may object that he "despises existence and life, [but in saying this, Plotinus says] he brings evidence against himself and all his own experiences. But if anyone is dissatisfied with life with which death is mixed, it is this kind of life he is dissatisfied with, not true life" (6.7.29). Or, "some cantankerous person" might say, "Really, you people, why do you use this pompous language up and down and all around, saying life is good, and intellect is good, and something transcending these?" (6.7.24). Or, another person may not be upset by Plotinus's arguments because "he does not know what they mean; he either hears only the words or understands each thing differently or is looking for something perceptible and locating the Good in property or something of the sort" (6.7.29). Perhaps Plotinus recalled Aristotle's description of Plato's only public lecture, "On the Good." The lecture was not a success. John Dillon writes, "The audience had come expecting, from the title, to hear something practical, such as how to become rich, healthy, or strong, and when Plato began to discourse on mathematics, geometry, and astronomy, and finally stated that the Good was the One, they incontinently left."[43]

Ultimately, Plotinus says, "what is really worth aspiring to is our selves, bringing themselves back for themselves to the best of themselves; this is the well proportioned and beautiful and the form which is not part of the composite and the clear, intelligent, beautiful life" (6.7.30). The beautiful life is made beautiful by light from its source.

Beauty

Plotinus contrasts the "beauties here" with those uncompromised by time. The one who seeks the source of sensible beauties will see that, in intellect, "all things are beautiful and true." "There" – an unfortunate locution that distorts the intimacy of Plotinus's universe – beauty "gains greater strength, since it is filled with the life of real being, and has become truly real itself also" (6.7.31). To make his point he exaggerates rhetorically between "the mud of bodies" and "the true beautiful things themselves." His purpose, however, is not to disparage the beauties "here," but, as he writes in *Ennead* 2.9.17, "*judging from them,*" to recognize their source:

> The productive power of all is the generator of beauty. Therefore the productive power of all is the flower of beauty, a beauty which makes beauty. For it generates beauty and makes it more beautiful by the excess of beauty which comes from it, so that it is the principle of beauty and the term of beauty. (6.7.32)

The beauty of intellect cannot be seen directly, for without matter it has no visible shape. Visible beauty mirrors but does not coincide with intellect's beauty. To mistake visible beauty for intelligible beauty is to "fall out of beauty into what is called beauty." Meta-beauty stands behind visible beauty, informing it and guaranteeing its reality. It is "a beauty which makes beauty" (6.7.32). "Whatever you bring into form and show to the soul, it seeks something else over it which gave it shape . . . The primarily beautiful, then, and the first is without form, and beauty is that, the nature of the Good" (6.7.33).

Recognizing the beauty of the Good in the people and things of the sensible world is a full-time job, but it is not a task that necessarily takes a person away from her ordinary activities. It is not an intellectual activity, strictly speaking. It is not a matter of seeing and subsequently interpreting what one sees. Rather, one sees this beauty, if at all, at the level of *perception*. It is a continuous contemplation by which "he no longer sees a sight, but mingles his seeing with what he contemplates, so that what was seen before has now become sight in him, and he forgets all other objects of contemplation" (6.7.35).

Plotinus distinguishes between intellect "in its right mind," that is, thinking and reasoning, and "Intellect in love" with its own source. The latter is the condition in which the soul is "simplified into happiness." Rational inquiry disappears and "the soul sees by a kind of confusing and annulling the intellect which abides within it" (6.7.35). At this level of sight, the Good rests on both aspects of intellect, uniting them and giving them "a blessed perception and vision" (6.7.35).

> The knowledge or touching of the Good is the greatest thing . . . We are taught about it by comparisons and negations and knowledge of the things which come before it and certain methods of ascent by degrees, but we are put on the way to it by purifications and virtues and adornings

and by gaining footholds in the intelligible and settling ourselves firmly there and feasting on its contents. (6.7.36)

There is certainly preparation for this vision, but there is also, and perhaps most difficult of all, letting "all study go. Up to a point one has been led along and settled firmly in beauty," but then one is "lifted on high by a kind of swell and sees suddenly, not seeing how, but the vision fills his eyes with light and does not make him see something else by it, but the light itself is what he sees . . . he himself is the ray" (6.7.36).

Plotinus complains again of the difficulty of speaking about this experience. Dropping his efforts to explain how the Good can be seen, Plotinus says the vision is "something like a touch," or contact (6.7.39). At their best his descriptions, he says, provide "words of encouragement." When one "goes on from substance and thought," one will come to "something wonderful . . . alone by itself" (6.7.40). As if he were suddenly addressing the postmodern self, glorying in unorganized multiplicity, Plotinus writes:

> "Know yourself" is said to those who because of their selves' multiplicity have the business of counting themselves up and learning that they do not know all of the number and kind of things they are, or do not know any one of them, not what their ruling principle is or by what they are themselves. (6.7.41)

Chance can never produce the spiritual world; nor is one's substantial connection with its power actualized by chance. "Self" is not created by happenstance and our reactions, but by purposeful committed engagement. The One is different. The One causes himself, "and himself from himself, and through himself; for he is primarily self and self beyond being" (6.8.15). What is effortless for the One is laborious for humans. To the extent that a person develops a nature that is not at the mercy of whatever happens,

> which has nothing of the other things which are attached to us by which we have to experience whatever happens by chance . . . when we ascend to this and become this alone and let the rest go, . . . we are more free and more independent . . . *we have become the true life itself or come to be in it*. (6.8.15)

Conclusion

Proposals for how to live a good life are perennial. I found one recently in my morning newspaper in an interview with a highly successful businessman. Questioned concerning the motivation for his successful career, he replied: "My feeling was why not lead the best life you possibly can, which means go and have a great career . . . Spend time with your friends, see the world, get drunk, eat well, and live in a great place."[44] This account of the "best life" shares a focus on pleasures with what may be the first recorded report in history on the good life. In the *Epic of Gilgamesh*, Siduri, winemaker to the gods who lives by the shining sea, remonstrates with Gilgamesh, who is desperately seeking immortality:

> Gilgamesh, where are you hurrying to? You will never find that life for which you are looking. When the gods created man they allotted to him death, but life they retained in their own keeping. As for you, Gilgamesh, fill your belly with good things; day and night, night and day, dance and be merry, feast and rejoice. Let your clothes be fresh, bathe yourself in water, cherish the little child that holds your hand, and make your wife happy in your embrace; for this too is the lot of man.[45]

In Plotinus's time, Epicureans were thought to represent the view that pleasures were the goal of human life.[46] But other prominent voices in mid-third-century Rome – Christian ascetics, philosophers, and Gnostics – focused on body from a different perspective and with a different agenda. They suggested that soul is best cultivated by minute and exacting attention to body and its needs and habits. Plotinus proposed that soul could be addressed directly. While he took for granted a certain well-defined philosophical lifestyle, he saw no need to talk about his social and personal practices as he discussed his philosophy. Instead he offered an integrated conceptual scheme and practice of contemplation designed to produce a conversion of the soul. In the first treatise he wrote he urged: "Shut your eyes, change to, and wake another way of seeing, which everyone has but few use" (1.6.8).[47] All of Plotinus's writings seek to motivate and enable that conversion.

7
Plotinus for the Present

Men build bridges and streets when there is already an amazing gold electric ring connecting every living being as surely as if we held hands, flippers and paws, feelers and wings.[1]

[We are] answerable for what we learn how to see.[2]

I hope it is by now evident that the *Enneads*, although they were shaped by and responded to a different time and society, contain some useful and usable ideas for the present. The value of a conceptual scheme or big picture that sets the lives of individuals and societies within what we might call a unified field cannot be exaggerated. An adequate orientation to the universe provides the security – Plotinus's "perfect safety" – that encourages a generous perspective based on a sense of kinship with other living beings. In this concluding chapter I examine some implications of the quickened sense of life Plotinus sought to make accessible. But first, because attractions, adopted uncritically, can become seductions, it is important to examine carefully and seriously the potential dangers of Plotinus's philosophy.

Plotinus on Body

Plotinus's alleged dualism is difficult to pinpoint and evaluate. He certainly distinguished body and soul, and he thought of soul as superior to body. Because soul can live without body – since soul *is* life – while body cannot live without soul's life; because soul unites all beings that share life, while bodies separate living beings; and because the source is greater than the object created, soul is superior to body. Clearly, if Plotinus's philosophy is to be useful for people who live at the beginning of the twenty-first century, we must be prepared to strengthen his sense of the interdependence of body and soul even while we accept his distinction.

Perhaps, however, a distinction inevitably creates a hierarchy in which one of the terms is considered inferior. Or, even if this logically *need* not be the case, is this a Western habit of mind that is so firmly established that such distinctions are best avoided? Can the life-giving capacity of soul be eulogized without implicit disparagement to body and the sensible? The way we respond to these questions will have a great deal to do with whether or not we find that Plotinus is useful for the present.

Plotinus's flexibility – some might label it inconsistency – in evaluating body might be taken as encouraging boldness in interpreting his philosophy in the context of our own needs. We have seen that Plotinus was a strong admirer of the sensible world in contexts in which he challenged Gnostic consignment of body to non-negotiable biodegradability. When his goal was to describe the unity and integrity of the universe he spoke of body as a necessary and beautiful reflection of the One. Elsewhere, in contexts in which he sought to inspire hearers and readers to "go on up" to identifying with soul, intellect and the One, he cautioned against becoming absorbed in the sensible and thus failing to recognize its source. When he aimed at generating motivation for contemplative ascent to the One, he spoke of body as the hindrance against which one must struggle. In these contexts his rhetoric was conventional and traditional among philosophers; it disparaged body.

Moreover, he wrote about body not only in different rhetorical contexts but also within a particular historical, social, intellectual, and personal context. Each of these contexts has been examined. In chapter 4 I analyzed the complex social, philosophical, and religious context within which Plotinus talked about the meaning and value of body. In chapter 5 I interpreted Plotinus's last statements on life, death, and body in the context of his own impending death. Here we can simply remind ourselves that it was not the healthy body, useful partner of the animating soul, that Plotinus found problematic. It was rather the inevitable reality of the vulnerable, ailing, moribund and finally lifeless body that prompted him to suggest that ultimate pleasure should not be sought in body, that body should be cared for but not indulged, and that although bodies are beautiful, beauty transcends body.

If physical experience is not as ambiguous for many or most contemporaries as it was for third-century people – who, after all, lacked antibiotics and anesthetic – it is perhaps because we experience unmitigated and unmanageable physical pain less frequently and more privately. Of course, pain remains a daily reality for many people, but until that pain is mine, or belongs to someone very close to me, I am likely to know pain only as a concept. Pain impresses our consciousness less because, unlike third-century colosseum culture, American society isolates from public view people who are in severe pain, the better to maintain the illusion that suffering is no longer necessary and inevitable. Our own experience and assumptions must be carefully scrutinized before we are in a position to judge the resentments of people of the past toward body.

Perhaps, however, it does not matter so much how heavily Plotinus's physical and social experience directed him often to find body one of the burdens as well as one of the graces of human life. What may matter more is whether a philosophy that *sometimes* disparages body is usable in our own time. Let's reconsider.

Plotinus and Dualism

Plotinus's primary dualism – the word is notoriously slippery and difficult to define – is that of the source and the multiple living beings generated by it.[3] Yet he does seem to have addressed the perennial difficulty of recalling attention to the transcendent source without cutting it off altogether from its creation.[4] He was unequivocally committed to the doctrine of the "one life extending unbroken through all the descending stages from the One [through intellect] to the soul or life-principle in plants," soil, and rocks. It is difficult to see how anyone who has read the *Enneads* attentively could charge Plotinus with the sort of dualism that separates the One from the many. And, as we have seen, soul and body display a similar resistance to separation, an interdependence.

Perhaps, however, Plotinus's separation and hierarchical ranking of intellect and the sensible is a greater problem. The practical effects of the devaluation of "matter" – which we usually confuse with what Plotinus called "body" – are evident in the careless use and abuse of the natural world in the West. I will return to this issue in what follows.

Yet Plotinus recognized and emphasized that body and the sensible are a necessary and beautiful articulation of intellect. *His purpose in distinguishing intelligible and sensible was to demonstrate their interconnection and interdependency, their unity.* For a unity is not a chaos or mixture, but a whole whose parts each contribute in definable ways to the cohesion of the whole. The idea of promiscuous "mixture" was repugnant to Romans (*mixtus*) and Greeks (*krasis*). In fact, the contents of the Roman sewer, the Cloaca were called *mixtus*.[5] Seeking to define and rank distinguishable entities, then, Plotinus followed (1) a deeply embedded philosophical tradition, (2) a social instinct in a rigidly stratified society, and (3) a broad consensus that mixture is abhorrent. Given these strong tendencies to differentiate and grade, rather than confuse, distinguishable entities such as sensible and spiritual, Plotinus's frequently voiced tender and poetic appreciation for body is all the more remarkable. It seems, then, that what we must primarily resist is not so much Plotinus's own view of the relationship of soul and body but interpreters' frequent caricatures of his teachings. Nonetheless, his sense of the poignant interdependence of soul/life and body is marred by passages in which he makes body foil for the greater worth and beauty of soul.

Plotinus on Moral Engagement

A critical appropriation of Plotinus must also acknowledge the inadequacy – indeed, the dangers – of his statements about moral concern. Although Plotinus's idea of the "strange sympathy" shared by all living beings supports concern about ecology, and social and economic justice, he explicitly advocated a nonchalant attitude toward suffering.[6] The "good and wise man," he wrote, leaves concern about poverty to others. He recognizes and accepts that "there are two kinds of life here below, one for the good and wise and one for the mass of men." The mass of men are on earth "to do manual work and to provide for the necessities of the better sort." Brushing aside the pains and damages of human life, *both his own and others'*, Plotinus tells his readers to consider the world a sports arena "where some win and others lose – what is there wrong with that?" Winners will not impress the "good and wise man," nor will losers worry him. All that is important for the good and wise man is to be "directed to the highest point and the upper region" (2.9.9). These words summarize Plotinus's guilt in contributing to the quietism that has often characterized Western contemplation.

More than seventeen centuries after Plotinus's death, I endeavor to see the world as Plotinus saw it. But my experience and my world are different from his in fundamental ways. In a world that is knit to-

gether by rapid transportation and communication, I have seen the
faces of people who suffer from economic, social, and political inequality. I have also seen and heard news media representations of
those who suffer from war, famine, and disaster. I cannot dismiss suffering children, women, men, and animals as "losers," no matter how
reassuring this might be. In his classroom, surrounded by his students,
Plotinus could apparently subsume suffering into his worldview more
easily than I can. Even if he did not see human suffering and death at
the colosseum, he accepted the attitudes and values of the colosseum
in his construction of suffering and injustice as a simple matter of
"winners and losers." While caring in practical ways for people in his
immediate vicinity who were in need, he apparently remained uncon-
cerned with suffering he had no ability to assuage. In this, of course,
he was a man of his time. He might (if he were our contemporary)
have been able to recognize the need for actively resisting social injustice as well as attempting to alleviate the need of individuals in his
immediate vicinity.

Clearly, Plotinus's philosophy could be read, and indeed, has been
read, as a rationale for ignoring blatant social and economic inequi-
ties. The fundamental incoherence of this attitude with the rest of
Plotinus's gentle philosophy is evident. It was also inconsistent with
his own practice of caring for orphans, helping those in need, and
counseling his friends. Why did he not simply regard all of these as
losers? Philosophies and theologies should articulate what philosophers and theologians know experientially. Rather than ignoring
Plotinus's elitist statements, it is important to see them as a cautionary
tale and to deplore the apparent ease with which a great philosophical
mind could casually incorporate the common prejudices of his society.

Yet Plotinus's philosophy actually did know better than to dismiss
"losers" as unworthy of concern. In our time, in a world fragmented by economic, political, geographical, and religious differences, Plotinus's description of an interconnected universe can help to
overcome attitudes based on isolation and insularity, encouraging that
"strange sympathy" for all living beings he described (4.9.3). His dynamic, intimately responsive, connected spiritual universe can serve as
a basis for social concern and action. To understand Plotinus's failure
to carry his vision to the point of working to alter the social, political,
and institutional conditions that create suffering is not to forgive that
failure, but to retrieve what is usable. It is to read both appreciatively
and critically.

A related problem in Plotinus's philosophy has to do with his assumption that the individual is the target of the philosophical life. In Plotinus's teachings, each person chips away at her/his own statue without apparent help (or hindrance) from others. In omitting relationship and community from his philosophy, he differs significantly from his mentor, Plato, who advocated both committed relationships in which the partners encouraged and stimulated each other to virtue, and communities in which philosophical issues were heatedly discussed.[7] A.H. Armstrong writes:

> In 1.6.9 [Plotinus] uses the metaphor of "working on the statue" from the *Phaedrus* with a very significant change. Plato showed the lover working on his beloved to make him more godlike, and becoming more godlike himself in the process. Plotinus exhorts the lover of absolute beauty to go on working *on "his own* statue" so as to make himself perfect and fit for the final vision . . . [F]or Plotinus the *eros* of aspiration to and union with the good is a solitary love, a love of one for One.[8]

In Plotinus's conceptual universe, the intimacy of each with all takes the place of community. Here again, Plotinus's philosophy does not reflect his practice. Porphyry's description of Plotinus's classroom in which serious issues were doggedly pursued, as well as his friendships, leaves no doubt that Plotinus lived in the midst of intense relationships and community. Yet in his philosophy, consanguinity has replaced conversation.

Plotinus's conceptual world in which nothing is distant from anything else may be much easier for twentieth-century people to imagine than it was for Plotinus's contemporaries. The "small world" has become a daily reality in technological societies in which news stories traverse the globe within seconds and it is possible to get up one morning in Boston and go to bed that night in Jerusalem. In Plotinus's small world, the other is not really other, and diversity is overwhelmed by unity. The philosophical moment in which the causes and effects of diversity are explored simply never occurs. This inadequacy in Plotinus's teaching must not be glossed over. I will return to it.

Feminism and Plotinus

We must also question Plotinus's philosophy from the perspective of one of the most important critical theories of the latter half of the twentieth century. Feminist and gender studies have led the way for a number of investigations of social and intellectual assumptions that had been largely unquestioned until our own time. In the latter half of the twentieth century, numerous scholarly studies have shown the dependence of Western philosophy and theology on elite male perspectives that position women at best as ancillary support, at worst as source of chaos, evil, and death.[9] How does Plotinus's work relate to the misogyny of Western philosophy and theology?

Evidence of his treatment of, and statements about, women is scanty. Porphyry describes women as Plotinus's students – apparently not a unique aspect of his school – and tells us that Plotinus lived in a woman's home. This could mean no more than, like other philosophical and religious organizations of late antiquity, women were permitted to be hangers-on and benefactors! However, it could also indicate that Plotinus intentionally practiced "counter-cultural" respectful attention to women as part of his philosophical commitments. There is some inconclusive but interesting evidence that the latter was the case.

One of Plato's primary metaphors was that of the philosopher as midwife (for example, *Theatetus* 149), assisting to birth insights already implicit in the minds of his conversation partners. Plotinus also used birth metaphors from time to time. In one important connection, he compared the process of achieving a unitive vision – surely his most valued experience – as similar to the process of labor and birth-giving, a process that oscillates between difficult and painful work and "patient waiting" (5.3.17; 5.5.8). But Plotinus may have been unique among philosophers of his time in speaking of labor and childbirth not, as Plato did, from the perspective of the midwife or the child struggling toward birth (*Epinomis* 973d), but from the perspective of the woman who gives birth.

His description of the rhythm of labor indicates a familiarity with birth-giving that would seem to depend either on attentive listening to women's narrations of their experience or on observation. That he uses birth-giving as metaphor for his most prized experience indicates, of course, that he recognized the similarity of these two processes in which activity and passivity are intertwined. In any case, he did not disparage physical birth-giving in relation to visionary experience. We might take the further step of collapsing his metaphor into actuality; at least for some women who describe their experience, giving birth results in a transformative unitive vision.[10]

A further indication of Plotinus's respect for women as childbearers is his insistence that mothers as well as fathers contribute form to the fetus. Plotinus's discussion of matter in *Ennead* 3.6. leads him to emphasize that "matter," though it is often called the mother of all things, should not be understood to describe the mother's role in conception as passive. Against "those who claim that the mother holds the position of matter in respect to her children in that she only receives [the seed] and contributes nothing to the children," he insisted that the mother contributes "because she is not only matter but also form" (3.6.19).[11]

It will still – and incontrovertibly – be objected that Plotinus spoke of women only as childbearers. Nor did Porphyry mention women as interlocutors rather than listeners in the classes he described.[12] In short, though Plotinus exhibited understanding and appreciation for conception and childbearing, it cannot be argued that he transcended the common gender assumptions of his time.

If Plotinus does not qualify as a forerunner of feminism, neither is he an adversary. Feminists often identify Platonism as the origin of concepts that have effectively disadvantaged, indeed oppressed, women: among them are dualism, hierarchy, and hatred for "the body."[13] In doing so, however, they implicitly accept the verdict of generations of male scholars from Porphyry forward who have identified these concepts as the cornerstones of Plotinus's philosophy. Plotinus is often hastily read in the light of a caricatured "Platonism."

Has Plotinus been read thoroughly and attentively by feminist scholars? Perhaps not, but why would they be inspired to do so? What body of scholarship on Plotinus might alert feminists, along with other critical readers, to the possibility that the *Enneads* might contain usable concepts? Some scholars have isolated Plotinus's "mystical" side (as opposed to his political side) as capable of retrieval.[14] But a long tradition of scholarship has admiringly read Plotinus as "otherworldly," body-denying, elitist, and uninterested in issues of social arrangements of equality and mutuality. In previous chapters I examined the proof texts by which those strains are usually documented, but when they are identified as key to Plotinus's philosophy, they dramatically distort his vision.

An example will help. At a 1984 symposium at the Free University of Amsterdam, the Dutch scholar A.P. Bos discussed the continuity of the assumptions and goals of Western science with those of Greek philosophy. He named "theoria," defined as "a form of flight from mortality and death," as "the mainspring of Greek philosophy." Greek philosophy, Bos writes, proclaimed that there is "warranted hope that it is possible to make a breakthrough and leave behind the limitations of everyday existence."[15]

If a flight from everyday existence were central to Plotinus, I would have little interest in retrieving his philosophy. Escape from the everyday is not usually a woman's fantasy or prerogative. Such escape is prohibited for most women not only by bodies that come to menarche, menstruate, bear children, and traverse menopause, but also by social roles that assign the everyday to their attention and care. However, I have argued throughout these chapters that Plotinus did not urge flight from everyday existence. His philosophy sought not to escape but to manage everyday existence most fruitfully. Rather, his philosophy is addressed to enabling flight from deadness, lethargy, and constriction of vision.

Bos writes, "I am of the opinion that [Platonism's] essence must be located in man's aspiration to leave behind the experiential situation of tension and struggle which results from never-ending differences of opinion, and to reach a level of knowledge and science which will once and for all put an end to all struggle and schism."[16] True, Bos claims to characterize "Platonism" rather than Plotinus specifically, but, as Platonism's foremost interpreter, Plotinus is included in his generalizations. Yet Plotinus believed that human access to the way the world is is only achieved by a fundamentally ineffable experience of vision/touch. From the perspective of Plotinus's philosophy, Bos's fantasy of unquestionable knowledge and absolute authority is exposed as a projection.

Second, Bos reads Plotinus as longing for the final demise of perspective. He continues his discussion of absolute knowledge: "Such knowledge will not be determined by a frame of reference dependent on individual experience or collective tradition, nor bound by factors of time and culture; it will be knowledge of the Truth, knowledge concerning reality as it *really is*."[17]

Moreover, such knowledge will not be influenced by the *relation* which the knowing subject has to the object of knowledge: "Only the pursuit of *rationality* enables man to aspire to liberation from the limitations of *relationality*."[18] Bos's non-inclusive language is oddly accurate in the passage; these aspirations belong to "man," not all men – perhaps not even many men – but to the universal subject, "man," constructed in Western universities. Unaware of his participation in a particular perspective, Bos deplores perspective. But surely, the cultivation of a relationship with the universe was essential to Plotinus. For him, as Pierre Hadot has so brilliantly demonstrated, philosophy was not a purely intellectual activity, but a way of life. The route to trustworthy knowledge was one of spiritual discipline, a committed refining of one's own beauty in preparation for recognizing the great beauty characteristic of the One.

Bos has accurately identified, not the essence of Platonic philosophy, but its reigning caricature, namely "flight from mortality and death," "leaving behind the limitations of everyday life," absolute authority, the disappearance of perspective, and liberation from relationality. This parody of Plotinus has achieved such consensus that it is difficult to read him freshly. C. Behan McCullagh describes a tendency endemic to scholarship when he writes, "It is interesting to note how, once a dominant pattern has been detected in a historical subject, it is difficult to see other patterns or to set it aside."[19]

Bos does not criticize these tenets, nor does he seek to read Plotinus for other than these most conventional insights. If these points were, in fact, the gist of what Plotinus had to say, they would be completely at odds with the most important insights, not only of feminist scholars, but of critical scholarship more generally.

In fact, if Plotinus's thought could be accurately characterized and summarized in this way, contemporary scholars should read Plotinus only for anachronistic interest. However, Bos's points represent, not the *Enneads*, but the consensus reading of a particular scholarly perspective. It is possible and fruitful, as I hope this book demonstrates, to read Plotinus with other interests than those of a fantasy of escape from the complexity of multiple perspectives – Plotinus's "richly varied" community of living beings – and the beauties and frustrations of relationship!

In short, to read Plotinus as he is read by some of his interpreters is to miss his usefulness for critical thought. For conceptual support and inspiration is available in Plotinus's writings for commitments to just social arrangements, equality and mutuality in relationships, the diversification of privilege, and pluralistic religious and social values. The *Enneads* can be read in ways that support these projects without falsifying Plotinus, or concealing aspects of his difficult philosophy that are deeply uncongenial to people with these commitments.

But why bother? Why not relegate Platonism to the dust-heap of ancient philosophies that can no longer attract critical thinkers? Why resurrect an ancient thinker from an alien culture whose values often seem so at odds with some of those of our own society?

Plotinus for the Present

I have indicated several discourses to which Plotinus can contribute. At this point I speak quite particularly from within and to a rather small discursive world perched on the side of a diverse society with multiple interests, fears, and longings ~ namely those arenas of the academic world in which worldviews are examined and criticized.

Important work has been done since the late 1970s to identify and challenge the complicity of conceptual schemes in creating and maintaining oppressive and exclusive institutions and political and social arrangements. Feminists, African Americans, gay men and lesbian women, and liberation theologians have met together to discuss and discern their identities and agenda. It has been of the greatest importance for these and other "special interest" groups – as they have been labeled by hostile witnesses – to have access to institutional time and space for these discussions. The criticisms these scholars have brought have also been of great importance to the health and vitality of academic institutions, for together they have decisively criticized a special interest group that, under the guise of impartiality and objectivity, has created and continues to dominate academic discourse. Marginalized people have moved "from margin to center" as they have brought mind-opening criticism to reigning scholarly assumptions.[20] Most, however, have not, to date, reached the senior ranks of the academic institutions that shape agenda for the future. There is a time-lag between the significance of their criticism and institutional change.

These scholars have called to the attention of the academic world the demonstrable ways in which intellectual interests, disciplines, and methods shape institutions. Thus far, critical scholars' work has been largely related to texts, authors, and events of the recent or distant past. They have focused on exposing and criticizing institutional structures and procedures that favor the status quo. They have not, thus far, presented worldviews designed to incorporate along with their most profound and trenchant criticism of mainstream academics a constructive vision capable of attracting a diverse audience.

It is unfair to imply that this should by now have been done. Critical scholars have spent their time not only in thought and the negotiation of ideas, but also in advocacy for social and economic justice. Moreover, the social and institutional conditions in which new, or fundamentally revised, worldviews can be established have not existed. The effective presentation of attractive theologies and worldviews requires multiple discussions, printed and oral, that specify and refine them. Our models of theological work are also to blame. Individual theologians and philosophers are almost invariably the focus of courses and books – Augustine, Luther, Calvin, Tillich, Aristotle, James or Whitehead. And so the extent to which those thinkers received many of their ideas, as well as the climate of reception that recognized the worth of their ideas, from their predecessors and colleagues has been concealed. Contemporary critical thinkers have made amazing progress in focusing and refining their projects in the short period of time in which they have had the (often grudging) support of universities and graduate schools. Their work is now at a point where in order to maintain its momentum, it needs to advance to the next phase.

If my analysis of the present academic moment is accurate, it is time to find, create, and compose worldviews that will attract diverse adherents. Tools and ideas must be sought and their unmarked and sometimes unintended allegiances made explicit and criticized. These ideas and tools must then be woven into worldviews capable of integrating self-critical and constructive elements. This, I believe, is the most serious challenge and task of the present.

At the risk of inviting a frequent criticism of Plotinus scholars, namely, that they tend to exhibit uncritical enthusiasm, I suggest that Plotinus has something to offer to that task. Beyond the example of a well-stocked mind and an unwearying commitment to intellectual work, Plotinus exemplifies some characteristics that make for effective communication. First, the compelling attractiveness of his vision, his imagining the real, is instructive. Plotinus's gentleness, remarked on by Porphyry, permeates his work. Even his polemical writings do not erupt into the charges of sexual misconduct and intellectual dishonesty we are so familiar with in his Christian contemporaries. Moreover, his inclusive generosity of vision is evident in his construction of a universe in which human beings hold "hands, flippers and paws, feelers and wings" with other living beings.

In addition, an intellectual discipline of imagining the real becomes, in Plotinus, a spiritual discipline, an art of life, a response to the ancient query, How should we live? Plotinus collapses the division of theory and practice, knowledge and spiritual discipline that vexes contemporary education. Plotinus saw that a vision constricted to the acquisition of sex, power, and possessions – the very objects to which Americans are directed by every media communication – cannot grasp the reality of the intimately connected universe. Plotinus's vision can help us to reconstruct "the good life" in ways that refocus our commitments and redirect our actions. Plotinus urged that the "richly varied" universe is to be enjoyed – loved – while and precisely because we see in it the one thing, the life and beauty that boils throughout. To go beyond criticism to attraction, we will need to catch Plotinus's vivid sense of beauty and the energy and passion with which he communicated what he saw.

Throughout these chapters I have discussed other aspects of Plotinus's ideas that enable reconstruction of the worldviews Western individuals and societies have inherited. I only summarize them here.

First, until the second half of the twentieth century, it has been impossible to identify and map with scientific precision the interconnectedness of living beings. Plotinus's notion of an interdependent web of sentient and non-sentient entities has been intuited rather than demonstrated. The intuition has been represented by a long tradition of authors who have frequently been labeled romantic, soft, or nature worshippers by "hard-headed" philosophers. But a sea-change for thought has occurred in our time, brought about by the scientific capacity to measure, and the technological capability to demonstrate, the tangible and intimate effects of such environmental crises as the disappearance of rain forests, the extinction of animal species, and pollution of air, water, and food. We consider each of these situations with alarm, but what is needed to energize our committed work on behalf of living beings and the earth is that we recognize the import of all the news *together*: the universe is utterly interdependent. This knowledge is no longer intuited or romantic, but concrete and documented, a fundamental fact of life at the beginning of the twenty-first century. Plotinus said it first:

> The All is a single living being which encompasses all the living beings within it; so it has one soul which extends to all its parts . . . This one universe is all bound together in shared experience and is like one living creature, and that which is far is really near . . . And since it is one living thing and all belongs to a unity nothing is so distant in space that it is not close enough to the nature of the one living thing to share experience. (4.4.32)

This recognition is the most important open secret of the universe. The universe continuously circulates gifts – of life, love, light, and nourishment, but damage and pain also circulate in the same way. The discovery of this secret can become the centerpiece of one's individual identity. This worldview, once a prerogative of mystics, now has obvious and crucially important implications for our efforts to protest and alter practices that damage the natural world and kill people.

Second, although I have suggested that Plotinus was uninterested in exploring the universe's diversity except as it demonstrates the richly various forms of the life common to all, he nevertheless provided a worldview congruent with a commitment to attention to diversity that surpasses his own. His insistence that our fundamental responsibility is to a "richly varied" community of living beings – not rational minds – offers an alternative to the coercive conceptions of social and religious unity the West has experienced.[21] Plotinus was the last important representative of the Platonic tradition who did not think of diversity as threatening unity.

Moreover, he shared with some Gnostic groups of late antiquity – like the North African Manichaeans, though for very different reasons – a sense of community with all living beings. His (in other respects) most articulate interpreter in the Christian West, Augustine of Hippo, imagined the community of moral concern very differently. Augustine pointedly stated his own exclusive interest in relationships among human beings and with God. An early treatise of Augustine's asks and answers the rhetorical question, With what are you concerned? He responds, "God and the soul." He asks again, "Nothing more?" and he answers, "Nothing more."[22] The West inherited, not Plotinus's view, but Augustine's argument that the community of human responsibility is that of rational minds.[23] In our world, threatened by extinction of species and ecological disaster, there is no doubt that Augustine's notion of community needs to be changed to Plotinus's.

Third, Plotinus offered a sophisticated critique of a phenomenon he calls "enchantment" (4.4.43). Enchantment comes in several varieties, some more pernicious than others. The most obvious enchantment occurs in magical rites. Sometimes it actually works because of "a natural concord of things that are alike and opposition of things that are different . . . in the rich variety of the many powers that go to make up the life of the one living creature" (4.4.40).

Another form of enchantment is more endemic and pervasive. In order to describe this more subtle form of enchantment, Plotinus contrasts choice and (irrational) enchantment. Plotinus's criterion is that "only that which is self-directed is free from enchantment." His high standard for "self-direction" is revealed by his statement:

Contemplation alone remains incapable of enchantment . . . No one who is self-directed is subject to enchantment: for he is one, and that which he contemplates is himself . . . But all practical action is under enchantment, and the whole life of the practical man: for he is moved to that which charms him. (4.4.43)

Psychology and of enchantment

What Plato meant when he spoke of philosophy as "practice for dying" may have been, at least in part, the ability, in the midst of life, to *see through* and *let go* of trained and repeatedly reinforced reactions. Plotinus also thought that one of philosophy's benefits is to provide a perspective from which to understand, and at least sometimes to resist, the creation and direction of desire through socialization. Awareness of one's own socialized responses supplies an increment of freedom and makes possible a chosen response. But recognition is only the first step, for the ability to make real choices is neither automatic nor easy. The difficulty of achieving some measure of freedom from socialization can only be seen by someone who has attempted to do so. Lacking a word for "socialization," Plotinus called it "enchantment."

Fourth, Plotinus can lend perspective to contemporary discussions of the fragmented self. The fragmented self is not new in the early twenty-first century. Living in the entertainment culture of mid-third-century Rome, Plotinus considered the unified self, far from being a given, to be *a project*. He pointed out that a well-known Socratic maxim addressed the scattered self:

unified self is not a given, a project

> "Know yourself" is said to those who, because of their selves' multiplicity have the business of counting themselves up and learning that they do not know all of the number and kind of things they are, or do not know any one of them, not what their ruling principle is or by what they are themselves. (6.7.41)

Plotinus realized that a unified self was the result of hard and committed work. Even then, the unified self is always merely "unified enough" to accomplish some of its dearest goals.

Fifth, Plotinus offers perspective on late twentieth-century interest in "the body." Although he wrote voluminously about body, he was ultimately interested in life, not body. He wrote about body because of its collaboration with life, but he thought it important to distinguish life from body. For Plotinus, body (without the presence of life) is the corpse that is buried at death.[24] Twentieth-century readers often confuse the "body" conceptualized by late antiquity with Descartes' "body," a body that has many physiological as well as psychological capacities. For example, Descartes' "body" can walk, sing, and feel; it can perform any feat not requiring the conscious engagement of intellect. If Plotinus were to drop in on a contemporary academic discussion of "the body" he might observe that the discussion is undermined by a conflation of body and life. No matter how frequent and loud the

Body has to have life

call for the "real body" to "please stand up," it is always a life-bearing body that rises.

"The body," is irreducibly a concept. The flesh cannot be made word and spoken without theoretical abstraction, no matter how determined we are to articulate the "real" body. Life is the broader category that integrates body and its animation, energy, and built-in trajectory. Life yields to fruitful analysis precisely because it acknowledges the rational forming principles by which the biological, psychological, and intellectual aspects of living beings are held in tension. Ultimately, neither Plotinus's concept of body nor that of Descartes can provide the strong sense of the intimate and mutual interdependence of body and soul that must inform our struggles on behalf of the well-being of the earth and all its inhabitants.

Plotinus's Worldview as Religion

Did Plotinus advance a specifically *religious* worldview? This depends largely on the definition of religion employed. Although early twenty-first-century scholars of religion do not agree on a single definition of religion, several recent proposals help to identify what may be thought of as the specific nature of Plotinian religiosity. If religion is about the activities of supernatural beings, as one definition states, Plotinus was famously disinterested, saying irreverently on the occasion of a religious festival, "[The gods] ought to come to me, not I to them."[25] If however, religion is about answering the question, "Can I trust the universe?," Plotinus was consummately religious.[26] His whole corpus seeks to answer that question in the affirmative. "The universe lies in safety," he said (3.4.4). Similarly, if we adopt William James's definition of religion: "religion is the sense of life by virtue of which [humanity] does not destroy [itself], but lives on," Plotinus offers a religious worldview.[27]

By most contemporary definitions, then, Plotinus offers a coherent religious system characterized by conceptual orientation within the universe and a practice of spiritual discipline—contemplation. To a cultural moment when theologians are puzzling about how to create a public conversation about worldviews across denominational and religious boundaries, Plotinus offers an inclusive theology that recognizes the dependence of all living beings on a transcendent creative and sustaining force. Acknowledging that human language and ritual forms at best merely point toward (but do not capture) our best guesses

about the nature of our lives' source, Plotinus feels free to use interchangeably, and as we have seen, often in rapid succession, personal
and impersonal expressions for "it."[28]

Plotinus's philosophical and religious interest lay in what is "within
our power."[29] He understood two interrelated spiritual disciplines as
"within our power," the practice of contemplation in which one imagines the real, and attentiveness to beauty, the mark of the presence of the
One, the great beauty (*mega kallos*: 1.6.9). Plotinus presents a secular
theology that could be attractive to numbers of Westerners who think of
themselves as "spiritual, but not religious." Theologian Charles Winquist
defines secular theology as "a thinking within the ordinariness of experience that makes a difference within the ordinariness of experience."[30]
Plotinus wrote: "We encounter the extraordinary with astonishment,
though we should be astonished at these ordinary things too" (4.4.37).

Plotinus also navigates effectively a problem endemic to religions,
namely, the problem of theodicy. In Christianity the question takes
this form: if God is omnipotent, why is there suffering? As discussed in
chapter 5, Plotinus answers that "providence is of the whole." Pain is
inevitable in a universe in which living beings struggle to grip and hold
life. Both gifts and pain circulate without planning or design. Each of
us has moments in which we "boil with life," "veins full of existence."[31] And we each, gracefully or gracelessly – the choice is ours –
also inherit pain and death when life "goes on" to other bodies, other
forms.[32] Plotinian prayer does not seek to harness the One's special
attention and protection; that concept of prayer makes little sense in a
Plotinian universe. Rather, prayer turns the person's attention toward
the choirmaster who directs the whole chorus. Its effects are on the
one who prays, not on the One who is always "there":

> In the order of its singing the choir keeps round the conductor but may
> sometimes turn away, so that he is out of their sight, but when it turns
> back to him it sings beautifully and is truly with him; so we too are
> always around him – and if we were not, we should be totally dissolved
> and no longer exist – but not always turned to him; but when we do
> look to him, then we are at our goal and at rest and do not sing out of
> tune as we truly dance our god-inspired dance around him. (6.9.9)

Plotinus's writings offer another correction to theological and philosophical conversation. In his article, "On Not Knowing Too Much
about God," the late A. Hilary Armstrong criticized "Christians' extreme addiction to the imposition of precise dogmatic statements as

truth about God in which all must believe."[33] Christians, he said, "tend to oversimplify issues, sharpen contrasts, and minimize any tendencies to agnosticism, tentativeness, and serious attempts to understand opposing points of view."[34] By contrast, Armstrong claimed somewhat idealistically, philosophy is conversational, open-ended, and exploratory. Armstrong puts his argument for religious humility well:

> Words and concepts are human things, part of the everlasting discussion, and the only faith which can remain unchanged and unperturbed through the discussion is one based on a dim awareness of the unthinkable and unspeakable reality which creates, stimulates, and eludes our minds as we discuss.[35]

"Precise dogmatic statements" are perhaps not presently quite as formidable an obstacle to dialogue as they were in earlier centuries. But we can still learn a great deal of value for our own conversations on matters of philosophy and theology from Plotinus's non-dogmatic, non-ideological stance. In a time in which vitriolic polemics were routine and rival religious and theological schools accused one another of everything from thinking wrong to eating babies, Plotinus's only polemical work was against Gnostic's exclusive claim to truth and their lack of appreciation for the universe as a whole. If our conversations are to address the pressing problems of our time, they must achieve a non-ideological generosity similar to that of Plotinus.

The accusation of being "ideological" is usually used by the "mainstream" to scold the marginalized. The ideological stances of the mainstream are more difficult to identify. Surrounded by institutions created especially to support and lend legitimacy to these perspectives, mainstream ideologies appear to be simply "normal" or "natural." Yet it does not take the proverbial rocket scientist (or in this case, a sophisticated Foucauldian analysis) to see that often the decisive difference between the self-interest of the marginalized and the self-interest of the mainstream is that while one has power, the other does not. When mainstream and marginalized perspectives come into fruitful dialogue it is because both are committed to "serious attempts to understand the opposing point of view."[36]

For this to happen, unusually large amounts of generosity are needed. Marginalized people for whom institutions have not changed, or have not changed *enough*, or rapidly enough, must exercise generosity in conversation with those they experience as oppressors. For the level playing field imagined by the privileged is, at best, temporary, artificial, and isolated from daily reality. And those who are privileged by social and institutional arrangements invariably feel that they are the wrong targets for marginalized people's legitimate anger. Are they not, after all, well-intentioned and generous in entering the conversation in the first place, in short, are they not among the "converted?" From the perspective of marginalized people, however, even if those who enjoy privilege have not themselves constructed the privileging institutions, even if they profess themselves willing to help dismantle them, they still presently benefit from them.

More than a determined willingness to *sit there*, listen, and talk is needed if conversations between privileged people and marginalized people is to achieve mutual understanding and institutional change.[37] A common worldview is needed. Something like Plotinus's concept of the one swirling universe, pulsing with life, can give an enhanced and expanded perspective that supplies the generosity needed for real conversation, conversation that is conducted simultaneously on intellectual and emotional levels. Philosophical discourse conceived as rational negotiation of ideas at the expense of emotions, commitments, and passionate interests, cannot provide the framework for conversation. The mutual recognition of heated interests must also inform mutual understanding. Plotinus's rejection of "rational minds" as the medium of community, and his insistence that "life" is the basis of the tie between living beings enables the engagement of lived experience as well as negotiation of the best of our ideas.

Having described some of the benefits Plotinus brings to discussion of religion, I must now suggest that a Plotinian "religion" has several important disadvantages. It lacks the ritual practices that, over a lifetime, shape the psyche. Even more significantly, it lacks community. Lacking these two vital ingredients of a religious practice, Plotinianism operates best in relation to a chosen religious practice and community. In such a context, Plotinian thought can correct a particular religion's claims to exclusive truth by picturing a more bountiful and comprehensive universe. In fact, the *Enneads* have been useful in this capacity to Christians in different historical settings throughout the common era.

Beauty and Responsibility

Plotinus's description of the connectedness of living things in a vast, interdependent, and beautiful universe challenges the individualism

Get this
book

Classical
Mediterrean
Spirituality

1986

Neoplatonism

that has characterized much of Western culture and philosophy since the Enlightenment. As Plotinus put it, "there is no [legitimate] place to draw a limit, to say, 'this and no further is I'" (6.5.7). A person's primary identity is with the universe, a finely textured relationship of parts to whole in which none of the parts could exist without the whole.

Moreover, the activity of perceiving beauty is, for Plotinus, receptive but not passive. Valuing contemplation as Plato and Aristotle did, Plotinus gave contemplation a more inclusive definition; for him, "every action is a serious effort towards contemplation."[38] What if participation in the great beauty were to be understood, then, not solely – or perhaps not even primarily – as what we (or Plotinus, in other moods) might call "contemplation" – solitary and individual – but as reflective activity in the world of bodies and society?

We must, however, continue to ask: what is the relationship between perceiving beauty and attention to social arrangements? For absorbing visions of beauty can be, and have been, compatible with the most egregious social injustice. Indeed, "Neoplatonism" has been repeatedly accused of contributing to the high value accorded contemplation in contrast to action, and to the strain of escapist mysticism within Christianity. The point of reading Plotinus both for the beauty and profundity of his vision *and* critically is that we must not import, along with Plotinus's inclusive philosophy, its potential seductions.

Clearly, articulations of beauty must be scrutinized and the essential question of the Holy Grail legend brought to them, "Whom does it serve?" The point of developing and exercising the ability to perceive beauty is not individual gratification. To hold together beauty and moral concern, then, requires both an energizing and compelling vision of an intimately interconnected world as the identity of the "real self," and continuous investigation and revision of the ways this vision is lived in "human, all too human" societies. Reading Plotinus we must, I believe, acknowledge both the beauty of Plotinus's enspirited universe and our need to take his suggestions further than he did himself.

If the universe is irreducibly interconnected for damage, it is also interwoven through veins of energy and delight. According to Plotinus, there is enough for all if we will use responsibly and help to circulate the universe's physical and spiritual resources. To recognize this is to work toward more equitable distribution of the earth's resources. It is also to recognize that we may finally abandon our frantic efforts to extract what we need from our families, lovers, and friends. The universe contains enough, and realizing this comes as an awareness of beauty, a relaxing. When individual isolation is overcome *on the level of perception*, one can only respond with gratitude and responsibility.

This knowledge is neither esoteric nor does it require philosophical training. But it is not evident to the sluggish eye. As Plotinus put it, the great beauty does not "go out" to confront anyone. Seeing it in our surroundings is the result of a spiritual discipline, a training of the eye together with a concentration and focus of the mind. There is something abundantly and compellingly energizing in those moments when we see the interconnectedness — what Plotinus calls the "unity" — of the universe and the consanguinity of living beings.

Notes

Preface

1 Elizabeth Cox, *The Ragged Way People Fall Out of Love* (San Francisco: North Point Press, 1991), p. 46.
2 Sections of this chapter are revised from chapter 2, "Beauty is Reality: Plotinus's *Enneads*," in my book *Reading for Life* (New York: Continuum, 1997).
3 *Enneads*, trans. A.H. Armstrong (Cambridge, Massachusetts: Loeb Classical Library, Harvard University Press, 1966–88).
4 Pierre Hadot, *Philosophy as a Way of Life* (Oxford: Blackwell, 1995), p. 201.

Chapter 1 Introduction: Seeing Double

1 *Enneads*, trans. A.H. Armstrong (Cambridge, Massachusetts: Loeb Classical Library, Harvard University Press, 1966–88).
2 Ibid.,6.5.8: "In the intelligible world the colour which blooms on the surface is beauty, or rather all is colour and beauty to its innermost part: for its beauty is not something different from itself, like a surface bloom."
3 Theologian Schubert M. Ogden makes the same point: "It is quite possible . . . to distinguish things without separating them and, therefore, to avoid separating things without identifying them. I should contend that the ability to do precisely this – to distinguish things, and hence neither to identify *nor* separate them – is of the very essence of analytical thinking . . . just as, conversely, either to confuse things that are really distinct or to disjoin things that are really connected is to default as a critical thinker": *The Point of Christology* (San Francisco: Harper and Row, 1982), p. 155.
4 In Carthage and Rome, Christians spoke Latin only after the early third

century: W.H.C. Frend, *The Rise of Christianity* (Philadelphia: Fortress, 1984), p. 338.

5   He criticizes Stoic materialism as well as the pre-Socratic philosophers' effort to find a fundamental material on which the universe is based (*Ennead* 2.4.1).

6   The phrase is taken from my book, *Reading For Life, Beauty, Pluralism, and Responsibility* (New York: Continuum, 1997).

7   A.H. Armstrong, "Plotinus and India," in *Plotinian and Christian Studies* (London: Variorum, 1979), I, p. 23.

8   C. Behan McCullagh argues that it is more accurate to claim that what one offers is a "fair" interpretation of a historical author, rather than a "true" interpretation. An interpretation is fair if it is balanced, supported by evidence, is not disprovable, and does not omit major evidence: *The Truth of History* (New York: Routledge, 1998), pp. 57–61.

9   Although he was probably born in Lycopolis, Egypt, Plotinus taught in Rome from the age of 40 until his death in 270 CE. He was probably a Roman citizen since all free persons were granted citizenship in 212 CE by the *Constitutio Antoniniana*.

10   Peter Brown, *The Body and Society: Men, Women, and Sexual Renunciation in Early Christianity* (New York: Columbia University Press, 1988).

11   Michel Foucault, *The Use of Pleasure* (New York: Pantheon Books, 1985); *The Care of the Self* (New York: Pantheon Books, 1986).

12   Teresa Shaw, *The Burden of the Flesh: Fasting and Sexuality in Early Christianity* (Minneapolis: Fortress, 1998); Judith Perkins, *The Suffering Self: Pain and Narrative Representation in the Early Christian Era* (New York: Routledge, 1995).

13   Peter Brown, *The Making of Late Antiquity* (Cambridge, Massachusetts: Harvard University Press, 1978), p. 34.

14   Keith Hopkins, "Murderous Games," in *Death and Renewal: Sociological Studies in Roman History* (Cambridge: Cambridge University Press, 1983).

15   Eusebius, *Ecclesiastical History* 6.43.11; *The Ante-Nicene Fathers*, Second Series, I (Buffalo: The Christian Literature Company, 1890), p. 288.

16   Brown, *Body*, p. 192.

17   Frend, *Rise*, p. 405.

18   Frend, *Rise*, p. 339.

19   Brown, *Body*, p. 191.

20   Frend, *Rise*, p. 413.

21   Robin Lane Fox, *Pagans and Christians* (New York: Knopf, 1987), p. 592.

22   Brown, *Body*, p. 192.

23   Frend, *Rise*, p. 346.

24   Ibid., p. 420.

25   Ibid., p. 320.

26 Ibid., p. 328.
27 Fox, *Pagans*, p. 30.
28 Ibid., p. 31.
29 Ibid., p. 30.
30 Ibid., p. 31.
31 Ibid., p. 30.
32 Martha Nussbaum, *The Therapy of Desire* (Princeton: Princeton University Press, 1994) distinguishes philosophical from religious interests, defining philosophy as "a reasoned procedure," and religion as "prayer and wishing." But this is a distinction without a difference, an artificial separation that is falsified by her own argument that philosophy is essentially about self-help, a category that encompasses both religion and philosophy. Curiously, she avoids comparing Stoic, Epicurean, and Skeptic philosophers with Christian or Jewish philosophers of similar education and skill. When she writes about the Christian teacher Clement of Alexandria, for example, she amalgamates his thought to Stoic philosophy without indicating that his interests were explicitly Christian. In short, Nussbaum does not allow the possibility of reasoned religious views: pp. 150, 426.
33 Ibid., pp. 3–4.
34 Ibid., p. 15.
35 Pierre Hadot, *Philosophy as a Way of Life* (London: Blackwell, 1995), pp. 64 and *passim*.
36 Ibid., p. 50.
37 Perkins, *Suffering Self*; Plotinus also considered physical health a balance of "too much" and "too little," but he did not advocate this as a model for spiritual healing (as, for example, Aristotle did in his concept of the golden mean in the *Nichomachean Ethics*).
38 Porphyry described Plotinus's polemical concerns as directed against "Christians and others" who alleged "that Plato had not penetrated to the depths of intelligible reality." Porphyry says that it was against these that Plotinus wrote the four-part treatise, "Against the Gnostics": *Life* 16.
39 Tertullian, *De resurrectione carnis* 8; *The Ante-Nicene Fathers* III (Buffalo: The Christian Literature Publishing Company, 1885), p. 551.
40 Foucault, *Use of Pleasure*, p. 27.
41 See also Pierre Hadot's criticism of Foucault's description of philosophical practice as a "relation to one's self, a culture of the self, or a pleasure taken in oneself." Hadot believes that emphasis on the self is misplaced. Rather, "the feeling of belonging to a whole, . . . both to the whole constituted by the human community and to that constituted by the cosmic whole . . . is an essential element." "Reflections on the Idea of the Cultivation of the Self," *Philosophy*, p. 208.
42 Ibid., p. 66.
43 Geoffrey Galt Harpham, *The Ascetic Imperative in Culture and Criti-*

cism (Chicago: University of Chicago, 1987).

44   Foucault, *Use of Pleasure*, p. 66.

45   A popular ancient and modern caricature of Epicurean identification of pleasure as the goal of life.

46   Margaret R. Miles, *Fullness of Life: Historical Foundations for a New Asceticism* (Philadelphia: Westminster, 1979).

47   Tertullian, *Apologia* 50; quoted by Perkins, *Suffering Self*, p. 35.

48   Gregory of Nazianzus, *De oratione* 6, cited by Herbert Musurillo, SJ, "The Problem of Ascetical Fasting in the Greek Patristic Writers," *Traditio* 12 (1956), p. 6.

49   However, the accuracy of labeling contemporary American society as "hedonistic" could certainly be questioned. Some of the practices that reach popularity among large groups within our society are harsher than any asceticisms practiced in late antiquity (for example, body piercing); other common social practices can become addictions that damage bodies far more than did ancient asceticisms (for example, smoking and excessive alcohol consumption).

50   Perkins, *Suffering Self*, p. 3.

51   A.H. Armstrong, "The Self-Definition of Christianity in Relation to Later Platonism," *Hellenic and Christian Studies* (London: Variorum, 1990), VIII, p. 75.

52   Brad Shore, quoting Donald Donham, in *Culture and Mind* (New York: Oxford University Press, 1996), p. 51.

53   Gnostic hymns are collected by C.R.C. Allberry, *Manichaean Psalmbook* (Stuttgart: Kohlhammer, 1938).

54   Walker Percy's phrase, *The Second Coming* (New York: Farrar, Straus, Giroux, 1980), p. 126.

55   A.H. Armstrong, "Platonic Mirrors," in *Hellenic and Christian Studies*, VI, p. 177.

56   Hopkins, "Murderous Games," p. 2.

57   Pliny, *Panegyric* 33; quoted by Hopkins, ibid., p. 2.

58   Ibid., p. 2.

59   Seneca, *Letters* 7.2ff; quoted by Hopkins, ibid., p. 3.

60   Augustine, *Confessions* 6.8; trans. Rex Warner (New York: Mentor–Omega, 1963), pp. 123–4.

61   Tacitus, *Dialogue on Oratory* 29; quoted by Hopkins, "Murderous Games," p. 2.

62   Hopkins writes, "In ancient times, amphitheaters must have towered over cities, much as cathedrals towered over mediaeval towns": "Murderous Games," p. 2.

63   Dio 68.15; quoted by Hopkins, "Murderous Games," p. 9.

64   Dio 59.10; quoted by Hopkins, "Murderous Games," p. 10. In targeting Christians for public execution in the amphitheaters of the empire, Nero may have been as concerned about acquiring human bodies for public torture and execution as he was about the potential harm to society of

Christian teaching.
65 Tacitus, *Annales* 1.76.
66 Christian affirmation of body is articulated specifically in beliefs in creation as "very good," in the Incarnation of God, and in the ultimate resurrection of body.
67 By Plotinus's time, the elite male project of self-construction based on physical practices was democratized. The Christian construction and "care of the self" overcame class affiliation but gendered assumptions were retained. They were both revealed and partially overcome within Christianity by the common understanding, often explicit in Christian literature, that the woman who sought self-definition on the basis of her religious choices had elected to "become male": see my *Carnal Knowing: The Female Body in Western Christianity*, chapter 3 (Boston: Beacon Press, 1988).
68 Perkins, *Suffering Self*, p. 3.
69 Origen, *Comm. in Ioannem* 1.37, quoted by Henry Bettenson, *The Early Christian Fathers* (Oxford: Oxford University Press, 1956), p. 210.
70 Porphyry, *Life* 11.
71 Plato, *Phaedrus* 275d–e.
72 One of Plotinus's most powerful metaphors – "emanation" – is central to his description of the informing activity of the One. See A.H. Armstrong, "'Emanation' in Plotinus," in *Plotinian and Christian Studies*, pp. 61–6.
73 At this point, the marked difference between Plotinus's "perennial philosophy" and that of Buddhist philosophy is apparent. For Plotinus it is the quality of sensible beauty that reveals the existence of a sustaining beauty; for Buddhism, the accurate view of the sensible world sees the inherent and ultimate corruption that testifies to the nothingness at the heart of all existing things.
74 S. MacKenna, *Plotinus: The Enneads*, third edition (London: Faber and Faber 1956).
75 Porphyry, *Life* 20.
76 *Life* 2; Armstrong suggests that Plotinus's final illness was a form of leprosy: *Enneads*, Vol. I, p. 5. See also M. Grmek in L. Brisson et al., eds, *La Vie de Plotin* II (Paris: J. Vrin, 1992), who says that Plotinus's final illness was diphtheria.

Chapter 2 Beauty: the Stepping Stone

1 William Carlos Williams, *Patterson* (New York: New Direction, 1963).
2 Peter Brown, *The Making of Late Antiquity* (Cambridge, Massachusetts: Harvard University Press, 1978), p. 28.
3 Ibid., p. 31.
4 Weinstock, *Journal of Roman Studies* (1961), pp. 209–10.

5 Peter Brown, *The World of Late Antiquity* (London: Thames and Hudson, 1971), p. 12.

6 Robin Lane Fox, *Pagans and Christians* (New York: Knopf, 1987), p. 573.

7 Peter Brown, *The World of Late Antiquity* (London: Thames and Hudson, 1971), p. 22.

8 Ibid.

9 Plotinus innovates by saying that the forms of individuals exist in intellect. Second-century Platonists had denied this.

10 See also 1.9.1. Plotinus believed in reincarnation, i.e. that the "manifold life that exists in the All circulates through the forms given it in Intellect." He speaks of death, then, as a "changing of body, like changing of clothes on a stage . . . [or as] a putting off of body, like in the theatre the final exit [of an actor]": 3.2.15.

11 A.H. Armstrong, "Gnosis and Greek Philosophy," in *Plotinian and Christian Studies* (London: Variorum, 1979), XXI, p. 115.

12 See also 4.4.27, where Plotinus says that stones "grow as long as they are attached to the earth but remain the size they were cut when they are taken away from it." For Plotinus, the capacity for growth is proof of life.

13 Plato, *Symposium* 210–12.

14 "Starting from individual beauties, the quest for the universal beauty must find him ever mounting the heavenly ladder, stepping from rung to rung – that is, from one to two, and from two to every lovely body, from bodily beauty to the beauty of institutions, from institutions to learning, and from learning in general to the special lore that pertains to nothing but the beautiful itself – until at last he comes to know what beauty is": *Symposium* 211c.

15 Armstrong wisely translates *epibathra* (literally "ladder") "stepping stone" in order to avoid the modern reader's insistence on noticing the rungs as a hierarchy of value rather than the uprights or sides of the ladder as holding together all entities in the All.

16 Wallace Stevens, "Sunday Morning," *The Collected Poems of Wallace Stevens* (New York: Alfred A. Knopf, 1978), p. 66.

17 According to Plotinus, authentic reality occurs when "substance and essence and the cause of existence are one": *Enneads* 6.7.22.

18 Armstrong's translation, "despising" for *huperophia*, literally "seeing over," overstates the dualistic tendency of this passage.

19 A.H. Armstrong explains that the term "emanation" refers to a doctrine, not to a specific word in the *Enneads*; he suggests that "procession" might serve as well or better; "'Emanation' in Plotinus," in *Plotinian and Christian Studies*, II, pp. 61–6.

20 Pierre Hadot, *Philosophy as a Way of Life*, trans. Michael Chase (Oxford: Blackwell, 1995); *Plotinus or the Simplicity of Vision*, trans. Michael Chase (Chicago: University of Chicago Press, 1993).

21 Ibid., p. 191.
22 Ibid., p. 192.
23 Ibid., p. 193, emphases in original.
24 Ibid, p. 64.
25 Iris Murdoch, *The Sovereignty of Good* (London: Routledge and Kegan Paul, 1970), p. 64.
26 On "birth pangs": *Enneads* 5.3.17; on "waiting patiently": 5.5.8; "One must not chase after [the vision], but wait quietly till it appears, preparing oneself to contemplate it, as the eye awaits the rising of the sun; and the sun rising over the horizon gives itself to the eyes to see."
27 Ibid., 1.6.5; The most humorous footnote I have ever seen in scholarly literature follows this sentence. Readers should know, A.H. Armstrong writes, that, although an earlier translator attributes this analogy to "a remark Heraclitus appears to have made," he thinks it is "at least possible that Plotinus might have thought of pigs at this point for himself, without any assistance from earlier philosophy." See also 3.5.1.
28 André Grabar, "Plotin et les origines de l'esthétique médiévale," *Cahiers archéologiques*, I: *Fin de l'Antiquité et Moyen Âge* (Paris: Van Oest, 1945).
29 Eric Alliez and Michel Feher, "Reflections of a Soul," *Fragments for a History of the Body* (New York: Zone, 1989), p. 66; compare *Ennead* 2.4.5.
30 Ibid.
31 Ibid., p. 67.
32 The ambiance of the figure makes it difficult to decide finally whether it is Jewish, Christian, or secular. Stevenson says that its community of origin was Gnostic, but does not explain why he thinks so; J. Stevenson, *The Catacombs* (London: Thames and Hudson, 1978), pp. 111–17. Frend also mentions the figures of the Tomb of the Aurelii as Gnostic, saying that they reveal "syncretism of Christian and Pythagorean themes, the pagan elements being absorbed into Gnostic Christianity and furnished with a new Gnostic significance." Neither author indicates how the art itself inspires these speculations; W.H.C. Frend, *The Rise of Christianity* (Philadelphia: Fortress, 1984), p. 280. Cf. Paul Corby Finney, "Did Gnostics Make Pictures?" *The Rediscovery of Gnosticism*, Vol. I, ed. B. Layton (Leiden: *Numen* Suppl. 41.1), pp. 434–54.
33 A.H. Armstrong, "Gnosis and Greek Philosophy," *Plotinian and Christian Studies*, XXI, pp. 113–14.
34 Martha Nussbaum, *Love's Knowledge, Essays on Philosophy and Literature* (New York: Oxford University Press, 1990), p. 37.
35 Seeing beauty translates instantly into energy. Augustine, a good Plotinian, wrote, "We are enflamed and we go!" ("Inardescimus et imus"): *Confessions* XIII.9, trans. Rex Warner (New York: Mentor-Omega, 1963), 322.
36 *Greater Hippias* 304e: trans. Thomas L. Pangle, *The Roots of Political Philosophy: Ten Forgotten Socratic Dialogues* (Ithaca, New York: Cornell

University Press, 1987), p. 339. See also: *Republic* 435c; 497d; *Cratylus* 348a–b; *Protagoras* 339ff.

37 Ian Hunter, "Aesthetics and Cultural Studies," in *Cultural Studies*, ed. Lawrence Grossberg, Cary Nelson, and Paula Treichler (New York: Routledge, 1992), pp. 348–64.

38 For a description of the villainizing of vision in the twentieth century, see Martin Jay, *Downcast Eyes: The Denigration of Vision in Twentieth-century French Thought* (Berkeley: University of California, 1994).

39 I have shown elsewhere that Augustine's description of the vision of God relies on this theory: Margaret R. Miles, "Vision: The Eye of the Body and the Eye of the Mind in St. Augustine's *De Trinitate* and the *Confessions*," *Journal of Religion* (April 1983). Ancient and medieval folk beliefs about the evil eye, in which a malign look can cause physical and/or spiritual damage, also rely on this model of vision.

Chapter 3 "Choice and Chance": Soul as Pivot of the Universe

1 Aristotle was the first philosopher to raise the question of how two distinct entities like body and soul could form a unity. Plato had assumed the connection, but in response to Aristotle's query, Plotinus addresses it explicitly. Stephen R.L. Clark usefully reminds readers of Plotinus that Plotinus could, and did, argue strenuously for his conclusions concerning body and soul; "Plotinus: Body and Soul," in *The Cambridge Companion to Plotinus*, Lloyd P. Gerson, ed. (Cambridge: Cambridge University Press, 1996), p. 277.

2 *Republic* 6, 509d.

3 Body is to be thought of more as an instrument – a lute – than a power tool. "He will care for and bear with [body] as long as he can, like a musician with his lyre, as long as he can use it; *Ennead* 1.4.16, trans. A.H. Armstrong (Cambridge, Massachusetts: Loeb Classical Library, Harvard University Press, 1966–88).

4 Plotinus accepted his society's view of reproduction, namely that the father supplies the essential part of the child. Compare, however, his insistence that both mothers and fathers provide the essential "soul" of the child (5.7.2).

5 Compare *Ennead* 6.9.5; 3.2.9.

6 Rainer Maria Rilke, *Duino Elegies* 4, trans. J.B. Leishman and Stephen Spender (New York: W.W. Norton, 1939), p. 33.

7 Here Plotinus is diametrically opposed to a Buddhist view of the beauty of the sensible world as *maya*, an illusory and deceptive screen that masks the reality of emptiness.

8 Augustine will make a similar claim about love in *De trinitate* and his homilies on the First Epistle of St. John: love, he says, is the particular and unique substance of God; humans, having no love of our own, par-

ticipate directly in God's substance when we love; Margaret R. Miles, "Vision: The Eye of the Body and the Eye of the Mind in Augustine's *De trinitate* and the *Confessions*," *The Journal of Religion* (April 1983).

9   What did Plotinus have in mind here? How could "a word spoken quietly act on something far off" in the third century? An emperor's decision affecting a distant army's maneuvers, perhaps? The spreading of a rumor? Religious ideas (like Christianity?) permeating societies across the known world? Ironically, twenty-first-century communications technology makes his point more accessible than it could have been in his own time.

10 Plotinus next turns to his great treatise "On the Good, or the One," *Ennead* 6.9. Although this topic follows from his insistence on a spiritual universe, I discuss it in chapter 6.

11 The phrase is Sarah Rappe's: "Self-knowledge and Subjectivity in the *Enneads*," in *The Cambridge Companion*, pp. 250–74.

12 Compare *Ennead* 4.3.11.

13 See *Lexicon Plotinianum*, col. 727 for a partial listing of Plotinus's uses of *oion* ("so to speak"), an all-purpose expression that he says should be taken with great seriousness (*Ennead* 3.9.6; 6.8.13); J.H. Sleeman and Gilbert Pollet, *Lexicon Plotinianum* (Leiden: E.J. Brill, 1980).

14 *Ennead* 4.3.8; S. MacKenna translates this passage: "We are what we look upon and what we desire;" *Plotinus. The Enneads*, third edition, revised by B.S. Page. (London: Faber and Faber, 1962).

15 Foucault's term, in *The Care of the Self* (New York: Pantheon, 1986), passim.

Chapter 4 Body in Third-century Rome

1   Keith Hopkins, "Murderous Games," in *Death and Renewal* (Cambridge: Cambridge University Press, 1983), 17; Thomas Wiedemann, *Emperors and Gladiators* (New York: Routledge, 1991), p. 131.

2   J.P. Toner, *Leisure and Ancient Rome* (Cambridge: Polity Press, 1995), p. 76.

3   Wiedemann, *Emperors*, pp. 1, 12.

4   Toner, *Leisure*, p. 38.

5   Wiedemann, *Emperors*, 88. The legal monopoly of the state in capital punishment had been established only in the second century; Hopkins, "Murderous Games," p. 28.

6   Shelby Brown, "Death as Decoration: Scenes from the Arena on Roman Domestic Mosaics," in *Pornography and Representation in Ancient Rome*, Amy Richlin, ed. (Madison: University of Wisconsin, 1995), pp. 180ff.

7   Hopkins, "Murderous Games," p. 26.

8   Paul Plass points out that *ordo* means both row of seats and social order. Strict seating arrangements in the colosseum replicated and reinforced

social order; *The Game of Death in Ancient Rome: Arena Sport and Political Suicide* (Madison: University of Wisconsin, 1995), p. 43.

9   Ibid., p. 23.

10 Wiedemann, *Emperors*, p. 1.

11 Toner makes the very important point that in studying history, "There is no state of 'understanding,' only constant effort against 'incomprehension:'" *Leisure*, p. 133.

12 For screen violence in relation to American society, see my *Seeing and Believing: Religion and Values in the Movies* (Boston: Beacon Press, 1996), chapter 9.

13 Similarly, Walt Disney, who has been called "the most influential American of the twentieth century," said that entertainment is "a vital public necessity – as important as food, shelter, and a job:" Steven Watts, *The Magical Kingdom: Walt Disney and the American Way of Life* (New York: Houghton Mifflin, 1997), pp. xv, 363.

14 These are Hopkins's suggestions about rationalizations of colosseum violence. He cites Tacitus (*Annals* I.76) for the view that colosseum performers are "worthless": "Murderous Games," p. 27.

15 K.M. Coleman, "Fatal Charade: Roman Executions Staged as Mythical Enactments," *Journal of Roman Studies* 80 (1990), p. 55.

16 Ibid., p. 45.

17 Ibid., p. 58.

18 Toner, *Leisure*, p. 39.

19 Ibid., p. 39.

20 Ibid., p. 42.

21 Ibid., p. 60.

22 Ibid., pp. 46, 44.

23 Pliny, *Nat.* 35.32; quoted in Toner, *Leisure*, p. 45.

24 Wiedemann, *Emperors*, p. 120.

25 David Potter, review of Thomas Wiedemann, *Emperors and Gladiators*, *Journal of Roman Studies* 84 (1994), p. 231.

26 Wiedemann cites R. Duncan-Jones, *Structure and Scale in the Roman Economy* (Cambridge: Cambridge University Press, 1990), chapter 6.

27 Wiedemann, *Emperors*, p. 142.

28 Seneca, *Letters* 7.3.

29 Toner, *Leisure*, p. 83.

30 Ibid., p. 35.

31 Plass, *Game of Death*, p. 43.

32 Toner, *Leisure*, p. 38.

33 Ibid., p. 59.

34 Augustine, *Confessions* II.6; trans. Rex Warner (New York: Mentor-Omega, 1963).

35 Toner, *Leisure*, p. 60.

36 Augustine, *Confessions* IX.12.

37 A.H. Armstrong writes, "Porphyry was . . . more inclined than his mas-

ter to follow Numenius in regarding this world as a place to escape from: "Dualism Platonic, Gnostic, and Christian," in *Plotinus Amid Gnostics and Christians* (Amsterdam: Free University Press, 1984), p. 48. Porphyry himself wrote refutations of Gnostic and orthodox Christian doctrine. Augustine undertook to answer several of Porphyry's teachings in *City of God* X.20ff; P. Hadot, "La Métaphysique de Porphyre en Porphyre," *Entretiens sur l'antiquité classique* T. 12 (Vandoeuvres-Geneve, 1966).

38 Brent D. Shaw suggests that a usual nursing period in late antiquity was about three years: "The Family in Late Antiquity: The Experience of Augustine," *Past and Present* 115 (November 1987), p. 42.

39 Porphyry and Plotinus use the same word (*aischunesthai*) *Life* 1.1: Ennead 3.2.3., trans. A.H. Armstrong (Cambridge, Massachusetts: Loeb Classical Library, Harvard University Press, 1966–88); J.H. Sleeman and Gilbert Pollet, *Lexicon Plotinianum*, col. 42 (Leiden: E.J. Brill, 1980).

40 A century later, Augustine criticized the aphorism attributed to Porphyry, "*omni corpus est fugiendum*" (*Retractationes* 1.4.3). John Rist calls Porphyry's representation of body "a partial reversion to a cruder dualism than the *Enneads* themselves are prepared to tolerate": "Plotinus and Christian Philosophy," in *The Cambridge Companion to Plotinus* (Cambridge: Cambridge University, 1996), p. 392.

41 Although Porphyry's statement has seemed to many twentieth-century authors a decisive condemnation of Plotinus, it is important to notice that Porphyry's intention was high praise for Plotinus.

42 This statement was discussed in chapter 2.

43 The *San Francisco Chronicle* (June 19, 1998; A2) gives an illustration: it was discovered that the popular author Carlos Castenada died secretly a month or so previously. His friends did not alert the media. Asked why, one of them said, "He didn't like attention. He always made sure people did not take his picture or record his voice. He didn't like the spotlight. Knowing that, I didn't take it upon myself to issue a press release."

44 A.H. Armstrong writes, "We have been, perhaps, inclined to pay rather too much attention to the first chapter of Porphyry's *Life* . . . and the many perfectly sincerely expressed, Phaedo-style Platonic commonplaces in the *Enneads* which seem to confirm that his attitude was that described by Porphyry, and to neglect somewhat a good deal in the *Enneads* which suggests a calmer, more benign, more tolerant attitude to his own body and to embodiment in general": "Gnosis and Greek Philosophy," in *Plotinian and Christian Studies* (London: Variorum, 1979), XXI, pp. 114–15.

45 Porphyry, *Life* 2.

46 In other contexts, Plotinus expressed a higher esteem of art. He recognized its potential for exhibiting the stronger realities informing the things depicted; see chapter 2.

47 Armstrong writes that, after studying Plotinus for forty years, he finds

Plotinus's concept of matter "the least coherent and satisfying part of his system:" "Plotinus's Doctrine of the Infinite," in *Plotinian and Christian Studies* (London: Variorum, 1979), V, p. 49.

48 *The Nag Hammadi Library*, James M. Robinson, ed. and introduction (San Francisco: Harper and Row, 1977), p. 3.

49 Ibid., p. 8.

50 Porphyry, *Life* 16.

51 R.T. Wallis, *Neoplatonism* (New York: Scribners, 1972), p. 39.

52 "Three Steles of Seth," trans. James M. Robinson and Frederik Wisse, *The Nag Hammadi Library*, p. 363.

53 Teresa M. Shaw, *The Burden of the Flesh: Fasting and Sexuality in Early Christianity* (Minneapolis: Fortress Press, 1998), pp. 237ff.

54 Charles Elsas has discussed Plotinus's "gnostic coloring," especially in Plotinus's first (chronological) treatise, 1.6. Elsas argues that Plotinus did not receive "the theory of a journey inward, and of meditation as a means of reaching our own personality" from Plato. The four great treatises of his middle period, culminating in 2.9, "Against the Gnostics," may represent Plotinus's working out of his own position against the Gnostic influences of his earlier period; T.D. Sinnige argues that Plotinus's attempt to provide a complete religious/philosophical system is itself influenced by Gnosticism; "Gnostic Influences in the Early Works of Plotinus and Augustine," *Plotinus Among Gnostics and Christians*, David T. Runia, ed. (Amsterdam: Free University Press, 1984), pp. 77ff.

55 John M. Dillon, in "An Ethic for the Late Antique Sage," distinguishes between an ethical stance and a philosophical ethics: *Cambridge Companion to Plotinus*, Lloyd P. Gerson, ed. (Cambridge: Cambridge University, 1996), pp. 315–35.

56 Plotinus's idea of providence is discussed in chapter 5.

57 A common caricature in late antiquity of Epicurus's teaching. Epicureans were the most misunderstood and misrepresented philosophers of the time, the scapegoats of other philosophers and religious teachers. In fact Epicurus taught that the greatest pleasure is absence of pain, a caution against the more flamboyant pleasures of sex and other appetites that, when overindulged, inevitably cause pain.

58 See Alain de Botton's description of Marcel Proust's indefatigable attention to detail: *How Proust Can Change Your Life* (New York: Pantheon, 1997).

59 For citation see chapter 7, note 1.

60 For example, Calvin makes God majestic and all-powerful by emphasizing the worthlessness of human beings.

61 Compare Herman Hesse's description of an experience of diversity in unity: "Siddhartha listened. He was now listening intently, completely absorbed, quite empty, taking in everything. He felt that he had now completely learned the art of listening. He had heard all this before, all these numerous voices in the river, but today they sounded different. He

could no longer distinguish the different voices – the merry voice from the weeping voice, the childish voice from the manly voice. They all belonged to each other: the lament of those who yearn, the laughter of the wise, the cry of indignation and the groan of the dying. They were all interwoven and interlocked, entwined in a thousand ways. And all the voices, all the goals, all the yearnings, all the sorrows, all the pleasures, all the good and evil, all of them together was the world. All of them together was the stream of events, the music of life. When Siddhartha listened attentively to this river, to this song of a thousand voices; when he did not listen to the sorrow or laughter, when he did not bind his soul to any one particular voice and absorb it in his Self, but heard them all, the whole, the unity; then the great song of a thousand voices consisted of one word: Om – perfection." *Siddhartha*, Herman Hesse (New York: New Directions, 1951), pp. 110–11.

Chapter 5 Providence: Does the One Care for Us?

1 On the safety of the universe, see also *Ennead* 6.4.5; 4.4.37; 4.5.7.
2 Two features of early Christians' experience prompted them to think of life as a quality distinguishable from body: persecution and Gnosticism; see my *Fullness of Life: Historical Foundations for a New Asceticism* (Philadelphia: Westminster, 1979).
3 Hans Zinsser, *Rats, Lice, and History* (New York: Bantam, 1935), p. 101.
4 Arthur E. R. Boak, *Manpower Shortage and the Fall of the Roman Empire in the West* (Ann Arbor: University of Michigan Press, 1955), p. 137.
5 Porphyry, *Life* 2.
6 Zinsser, *Rats*, pp. 101–2.
7 Cyprian, *De mortalitate* 14; Vegetius's *De re militari* (dedicated to Valentinian, ca. 257 CE) describes a plague in the army caused by corrupt drinking water. "When once the disease attacked a man, it spread rapidly over all his frame. A burning fever and thirst drove men to the springs and wells; but water was of no avail when once the disease had attacked a person. The disease was very fatal. More died than survived, and not sufficient people were left to bury the dead." Quoted by Zinsser, who comments: "Throughout the early Christian period, every great calamity – famine, earthquake, and plague – led to mass conversions . . . Christianity owes a formidable debt to bubonic plague and to smallpox": *Rats*, p. 103.
8 Zinsser, *Rats* (quoting Haeser), p. 104.
9 Robin Lane Fox, *Pagans and Christians* (New York: Alfred A. Knopf, 1987), p. 505.
10 W.H.C. Frend, *The Rise of Christianity* (Philadelphia: Fortress Press, 1984), p. 404.

11 Fox, *Pagans*, p. 502.
12 Porphyry, *Life* 9.
13 Fox, *Pagans*, p. 499.
14 Porphyry, *Life* 2: A.H. Armstrong, *Plotinus* (Cambridge, Massachusetts: Loeb Classical Library, Harvard University Press, 1967), Vol. III, note 31, p. 5.
15 Ibid., "Introductory Note," p. 38.
16 Compare *Ennead* 6.8.17, where Plotinus discusses how providence creates: "We affirm that each and every thing in the All, and this All here itself, is as it would have been if the free choice of its maker had willed it and its state is as if this maker proceeding regularly in his calculations with foresight had made it according to his providence ... So that if someone calls this disposition of things providence, he must understand it in this way, that Intellect is there standing still before this All, and this All here is from and according to Intellect."
17 Rilke, *Duino Elegies*, 2nd elegy, trans. J.B. Leishman and Stephen Spender (New York: W. W. Norton, 1939), p. 33.
18 Michael F. Wagner, "Plotinus on the Nature of Physical Reality," *The Cambridge Companion to Plotinus*, Lloyd P. Gerson, ed. (Cambridge: Cambridge University Press, 1996), p. 158.
19 Plotinus uses apparently interchangeably locutions of space and time: entities may be "higher" and "lower," or "beginning" and "end," "before" and "after."
20 Similarly, the seventeenth-century author, Thomas Traherne, wrote: "One wry principle in the mind is of infinite consequence": *Centuries* (New York: Harper, 1960).
21 In a similar insight, Ludwig Wittgenstein wrote, "it is what one might call the experience of feeling absolutely safe. I mean the state in which one is inclined to say, 'I am safe, nothing can injure me whatever happens'": "Lectures on Ethics," *Philosophical Review* (January 1965), pp. 3–26.
22 Albert Camus's protagonist in *L'étranger* recognizes the world's benign indifference just before his execution: "Je m'ouvre pour la première fois à la tendre indifférence du monde" (Paris: Gallimard, 1942).
23 I note that I have slipped from impersonal language – "one" and "human beings" – to speaking personally – "I" – as Plotinus and Greek philosophy itself frequently did: A.H. Armstrong, "Plotinus's Doctrine of the Infinite and Its Significance for Christian Thought," in *Plotinian and Christian Studies* (London: Variorum, 1979), V, p. 57.
24 Augustine, *In Ps.* V. 10.
25 See also *Ennead* 4.4.39; 45.
26 Plotinus's treatise "On Virtue" supports Porphyry's report of Plotinus's sexual asceticism. The soul, Plotinus says "collects itself in a sort of place of its own away from the body." As much as possible it gets rid of both pleasures and pains, and "gets rid of passion (*thumos*) as completely as

possible . . . What about desire? . . . It will not itself have the desire of food and drink for the relief of the body and certainly not of sexual pleasures either;" *Ennead* 1.2.5. See also 6.7.30, where Plotinus says that it is "clear to everyone that no one would think that bodily pleasure could possibly be mixed with intellect."

27 John M. Dillon characterizes Plotinus's ethical system as "uncompromisingly self-centered and other-worldly": "An Ethic for the Late Antique Sage," in *The Cambridge Companion to Plotinus* (Cambridge: Cambridge University, 1996), p. 331.

28 J.P. Toner, *Leisure and Ancient Rome* (Cambridge: Polity Press, 1995), p. 48.

29 Ibid., p. 52.

30 Porphyry, *Life* 2.

31 This, however, is picture-language and not an accurate representation of the case. In *Ennead* 6.5.8–9 Plotinus pointedly contradicts the picture he presents here: "For, I think, it is probable, and indeed necessary, that the ideas are not placed separately on one side and matter a long way off on the other and then illumination comes to matter from somewhere up there: I am afraid this would be empty words . . . But we must . . . not assume that the form is spatially separate and that the Idea is reflected in matter, from every side grasping (and again not grasping) the idea, receives from the form, over the whole of itself, by its drawing near to it all that it can receive, with nothing between . . . One and the same life holds the sphere."

32 A.H. Armstrong, *Plotinus*, "Introductory Note," Vol. I, p. 267.

33 Although Plotinus refers to "soulless things," he immediately undermines this misleading locution by stating that in fact "soulless things" do not lack soul inasmuch as "each particular thing is one somehow and is existent somehow": 1.7.2.

Chapter 6 "Go On Up": the One and Contemplation

1 *Ennead* 4.9.4: trans. A.H. Armstrong (Cambridge, Massachusetts: Loeb Classical Library, Harvard University Press, 1966–88).

2 Martha C. Nussbaum, *The Therapy of Desire* (Princeton: Princeton University Press, 1994), p. 347.

3 Walker Percy's phrase, *The Second Coming* (New York: Farrar, Straus, Giroux, 1980), p. 126.

4 John Rist, "Plotinus and Christian Philosophy," in *The Cambridge Companion to Plotinus*, ed. Lloyd P. Gerson (Cambridge: Cambridge University, 1996), pp. 386ff.

5 John Kenney comments, "If we realize that monotheism as a core religious intuition can admit of a range of possible interpretations other than the one we naturally assume, then we will be free from a habit of mind that can blinker our assessment of classical religious thought and,

indeed, that of other non-Western traditions"; "Monotheistic and Poly-theistic Elements in Classical Mediterranean Spirituality," in *Classical Mediterranean Spirituality*, ed. A.H. Armstrong (Vol. 15 of *World Spirituality*: New York: Crossroads, 1986), p. 270.

6   Armstrong notes the possible exception of *Ennead* 6.8 in which Plotinus speaks of the One as something like a "personal God": "Two Views of Freedom," *Studia Patristica* XVIII (Oxford: Pergamon Press, 1982), pp. 397–406. Rist also remarks that *Ennead* 6.8 may refer to "what can crudely be called the mainline Christianity of his day": "Plotinus and Christian Philosophy," p. 394.

7   The *Enneads* were probably first published in 301 CE during the persecution of Christians under the emperors Maximian and Diocletian.

8   W.H.C. Frend, *The Rise of Christianity* (Philadelphia: Fortress, 1984), p. 320.

9   Tertullian, *De carne Christi* X, *The Ante-Nicene Fathers*, III (Buffalo: The Christian Literature Publishing Company, 1885), p. 530.

10   Tertullian, *De resurrectione carnis* VIII, Ibid., p. 551.

11   Irenaeus, *Adversus haereses* IV. xviii.5, *The Ante-Nicene Fathers*, I, p. 486.

12   Origen, *De principiis* III.vi.5, trans. G.W. Butterworth (Gloucester, Massachusetts, 1973), p. 251.

13   Origen, "Dialogue with Heraclides," in *Alexandrian Christianity* (Philadelphia: Westminster Press, 1954), p. 454.

14   For discussion of early Christians' views on body and interest in life, see Margaret R. Miles, *Fullness of Life* (Philadelphia: Westminster Press, 1981).

15   Irenaeus, *Ad. haer.* IV.20.6, *Ante-Nicene Fathers* I, p. 489.

16   Origen, *Comm. in Matt.* xvi.8, in Henry Bettenson, *The Early Christian Fathers* (New York: Oxford, 1969), p. 224.

17   Pierre Hadot has questioned Foucault's emphasis on the individualism of philosophical exercises that established a relation of "oneself to oneself." He agrees that ancient philosophers were interested in practical exercises to shape and define the self, that is, in spiritual disciplines. But "the feeling of belonging to a whole is an essential element: belonging, that is, both to the whole constituted by the human community, and to that constituted by the cosmic whole." He quotes Seneca as advocating "plunging oneself into the totality of the world": *Philosophy as a Way of Life* (Oxford: Blackwell, 1995), p. 208.

18   Michel Foucault, *The Use of Pleasure* (New York: Pantheon, 1985), p. 10.

19   Michel Foucault, *The Care of the Self* (New York: Pantheon, 1986), p. 43.

20   Ibid., p. 56.

21   Ibid., p. 63.

22   Foucault, *Use of Pleasure*, p. 244.

23 Diogenes Laertius, *Lives of the Eminent Philosophers* VI.2.70; Foucault, *Use of Pleasure*, p. 72.

24 Evagrius Ponticus, *The Praktikos*, trans. John E. Bamberger (Kalamazoo, Michigan: Cistercian Publications, 1970), p. 61.

25 Palladius, *Lausaic History* VI, ed. J. Armitage Robinson (London: Chatto and Windus, 1907), p. 87.

26 Evagrius Ponticus, *Praktikos*, 11.

27 Origen, *Comm. in Ioannem* i.37, in Bettenson, *Early Christian Fathers*, p. 210.

28 Irenaeus, *Adv. haer.* V.xii.6, *Ante-Nicene Fathers* I, p. 539.

29 Augustine, *De gen. ad litt.* XII.35.68, *Patrologia Latinae*, p. 483.

30 Plato: "I strain after images": *Republic* VI, 488a.

31 Discussed in chapter 2.

32 See also *Enneads* 4.8.1.

33 Cf. *Ennead* 6.8.21: "When you speak or think of him, put away all the other things."

34 "Outside" and "inside" are puzzling concepts in Plotinus's usage. "Inside" refers to whatever is simple, unified, and invisible; "outside," to visible phenomena and body. But why are these "outside" the presence of the One? The answer, I believe, is that they are not, ultimately, outside in that sense. They simply lie closer to the only "outside" of the universe, namely matter.

35 Henry J. Blumenthal agrees with others who have argued that "this passage is really about what happens when we attain to Intellect," not the One: "On Soul and Intellect," in *The Cambridge Companion to Plotinus* (Cambridge: Cambridge University Press, 1996), pp. 82ff. See also F.M. Schroeder, *Form and Transformation: A Study in the Philosophy of Plotinus* (Montreal: McGill-Queen's University Press, 1992), pp. 4–5; and Dominic O'Meara, *Plotinus: An Introduction to the Enneads* (Oxford: Oxford University Press, 1993), pp. 104–5. However, what Blumenthal calls the "traditional view" is also represented by excellent scholars: J.M. Rist, *Plotinus: The Road to Reality* (Cambridge: Cambridge University Press, 1967), p. 56; and Pierre Hadot, "Neoplatonist Spirituality," in *Classical Mediterranean Spirituality* (New York: Crossroad, 1986), p. 233.

36 See Augustine, *Confessions* 13.9 for a description that brings together the same themes and metaphors of fire and weightlessness in the context of love of God: "inardescimus et imus"; "we are enflamed and we go"; trans. Rex Warner (New York: Mentor-Omega, 1963), p. 322.

37 Augustine wrote of a similar experience, "Cessavi de me paululum": "I relaxed a little from myself," *Confessions* 7.14, ibid., p. 152.

38 Armstrong "Introductory Note," *Plotinus* (Cambridge: Massachusetts: Loeb Classical Library, Harvard University Press, 1988), Vol. 7, p. 79.

39 Compare Porphyry's description of Plotinus's appearance when engaged in philosophical inquiry: "When he was speaking his intellect visibly lit

up his face; there was always a charm about his appearance, but at these times he was still more attractive to look at: he sweated gently, and kindliness shone out from him, and in answering questions he made clear both his benevolence to the questioner and his intellectual vigour": *Life* 13.

40   Armstrong, *Plotinus*, Vol. 5, note 1, p. 258.

41   E.J. Emilsson comments: "On an epistemological level [this] means that for a mind without access to the archetype everything it encounters becomes entirely devoid of meaning: "Cognition and its Object," in *The Cambridge Companion to Plotinus* (Cambridge: Cambridge University Press, 1996), p. 239.

42   Plotinus's monotheistic universe is not incompatible with a plurality of gods, each "different in their powers," but "by that one manifold power they are all one" (5.8.9). See also A.H. Armstrong's "Some Advantages of Polytheism," in *Hellenic and Christian Studies* (London: Variorum, 1990), I.

43   John Dillon, *The Middle Platonists, 80 BC to AD 220* (Ithaca, New York: Cornell University Press, 1977), p. 9.

44   *San Francisco Chronicle*, 2 July 1998, E1.

45   *The Epic of Gilgamesh*, trans. N.K. Sanders (Baltimore: Penguin, 1960), pp. 52–3.

46   Then, as now, Epicureans were misunderstood and caricatured. They understood pleasure as absence of pain rather than any of the more exuberant pleasures of table and bed, and they ruled out any "pleasure" whose indulgence was likely to create pain. Drunkenness, one of the staples of our contemporary description, was disqualified on these grounds!

47   Similarly, Plato spoke of "an art of the speediest and most effective shifting or conversion of the soul, not an art of producing vision in it, but on the assumption that it possesses vision but does not rightly direct it and does not look where it should, an art of bringing this about": *Republic* 519a.

Chapter 7 Plotinus for the Present

1   Maxine Hong Kingston, *China Men* (New York: Knopf, 1980), p. 92.

2   Donna Haraway, "The Persistence of Vision," in *Writing on the Body*, Kate Conboy, Nadia Medina, and Sarah Stanbury, eds. (New York: Columbia University Press, 1997), p. 285.

3   Paul Churchland offers multiple definitions of "dualism": *Matter and Consciousness* (Cambridge, Massachusetts: MIT Press, 1984).

4   A.H. Armstrong, "Introductory Note," *Plotinus* (Cambridge, Massachusetts: Loeb Classical Library, Harvard University Press, 1984), Vol. V, p. 56.

5   Emily Gowers, "The Anatomy of Rome from Capitol to Cloaca," *Jour-*

nal of Roman Studies 85 (1995), p. 30. On discussions of mixture in antiquity, see also M.R. Miles, *Augustine on the Body* (Missoula, Montana: Scholars Press, 1979), pp. 80–4.

6 It is worth noting that, until the eighteenth century, few believed that the social and political inequalities of human life could be changed; see John Hick, *An Interpretation of Religion* (New Haven: Yale University Press, 1989), p. 305.

7 Plato, *Phaedrus* 252d.

8 A.H. Armstrong, "Platonic *Eros* and Christian *Agape*," in *Plotinian and Christian Studies* (London: Variorum, 1979), IX, 112, emphases in original.

9 See my *Carnal Knowing: Female Nakedness and Religious Meaning in the Christian West* (Boston: Beacon, 1989).

10 Rachel C. Rasmussen, "Crown of Creation: Toward a Theology of Birth," unpublished dissertation, Harvard Divinity School, 1997, Ann Arbor, Michigan: UMI Dissertation Information Services. See also: Patricia Bernstein, *Having a Baby: Mothers Tell Their Stories* (New York: Simon and Schuster, 1993); Janet Ashford, ed., *Birth Stories: The Experience Remembered* (Trumansburg, New York: Crossing, 1984); Ina May Gaskin, *Spiritual Midwifery* (Summertown, Tennessee: Book Publishing, 1977).

11 Aristotle also held this view "with some refinements and modifications": Armstrong, *Enneads* Vol. 3, note 1, p. 286.

12 Porphyry, *Life* 9. Apparently this was not a unique feature of Plotinus's school. Eusebius mentions that women also attended Origen's classes; *Historia Ecclesiastica* 6.8.2.

13 "The body" – a generic, universal body – is an entity that, like matter but in a different sense, is never seen. Not only are bodies male and female, but they are also always and irreducibly socialized to a particular gender as well as other important variables. See Judith Butler, *Gender Trouble: Feminism and the Subversion of Identity* (New York: Routledge, 1990), and *Bodies That Matter: On the Discursive Limits of "Sex"* (New York: Routledge, 1993). According to Ruth Hubbard, even bodies' physiology is gendered: "Constructing Sex Difference," *New Literary History* 19, 1 (Autumn 1987), p. 131.

14 See, for example, Alliez and Feher, "Reflections of a Soul," in *Fragments for a History of the Body*, part II (New York: Zone, 1989), p. 47. We should not, however, place too much emphasis on Plotinus's "mysticism"; Plotinus only uses the word twice and that in the context of speaking about rites of the mystery religions (*Enneads* 5.1.7; 6.9.11). Freighted as the word is in contemporary usage, it is difficult to use it to convey Plotinus's sense of a vision of a *reality* more immediate and (in a sense) ordinary than the everyday.

15 A.P. Bos, "World-views in Collision: Plotinus, Gnostics, and Christians," in *Plotinus Amid Gnostics and Christians* (Amsterdam: Free University Press, 1984), p. 13.

16 Ibid., p. 13.
17 Ibid., emphasis in original.
18 Emphasis in the original; ibid., p. 14.
19 C. Behan McCullagh, *The Truth of History* (New York: Routledge, 1998), p. 123.
20 This is the title of bell hooks's book, *Feminist Theory: From Margin to Center* (Boston: South End Press, 1984).
21 *Ennead* 4.4.40, trans. A.H. Armstrong (Cambridge, Massachusetts: Loeb Classical Library, Harvard University Press, 1966–88).
22 Augustine, *Soliloquies* I.2.
23 For Augustine's concept of the community of rational minds, see my article "'*Jesus patibilis*': Augustine's Debate with the Manichaeans," in *Faithful Imagining: Essays in Honor of Richard R. Niebuhr*, Sang Lee and Wayne Proudfoot, eds. (Missoula, Montana: Scholars Press, 1995).
24 Discussing late antiquity's concept of body, Gareth B. Matthews writes that body is "the 'part' of a man that is buried at death": "The Inner Man," *Augustine: A Collection of Critical Essays*, R.A. Markus, ed. (New York: Doubleday, 1972), pp. 87–8.
25 Porphyry, *Life* 10. For the definition of religion as "a system of beliefs and practices that are related to superhuman beings," Hans Penner, "Holistic Analysis: Conjectures and Refutations," in *Journal of the American Academy of Religion* LXII, 4 (Winter 1994), p. 990.
26 Susan Thistlethwaite, "Settled Issues and Neglected Questions: How is Religion to be Studied?" *Journal of the American Academy of Religion* LXII, 4 (Winter 1994), p. 1043.
27 William James, *The Varieties of Religious Experience: A Study in Human Nature* (New York: Collier Books, 1962), p. 5.
28 For example, *Ennead* 6.9.6. Plotinus supplied Augustine with a similar ability to personalize – or not – language about God: "Only they can think of [God] without absurdity who think of [God] as life itself": *On Christian Doctrine*, trans. D.W. Robertson, Jr. (New York: Bobbs-Merrill, 1958), p. 12.
29 Pierre Hadot, *Philosophy as a Way of Life*, trans. Michael Chase (London: Blackwell, 1995), p. 84.
30 Charles Winquist, "Theology: Unsettled and Unsettling," in *Journal of the American Academy of Religion* LXII (Winter 1994), p. 1028.
31 Rainer Maria Rilke, *Duino Elegies*, 7th elegy, trans. J.B. Leishman and Stephen Spender (New York: W.W. Norton, 1939), p. 61.
32 Body deserts soul/life (*Ennead* 1.9.1), and not vice versa because "soul is not in body, but body in soul" (*Ennead* 6.5.9).
33 A.H. Armstrong, "On Not Knowing Too Much About God," in *Hellenic and Christian Studies* (London: Variorum, 1990), p. 130.
34 Ibid., p. 131.
35 A.H. Armstrong, "The Escape of the One," p. 88.
36 A.H. Armstrong, "On Not Knowing Too Much About God," *Hellenic*

and Christian Studies XV, p. 131.

37   For a description of the essential components of fruitful conversation
      among people of diverse perspectives, see my article, "Hermeneutics of
      Generosity and Suspicion: Theological Education in a Pluralistic Setting,"
      in *Theological Education* XXIII (Supplement, 1987), pp. 34–52.

38   Plotinus differentiates compulsive action, which "drags contemplation
      more towards the outer world," from voluntary action, but ultimately,
      "all things aspire to contemplation . . . and all attain to it as far as poss-
      ible for them in their natural state": *Ennead* 3.8.1.

Bibliography

Translations of Plotinus and Plato

I have used throughout A.H. Armstrong's translation of the *Enneads* for The Loeb Classical Library (Cambridge, Massachusetts: Harvard University Press 1966–88). Armstrong based his translation on the critical edition of the Greek text of Plotinus by P. Henry and H.-R. Schwyzer, *Plotini opera* (Oxford: Clarendon, 1964–1977). I have sometimes altered Armstrong's translation slightly on the authority of J. Sleeman and G. Pollet, *Lexicon Plotinianum* (Leiden: E.J. Brill, 1980). Quotations from Plato are from the English translations edited by Edith Hamilton and Huntinton Cairns, *Plato: The Collected Dialogues*, Bollingen Series 71 (Princeton: Princeton University Press, 1961). Translations of other ancient authors are indicated in the notes.

Select Bibliography

Alliez, Eric and Michel Feher. 1989. "Reflections of a Soul," *Fragments for a History of the Body*. New York: Zone.

Armstrong, A.H. 1990. *Hellenic and Christian Studies*. London: Variorum.

—— 1986. *Classical Mediterranean Spirituality*. Edited by A.H. Armstrong. New York: Crossroads.

—— 1981. *Neoplatonism and Early Christian Thought*. London: Variorum.

—— 1979. *Plotinian and Christian Studies*. London: Variorum.

—— 1970. "Plotinus," *Cambridge History of Later Greek and Early Medieval Philosophy*. Cambridge: Cambridge University Press.

Barnes, J. 1982. "Medicine, Experience, and Logic," in *Science and Speculation*. Edited by J. Barnes et al. Cambridge: Cambridge University Press.

Barton, Carlin A. 1993. *The Sorrows of Ancient Romans*. Princeton: Princeton University Press.

Best, Steven and Douglas Kellner. 1997. *The Postmodern Turn*. New York:

Guilford Press.

Boak, E.R. 1955. *Manpower Shortage and the Fall of the Roman Empire in the West*. Ann Arbor: University of Michigan Press.

Brown, Peter. 1988. *The Body and Society: Men, Women, and Sexual Renunciation in Early Christianity*. New York: Columbia University Press.

—— 1978. *The Making of Late Antiquity*. Cambridge, Massachusetts: Harvard University Press.

—— 1971. *The World of Late Antiquity*. London: Thames and Hudson.

Churchland, Paul. 1984. *Matter and Consciousness*. Cambridge, Massachusetts: MIT Press.

Coleman, K.M. 1990. "Fatal Charades: Roman Executions Staged as Mythical Enactments," *Journal of Roman Studies* 80, 44–73.

Dillon, John. 1977. *The Middle Platonists*. Ithaca, NY: Cornell University Press.

Elsas, Charles. 1975. *Neuplatonische und Gnostische Weltablehnung in der Schule Plotins*. Berlin and New York: Walter De Gruyter.

Finney, Paul Corby. n.d. "Did Gnostics Make Pictures?" *The Rediscovery of Gnosticism* I. Edited by Bentley Layton. Leiden: *Numen* Suppl. 41.1.

Foucault, Michel. 1986. *The Care of the Self*. New York: Pantheon.

—— 1985. *The Use of Pleasure*. New York: Pantheon.

Fox, Robin Lane. 1987. *Pagans and Christians*. New York: Knopf.

Frend, W.H.C. 1984. *The Rise of Christianity*. Philadelphia: Fortress Press.

Garnsey, Peter. 1988. *Famine and Food Supply in the Graeco-Roman World*. Cambridge: Cambridge University Press.

Gerson, Lloyd P. 1996. *The Cambridge Companion to Plotinus*. Cambridge: Cambridge University Press.

Gowers, Emily. 1995. "The Anatomy of Rome from Capitol to Cloaca," *Journal of Roman Studies* 85, 23–32.

Grabar, André. 1945. "Plotin et les origines de l'esthétique médiévale," *Cahiers archéologiques* I. Paris: Van Oest.

Hadot, Pierre. 1995. *Philosophy as a Way of Life*. Trans. Michael Chase. Oxford: Blackwell.

—— 1993. *Plotinus or the Simplicity of Vision*. Trans. Michael Chase. Chicago: University of Chicago Press.

—— 1986. "Neoplatonist Spirituality," *Classical Mediterranean Spirituality*. Edited by A.H. Armstrong. New York: Crossroad.

—— 1981. *Neoplatonism and Early Christian Thought*. London: Variorum.

Harpham, Geoffrey Galt. 1987. *The Ascetic Imperative in Culture and Criticism*. Chicago: University of Chicago.

Hopkins, Keith. 1983. *Death and Renewal*. New York: Cambridge University Press.

Hunter, Ian. 1992. "Aesthetics and Cultural Studies," *Cultural Studies*. Edited by Lawrence Grossberg, Cary Nelson, and Paula Treichler. New York: Routledge.

Jay, Martin. 1994. *Downcast Eyes: The Denigration of Vision in Twentieth-*

century French Thought. Berkeley: University of California Press.

Jones, A.H.M. 1964. *The Later Roman Empire*, 3 vols. Oxford: Blackwell.

Katz, Joseph. 1954. "Plotinus and the Gnostics," *Journal of the History of Ideas* 15, 289ff.

Liebeschutz, J.H.W.G. 1979. *Continuity and Change in Roman Religion*. Oxford: Clarendon.

Long, A.A. 1974. *Hellenistic Philosophy*. New York: Scribners.

MacMullen, Ramsey. 1990. *Changes in the Roman Empire*. Princeton: Princeton University Press.

McCullagh, C. Behan. 1998. *The Truth of History*. New York: Routledge.

McNeill, William. 1976. *Plagues and People*. New York: Anchor Doubleday.

Miles, Margaret R. 1997. *Reading For Life: Beauty, Pluralism, and Responsibility*. New York: Continuum.

—— 1995. "'*Jesus patibilis*': Augustine's Debate with the Manichaeans," *Faithful Imagining: Essays in Honor of Richard R. Niebuhr*. Edited by Sang Lee and Wayne Proudfoot. Atlanta: Scholars Press.

—— 1988. *Carnal Knowing: The Female Body in Western Christianity*. Boston: Beacon Press.

—— 1983. "Vision: The Eye of the Body and the Eye of the Mind in St. Augustine's *De trinitate* and the *Confessions*," *Journal of Religion* 63, 2, 125–42.

—— 1979. *Fullness of Life: Historical Foundations for a New Asceticism*. Philadelphia: Westminster Press.

Murdoch, Iris. 1970. *The Sovereignty of Good*. London: Routledge and Kegan Paul.

Nussbaum, Martha C. 1994. *The Therapy of Desire*. Princeton: Princeton University Press.

—— 1990. *Love's Knowledge: Essays on Philosophy and Literature*. New York: Oxford University Press.

O'Meara, Dominic J. 1995. *Plotinus: An Introduction to the Enneads*. Oxford: Clarendon.

Pangle, Thomas, editor. 1987. *The Roots of Political Philosophy*. Ithaca: Cornell University Press.

Perkins, Judith. 1995. *The Suffering Self: Pain and Narrative Representation in the Early Christian Era*. New York: Routledge.

Plass, Paul. 1995. *The Game of Death in Ancient Rome: Arena Sport and Political Suicide*. Madison: University of Wisconsin Press.

Rist, John. 1996. "Plotinus and Christian Philosophy," *The Cambridge Companion to Plotinus*. Edited by Lloyd P. Gerson. Cambridge: Cambridge University Press.

Robinson, James M., editor. 1977. *The Nag Hammadi Library*. San Francisco: Harper and Row.

Runia, D.T. 1984. *Plotinus Among Gnostics and Christians*. Amsterdam: Free University Press.

Schroeder, F.M. 1992. *Form and Transformation: A Study in the Philosophy of Plotinus.* Montreal: McGill–Queen's University Press.

Shaw, Teresa. 1998. *The Burden of the Flesh: Fasting and Sexuality in Early Christianity.* Minneapolis: Fortress Press.

Shore, Brad. 1996. *Culture and Mind.* New York: Oxford University Press.

Sleeman, J.H. and Gilbert Pollet. 1980. *Lexicon Plotinianum.* Leiden: E.J. Brill.

Stark, Rodney. 1996. *The Rise of Christianity.* Princeton: Princeton University Press.

Stevenson, J. 1987. *The Catacombs.* London: Thames and Hudson.

—— 1987. *A New Eusebius.* London: SPCK, 2nd edition.

Szlezák, T. 1977. *Platon und Aristoteles in der Nuslehre Plotins.* Basle and Stuttgart: Schwabe.

Toner, J.P. 1995. *Leisure and Ancient Rome.* Cambridge: Polity Press.

Tuana, Nancy, editor. 1994. *Feminist Interpretations of Plato.* University Park, Pennsylvania: Pennsylvania State University Press.

Veyne, Paul. 1976. *Le pain et le cirque.* Paris: Éditions du Seuil.

Wagner, Michael. 1996. "Plotinus on the Nature of Physical Reality," *The Cambridge Companion to Plotinus.* Cambridge: Cambridge University Press.

Wallis, R.T. 1972. *Neoplatonism.* New York: Scribners.

Wiedemann, Thomas. 1991. *Emperors and Gladiators.* New York: Routledge.

Zinsser, Hans. 1935. *Rats, Lice, and History.* New York: Bantam.

Index of Passages, Plotinus

Index of Names and Subjects